HISTORY AND EVOLUTION

SUNY Series in Philosophy and Biology
David Edward Shaner, Furman University, editor

HISTORY AND EVOLUTION

edited by

Matthew H. Nitecki

and

Doris V. Nitecki

State University of New York Press

Published by
State University of New York Press, Albany

© 1992 State University of New York

Printed in the United States of America

For information, address State University of New York Press,
State University Plaza, Albany, N.Y., 12246

Production by Marilyn P. Semerad
Marketing by Bernadette LaManna

Library of Congress Cataloging-in-Publication Data

History and evolution / edited by Matthew H. Nitecki and Doris
  V. Nitecki.
      p.   cm. — (SUNY series in philosophy and biology)
    "Proceedings of the Spring Systematics Symposium held at the Field
  Museum of Natural History in Chicago in May, 1989"—Pref.
    Includes bibliographical references and index.
    ISBN 0-7914-1211-3 (hardcover). — ISBN 0-7914-1212-1 (paperback)
    1. History—Philosophy—Congresses.   2. Evolution (Biology)-
  -Philosophy—Congresses.   3. Human evolution—Philosophy-
  -Congresses.   I. Nitecki, Matthew H.   II. Nitecki, Doris V.
  III. Series.
  D16.8.H6242   1992
  901—dc20   92-724
                                                               CIP

10   9   8   7   6   5   4   3   2   1

Table of Contents

Preface

The studies of evolutionary biology and human history face similar kinds of problems and deal with similar processes. Evolution and history have two general aspects: one, the sum total of past biological or human events, and two, the interpretation and chronological synthesis of these events. Both disciplines deal with similar questions in similar ways. Some questions of methodology lie in the realm of the philosophy of history and of science, while others are more pragmatic. But do the methods used in evolutionary biology and history produce comparable knowledge, and are the differences and similarities between these disciplines real? There exists an enormous historical literature greatly concerned with the nature and limits of historical interpretations. On the other hand, although there is an increasing amount of analysis of the historical events in evolutionary biology, there is relatively little large-scale theory of the historical analysis of evolution. The common opinion among historians is that science and history are distinctly separate disciplines and that the methodology is not applicable from one to the other. Yet history, as practiced by a historian or a paleontologist, is a narrative (whether or not scientifically testable) of events, usually chronological. Historical narratives apply equally well to human events and to paleontological questions. This volume examines the philosophy of historical and evolutionary studies; the objectivity and meanings of human and evolutionary histories; the evolutionary approaches to and the analysis of history, historical approaches, and utilization of evolution; the logic of historical and evolutionary thinking and explanations; the identification of similarities, differences, and common problems of evolutionary biology and history; and what constitutes the major historical and evolutionary events.

This book represents the proceedings of the Spring Systematics Symposium held at the Field Museum of Natural History in Chicago in May, 1989.

The topic of this volume, easy at first sight, goes well beyond the competence of any single writer and demands contributions and help from many specialists from across many disciplines, and this we got. We are particularly grateful to Professor Robert Richards for his wise counsel and professional advice during all stages of the preparation of the symposium and this volume. We are also most thankful to the following who helped in many ways: Bret S. Beall, Kristine Bradof, Sophia Brown, William Burger, Glen H. Cole, Mikhail A. Fedonkin, John J. Flynn, Jack Fooden, Philip D. Gingerich, Jan Goldstein, David Hull, Richard G. Klein, Russell S. Lande, Scott Lidgard, Bruce D. Patterson, Moishe Postone, David M. Raup, Olivier Rieppel, Alexander Rosenberg, Lawrence Rothfield, J. John Sepkoski, Jr., Phillip R. Sloan, Elliott Sober, Adam Urbanek, George C. Williams, William Wimsatt, and two anonymous reviewers.

M.H.N.
D.V.N.

INTRODUCTION

History: La Grande Illusion

Matthew H. Nitecki

The earth has journeyed in its orbit around the sun, literally from time immemorial, and the planetary revolutions, like earth's seasons, have followed one another. Large and small cycles were smeared out by the monotony of the planet's never-disturbed progressions. For billions of years neither the earth nor its motions could be described as having any history or any evolution. The multitudes of life forms succeeded one another, sometimes with very minor morphological variations and changes, but mostly generations were indistinguishable from one another. Neither the planet, its life, nor its rocks appeared to have aged, only one form of life or one kind of rocks followed the change, or disappearance, of another. Neither history nor evolution were born yet, and neither do our models allow life without evolution, or history without humans.

When humans began to think of the past, they began simultaneously to object to it, and to superimpose on it the endless cycles of eternal returns. The past was sacred, heroic and always returning, and history was a word whose meaning has long eluded man. The past became prophets' foreknowledge of the future, and thus the necessity of history was born. Written history started when man began to write, to fit past events into calendars, and to break up calendars into periods. Once the Bible was written it became a document of history. Events in the Judeo-Christian tradition were arranged in linear form rather then being interpreted as cyclic as in the Mayan calendar. And ever since its birth, history continues to be of paramount importance to us all: to each individual, to each profession, to each decade, and to each century history presents its own picture of the past. This is so because each time and each culture paints or distorts the pictures of history differently. Through historical imagery each epoch apprehends and defines its own life.

Astronomers today (just like ancient, scholastic and Middle Ages astronomers) tell us that before the Big Bang (creation) there was no time and no history, and that the future will be either cyclic or history will cease in the red-heat death of the universe (or the realm of the netherworld). These cosmological initial and terminal events mark the symbolic life-span of earth history as interpreted by mankind, and since history is human invention, there was no history before us, nor will there be any after us. I believe this to be fundamentally correct. Yet I see something basically wrong, or to put it mildly, something religious in this science which attempts to lead us to the pre-time, pre-space, pre-beginning, even pre-here, pre-there and pre-nothing. Surely this is either the great error, or the great myth – but a myth that, perhaps as the Russians say, is a fragment of former truth!

There are many interpretations of evolutionary history and human history. To some the entire history of life or of man is a steady consequence of organismal relationships embedded in variation and competition; others interpret history as periods of stasis interrupted by catastrophes or events of unusual significance. The data to support the paleontological interpretations of history as either gradual or catastrophic are still controversial, and the genetic data are just emerging. History attempts to explain by means of models. Unfortunately making models simplifies and narrows the field of vision. And here is the problem of how to enlarge our understanding while making models. But this is the fate of all treatments of ideas including those in science. Events narrated in history and in evolution do not necessarily correspond to the real events occurring in history or in nature. Instead, both are based on models.

Our models about evolution reflect our politico-social milieu, and may be rooted in what appear to be just slogans, advertising jargons claiming, perhaps, more than they can prove. It is unreasonable to claim that natural science is "objective" while the "mental sciences" such as history are not. Some might claim that historians must reflect their own cultures in their narratives, while scientists tell completely objective tales. But no intellectual discipline escapes the impact and delusions of its own time. For example, any North American geologist promulgating continental drift would have been denied tenure before World War II, the time of skepticism about continental drift; neither would Lamarckian evolutionary biologists be more successful today. Both evolutionary biology and history are equally subjective activities because both are influenced by the training and social standing of their respective practitioners; yet both claim to reach beyond their immediate circumstances. But the biggest danger with models is that the ideas of a selected few individuals stand for the knowledge at large, and make these selected ideas and selected people represent the status quo of the profession. Those are really only symptoms of a larger universe, in which ad hoc theories, when they materialize, alter our science. All of us will go on defending our models irrespective of how correct they are. We must beware of not confusing the model with the reality.

What we are doing when teaching Darwin's biotic history to our biology students is pure history. It is possible that the biggest difference between evolutionary biology (at least its historical aspects) and history is linguistic, and not a cosmic battle between science and nonscience. If we substitute the English word *science* with the German *Wissenschaft*, or Russian *nauka*, then the differences between these disciplines become less significant. To a German or a Russian both history and biology are *Wissenschaften* or *nauki*, and thus both disciplines have an equal claim to the place in their respective Academies of "Sciences." In this light the differences and similarities between evolution and history are simply the differences between the *Naturwissenschaft* and *Geisteswissenschaft*. The *Naturwissenschaft* appears to depend less on narrative than does the *Geisteswissenschaft*, although paleontology, geography, or cosmology certainly tell stories. This is not to say that there are no differences; history (like such sciences as sociology and anthropology) deals with human actions and events within social and institutional frameworks, with ideas, thoughts and emotions, and, above all, with human problems. Change, however, has an additional meaning to the evolutionary biologist. The stability of life is maintained by the continuous cybernetic changes, or adjustments of organisms to the environment. And this homeostasis consists of stability and novelty, which, in order for an organism to survive, must always tend to equilibrium. However, few intellectual disciplines (e.g., Freudianism, relativity theory, etc.) are associated with a single theory more than the study of evolution. But the study of history is a discipline seemingly in search of, so far, very elusive theories or law.

Methodologies of Historical Explanations

The common element of evolutionary biology and history is the concept of *change* through time. Historians and evolutionary biologists seek to picture changing and dynamic processes, as they desire to reconstruct life from the remains of death. The historian gathers the extant fragments of past events, and imaginatively rebuilds those events from a few documents, some old letters, or from the pieces of cracked pottery. The evolutionist, such as the paleontologist, does precisely the same. From rock splinters bearing the dull imprint of once vivid organisms, one brings back to conceptual life whole populations – teeming hordes of strange creatures. Out of historical evidence the past is made present, whether the past is Caesar crossing the Rubicon or a trilobite crawling across the bed of a Paleozoic sea. In both cases historical explanations are similar and either none is, or both are, equally "good science," and the methodologies of general history and evolutionary biology are homologous. Although it could be considered that history and evolutionary biology are conceptually different (as evolution as a natural process occurred regardless of whether humans arose to interpret it, whereas human history is processionally and conceptually dependent on the existence of humans), nevertheless, both seem to be involved in the construction of narratives based on historical artefacts, necessitating the interpretation of their significance and the synthesis of these into an explanatory narrative which might appeal to single or multiple causes. The primary difference in most general methodology would seem to lie in the kinds of "documents" utilized and the different character of the causes; the first often deal with such issues as human intentionality, political events, and economics and sociology, and the other appeals to genetics, interaction of species, geological changes and so on. In this aspect we are concerned with the communality of methods in spite of the split of disciplines into departments of science and humanities, and hence a dialogue across normal disciplines results.

Robert Richards is one of the philosophers, scientists and historians mutually concerned to explore the common problems and methodologies involved in standard historical disciplines and the historical sciences. In this volume, he is primarily interested in the structure of historical narrative and explanations, which he finds not only explanatory, but the most fundamental sort of explanation to be found in science. He argues against Hempel's interpretations (for a different view on Hempel see Hull, this volume). To Richards history is scientific because it explains, and thus history is "explanation science." Richards dissects Darwin's narrative, and shows how various devices of the narrative provide an explanation.

This aspect of the numerous parallels in the issues confronted by the historian and natural scientist engaged in historical reconstruction of the past is emphasized by Rachel Laudan. To her the great similarity among all historical sciences is that they have a common goal of seeking a reliable knowledge of the world. She assesses the problems of historical sciences, and notes that evolutionary biology and history are similar in these aims. Although we cannot experiment on the past, the differences between the historical and nonhistorical sciences have been exaggerated. Although she demonstrates that not all historical sciences are the same, and that the lessons from the philosophy of history are limited, nevertheless, by examining chronology and interpretive history she declares that "from an epistemic point of view there is absolutely nothing special about the past."

David Hull is not satisfied with the Covering-Law Model of Scientific Explanations, and feels a need for a unique historical form of explanation, one concerned with particular events. Basing his conclusion on analysis of historical reconstructions and explanations and on historical entities (which he argues are particulars), Hull proposes the Particular-Circumstance Model of Scientific Explanations.

Marc Ereshefsky argues that the distinction between evolutionary biology and such nonhistorical sciences as physics and chemistry are not clear, and that in both evolutionary biology and experimental sciences there is a temporal ordering of events, the use of how-possibly explanations, the uniqueness of events, and the reliance on particular-circumstance explanations. However, evolutionary biology differs from all other sciences, since it deals with biological taxa, which as historical entities, transmit information from one generation to another. In this aspect evolutionary biology is similar to human history, which is concerned with social groups that also transmit information. The differences between the disciplines may be of degree only. While taxa faithfully transmit information via the physical transfer of hereditary material, in history information is transmitted much less predictably or "faithfully" via culture/society. Ereshefsky sees evolutionary theory as a methodologically, but not ontologically, distinct historical discipline. Both are sciences without laws, whether or not they are actually attempting the discoveries of laws, and whether or not the natures of the underlying processes are comparable. The aim of both is not the judgment, but the understanding of the past.

Richards, Laudan, Hull and Ereshefsky lay the most general issues at stake before the reader, and they also raise some immediate cautions about overly ambitious use of analogies and the possible pitfalls awaiting those who see easy parallels between the enterprise of the historian and that of the natural scientist.

Historical Explanations and Evolutionary Biology

History, meaning either "written history" or "past events," surely must have been developing prior to Darwin. No one, absolutely no one, can visualize the hominid history otherwise than evolving – not emerging or progressive, but evolving. Most evolutionary biologists, including paleontologists and paleoanthropologists, assume that this evolving process is controlled by natural selection. Historians, irrespective of any claims to the contrary, are equally constrained by evolutionary theory.

Darwin's evolution asserts that the biological world is discontinuous, changing and dynamic, that is, discontinuous morphologically at any time but continuously and gradually changing in (pre-punctuated equilibria) uniformitarian time. Human history must also be discontinuous, changing and dynamic if it is not to become continuous, unchanging and static. This is of great significance, for if Darwin's claim is right then history must be fundamentally related to evolutionary biology, and historical events cannot be different from other universal events in nature, and must be subject to the same considerations.

A common wisdom claims that no two things are ever identical, hence it seems unnecessary to show the difference between entities to demonstrate their individuality. However, we need to classify things, to arrange them in some orderly fashion, if possible, to set their hierarchical relationship. History and evolutionary biology are not identical, there are differences between them. Indeed, they are separate and well-developed disciplines. However, they are retrospective, closely related and similar sciences; they are the maps of past life (however incomplete), telling us where we came from. Perhaps the very nature of the topic makes us in some way critics of the received view of history.

In history and in evolutionary biology time is lumped into "periods": Medieval, Elizabethan, Tertiary or Burgess Shale. The visions that historians and paleontologists have about their systems are similar. Gibbon's unified temporal period of the Roman Empire is comparable to Murchison's Great Silurian System. A striking difference between history and evolutionary biology, of course, is in the time scales used. While physicists usually deal with ahistorical events, (or rather with the laws governing these events), evolutionary biologists are concerned (in addition to the biological "laws") with the nonhuman living world of millions of years, and historians with the human world of shorter duration. However, even historical time is sufficiently long for recognition of long term evolutionary phenomena such as natural selections, extinctions, etc.

Douglas Futuyma, in his discussion of issues in reconstruction of phylogenies, argues that our historical thinking influences our evolutionary thinking, and that the history learned from paleontological and phylogenetic analyses influences history at the population level. Thus, learned history further influences the interpretation of functional characters and our understanding of rates and directions of evolution. Gene flow may also explain the hypothesis of punctuated equilibria of certain characters. To Futuyma, historical evolutionary biology explains major macroevolutionary phenomena, and thus evolutionary studies are basically studies of history. History of population distributions and movements is needed to understand evolutionary development more precisely.

David Kitts wants to confirm evolutionary theories by paleontological data. He first considers historical inferences, and then turns to geology and paleontology for particular events to test the general evolutionary hypotheses. He warns us to be careful "that the hypotheses to be tested [have] not been presupposed in inferring the event to be employed in its test." He also pleads that the theory to be tested and procedures used to infer the events be very clearly formulated to determine which features of the fossil record are to be counted as positive, and which as negative. He also requires that it be clear whether the hypothesis will be tested or presupposed. He scrutinizes the success of theoretical paleontologists in their attempts to overcome these difficulties.

Futuyma and Kitts specifically address the most general issues from the standpoint of historical science proper. They display the relevance of general issues in historical explanation to the questions of historical science, and they display in more detail the way in which there are meaningful connections between disciplinary approaches.

Historical Science and the Philosophy of History

The analogy of history and evolutionary biology is united by a more general concern with the unity of processes found in human and natural science. The chapters by Ruse, Boyd and Richerson, Allen, and Slobodkin deal variously with the philosophy of history, and are concerned with understanding the process of historical development itself. They successfully ask whether history progresses and what are the criteria of scientific progress. They also show that there are parallels between the dialectic of Marx and Darwin's natural selection; that there are historical laws which also govern the development of the sciences; that such laws govern human history and evolutionary biology; that there are similar processes at work in society and the natural world.

Michael Ruse in his chapter on progress in science analyzes the parallel between the history of society, history of science, and phylogeny. All three, he maintains, assume progressive development, passing from a primitive to a more advanced stage. Though progressiveness is now routinely rejected in evolutionary biology, general history and history of science, Ruse argues that the assumption covertly quickens all of these disciplines.

Whether there is direction to human history depends on whether there is a purpose, or meaning, in history, because it is purpose that gives direction to history. Nonhuman history may have a direction – that is, increase of entropy in cosmological change – however, that does not mean that it has a purpose. There is a general consensus among historians and evolutionary biologists that neither history nor evolutionary biology claims to foretell the future. However, are we really unable to predict the future? It seems that on the one hand we loudly deny any ability to tell the future (and laugh at Marxists, utopias, and dreams), and on the other we are deftly doing just that. The most recent paleontological arguments about periodicities of mass extinctions, are very strong statements proclaiming knowledge of the future. Likewise, the rise and fall of Great Powers, and the demise of Republican exuberances are equally strongly, and often wrongly, predicted by historians.

The reason why past events and evolutionary events had, and still are considered by some to have, a direction is because history was once interpreted as nonscientific and controlled by divine providence which became its law. All biologists believe that nature is explainable without recourse to explanation via divine intervention. Without such belief there would be little merit in doing science. If nature is explainable, so must be man, since man is also part of nature. Thus, human history must also be explainable. This, however, does not imply existence (or absence) of laws. Definitely, no universal laws have been found in history or in evolutionary biology. There are, however, plenty of theories.

The predictions of the future, except those based on testable and verified natural laws, are possible candidates of failure, for example, the population bomb, the greenhouse effects, the predictions of the School of Rome, the fall of the Great Powers, the nuclear winter scenarios, etc. However, the new temper in biology away from the pure descriptive studies, and in history from descriptions of battles and lives of rulers demands us to quantify processes and patterns. These "philosophical" departures from traditional studies and our new abilities to accumulate great amounts of data may allow us to predict future events. However, if evolution teaches us anything it is that we are ignorant of effects that will or could wipe out the human species. Of course this does not mean that there are no reasons for optimism about the human fate and thus the fate of "history."

Robert Boyd and Peter Richerson try to understand the relation of cultural evolution to microevolutionary dynamics. In other words can we explain macroscopic behavior by microscopic effects? They argue that we can. The behavior of a population is the sum of behavior of individuals of this population, and thus by explaining the behavior of individuals (in the evolutionary or historical sense) we can explain the characteristics of the population. Boyd and Richerson utilize statistical mechanics and thermodynamics as sources of theoretical analogies. Thus, organic evolution and analogous cultural evolution result from microevolutionary processes in the course of historical events.

Garland Allen compares Darwin's evolutionary theory with Marx's ideas on the development of society. According to Allen both organic evolution and socioeconomic processes are historical transactions subject to laws. The laws in evolutionary biology and in history are similar, but are different from laws in physics. I fully agree with Allen that history can be as scientific as evolutionary biology, and that although historical development does not share the same mechanisms, the two disciplines are nevertheless very similar. Whether Allen is right that dialectical materialism was implicit in Darwinism and explicit in Marxism, is in a way irrelevant – what is of great interest is that Marxism, however now discredited, can be of value in studies of modern evolutionary theory.

Marx sees the Golden Age, and, therefore, the meaning and direction in history. Darwin sees similarly that "forms even more perfect will evolve." Both men reflect deep feelings of seeing the benevolence and beauty in the universe. Both wonder at the marvels of nature. The opposite of this view is the pessimism manifested in the objection to the idea of progress, in the desire to shut the eyes, to the *axis mundis*, or *axis vitae*, or to become antihistorical, or at least ahistorical.

Lawrence Slobodkin is interested in the nature of science, and more specifically the features of its evolution, and particularly the evolution of natural laws. He sees laws evolving, in that scientists apply new laws to newly observed phenomena, and broaden their application. In other words science and the laws that science describes, as well as the universe, are subject to change with time. Thus the laws evolve! He shows how evolution can be used to explain the ontogeny of science (its birth, maturity and extinction), and this to him constitutes the historical sequence of development. Thus, evolutionary biology itself is a historical phenomenon.

Dawkins claims that evolution itself evolves. I agree, and I add that natural laws must also evolve. But this is correct *only when we accept that history and the study of evolution are cultural phenomena that follow the principle of the hermeneutic circle.* It is then that Darwin will be given greater credit; when his theories are correctly expanded to the nonbiological realm, as is continuously done, and when it is accepted that the universe indeed evolves then the very properties of the universe must also evolve. Therefore, although our concept of laws may require them to be fixed, I believe that laws cannot be fixed forever. And if laws change why not time itself? If it is true that in our model the universe as a whole evolves, then the temporal and spatial parts of the universe must also evolve. Hence history evolves. Or to be more exact, if life evolves, there is absolutely no reason to assume that man does not; hence human history cannot be different from histories of other organisms.

This specialization (or fragmentation) of the field – this niche partitioning – a necessary by-product of the increase of knowledge (or its classifications), requires the synthesis (or unification) of these various disciplines, particularly the synthesis of history and evolutionary biology – in effect, an opposite to the fashionable specialization so prevalent now in history and in evolutionary biology. This is not to say that there is anything wrong with specialization per se. Specialization results from the increasing complexity of life itself; for example, the modern army's tank driver is as much a soldier as the nineteenth-century Hussar. In the same way a specialist in ideas of antiquity and one specializing in World War II are as much historians as the student of trilobites. *All are specialists of history.*

Sense of Meaning

History as a discipline and as a popular subject is blossoming as never before; witness Paul Kennedy's *The Rise and Fall of the Great Powers* on the best seller's list, and the popularities of the history book clubs. The field is alive, and even new subdisciplines are born (e.g., history of geology), but above all there is a great understanding among historians that history must be related to the general process of extant human life. It is in this sense that history acquires a practical aspect. History, and for that matter all science, is not an activity unconnected with the present. On the contrary it lives, grows and serves today's life, and is at the same time nourished by it, it is dependent on it and draws the inspiration from today's activities. Evolutionary theories and explanations may come and go, and historical fashions may change. Most of our actions are independent of our intellect, however "thoughtful, premeditated" actions are clearly tied to our present conditions. Thus it is the dictates of our present life that are central to all our sciences. This is the reason why the interpretation of the past, and thus the past itself, is continuously changing. History and evolutionary biology change continuously and reconstruct the past according to the demands of the present. *Autre temps autre moeurs.* In this sense these activities have a life of their own. Thus we continuously manufacture a new history of human life and of the organic world. In a very profound sense both human and biological histories create their own subject matter.

It seems that there is plenty of history to go around; everyone speaks history. We even have a return to roots, to individual histories of one's own families. Books on history and histories abound and yet we live in the world of an ahistorical desert and there is some antagonism toward considerations of what history is. What we talk about instead are the historical facts and narratives, but we are forbidden to talk about the *sense* of history. Sense of history is a taboo, a something akin to the soul of history, the direction of the historical processes, some mysterious religious spirit. However, we cannot reject the sense of history any more than we can reject the sense of life itself. As much as sense of our individual life has deep meaning in, and for, our own life, sense has also a deep meaning in history. In our blind and premature rejection of sense and meaning in history, we play games of "rationality" and reject these concepts as romantic and nonscientific. To say that history has no meaning is as meaningless as to say that life of individuals has no meaning. Religion has neither a patent on the meaning of life nor a patent on the ethics of life. If the life of individual has meaning, why should a life of society, or history, or evolution, be without it?

I think it was psychoanalysis that has forced upon us an unescapable conclusion that history explains our present condition. Thus history really defines modern humans, the *Homo sapiens historicus.* In this sense history has a meaning, just as psychoanalysis has meaning. This meaning is the explanation of the present human condition, its origins, and manifestations.

Are there deeper needs that historians satisfy? Surely the purpose of history is not only collecting of historical facts, a purpose a classical systematist would propose, and claim a legitimate and useful science. History, like evolutionary biology, must explain human life, must help in understanding human life, and by this process of understanding allow us to behave and act rationally, and to plan for the future. Planning for the future is not yet an entirely discredited idea – it is a necessity. To understand individual life we must dig into the previous experiences, to understand larger units of life we must do likewise. In spite of Popper we must try to shape and control future events – it is nonsense to think otherwise. Without planning for the future, history becomes only an intellectual game, of little importance outside the Academe. But history has two meanings, one the study of the past human life, the other that past life itself. But are there really any differences between these two concepts? I think not. The so-called past life is nothing else but our understanding of that life.

If we accept psychoanalysis as a valid method with which to dig into the past of an individual for the explanations of the meaning of human life then we must also accept history's "sense" for the same purpose of digging into the past of humanity. The basis of history, as the bases of all knowledge, is imagination that must not be restrained by any a priori rejections. After all history has an incredibly powerful influence on our present life. We are unable to make legal judgments without consulting the Constitution, which has the transcending power of history over the American lives. Should we, therefore, not attempt to see life through the glasses of history? Should we not concentrate on history more, and go in depth into our own historical past for strength, understanding, and guidance? Evolutionary theories come and go, historical fashions change, yet history will never go away, but instead will haunt us with offers of explanations and guidance.

METHODOLOGIES

OF

HISTORICAL EXPLANATIONS

The Structure of Narrative Explanation in History and Biology

Robert J. Richards

> Cut us off from Narrative, how would the stream of conversation, even among the wisest, languish into detached handfuls, and among the foolish utterly evaporate!
> – Thomas Carlyle, *On History*

Had Darwin been the type, more perhaps like Huxley, to whoop with a battle cry that would marshal naturalists of his time and ours to the colors of his theory, it might have been "Biology is – well, if not destiny – biology is history." For Darwin to ally biology with the forces of history was a shrewd strategy for the midnineteenth century, a time when the discipline had been served by extraordinary intellects: Jules Michelet and Alexis de Tocqueville in France; Alexander von Humboldt, Leopold von Ranke, Jacob Burkhardt, and Wilhelm Dilthey in the German states; William H. Prescott and Henry Adams in America; and in England, Thomas Carlyle and Thomas Babington Macaulay. Darwin had read most of these historians, as well as the earlier histories of Edward Gibbon, James Boswell, and David Hume, along with numerous figures of lesser light. In the lists of Darwin's reading notebooks (1988), after the various works in the biological sciences, the next largest category of books is history. Darwin's science as well as his delight was history.

Philosophers of science and their *beau ideal*, the physicist, have never been very good at history, for that discipline requires an expansion of intellectual power and its penetration into fields afar to touch hidden connections, not the contraction of intellect into a narrow shaft of insight that bores down along prescribed mathematical lines. From the confined perspective of most philosophers and physicists, though, history has seemed to be the pursuit of pedestrian minds, grubbers of disparate detail who rarely raise their

heads to gaze upon empyrean heights where facts reach to general law.
When history pretends to science, it can only lead to mischief, or so sugges-
ted the doyen of philosophers of science, Karl Popper, in his 1944 tract *The
Poverty of Historicism*. There he maintained:

> We must reject the possibility of a theoretical history; that is to
> say, of a historical social science that would correspond to
> *theoretical physics*. There can be no scientific theory of histori-
> cal development serving as a basis for historical prediction.
> ([1944] 1966:vii)

Popper rightly worried about the pretensions of grand historical schemes
(e.g., Marxism), but in a fit of logical fret, he rejected all considerations of
history as a science. In the 1970s, then, when he discovered evolutionary
biology, it is no wonder that he found not a science, but metaphysics – that
is, a research program into history that, while very suggestive, failed the test
of true science. As he put it in 1974: "Darwinism does not really *predict* the
evolution of variety. It therefore cannot really *explain* it" (1974:136).
Though friends have since convinced Popper (1978) that he should admit
evolutionary biology into the temple, yet there is no good reason why he
should have succumbed to ecumenism. Evolutionary biology still does not
meet the logical criteria that Popper proposed for science. That is because
it is historical and suffers from the presumed disabilities of all history attempting to pass as science.

The most logically acute effort to demonstrate the poverty of history,
a challenge whose power has not withered in this postmodern age, has been
Carl Hempel's (1942) paper "The Function of General Laws in History."
Briefly, Hempel, the logical positivist, argued that any presumptive science
must display in its putative explanations a certain logical form, called the
nomological-deductive pattern (see also Hull, this volume). This covering
law model of explanation, as it is called, continues to dominate considerations in philosophy of science. Its power flows from sources of cogency,
grace, and elegance; and any alternative theory of explanation must still
attempt to weaken its countervailing force.

If I wished to explain scientifically – and, indeed, there is no other
way to explain but scientifically, according to Popper and Hempel – why, for
instance, object **A** conducts electricity, I would do so by specifying the bound-

ary condition, to wit, "**A** is a piece of copper," and a relevant law, in this case "All copper conducts electricity." The relationship between the so-called "explanans," the law and the boundary conditions, and that which is to be explained, the "explanandum," namely, the fact that object **A** conducts electricity, is that of logical deduction. From the premises "All copper conducts electricity" and "Object **A** is a piece of copper" I can deductively derive the conclusion "Object **A** conducts electricity" – and that is what it is to explain something, to deduce it logically, to bring it under a covering law. For Hempel, this logical pattern meant, of course, that what was an explanation of an event that had already occurred, could serve also as the means of predicting an event which had yet to occur. It follows from this analysis that if the logical pattern of explanation cannot permit prediction, then neither can it support explanation. This is the so-called "symmetry thesis."[1] Hempel noticed that respectable historians – which, of course, excluded Marxists – did not propose any large-scale general laws of historical processes. But without laws, historical accounts could at best be explanation sketches, not real explanations. Most written histories, he suggested, were rife with explanation sketches, but failed to explain anything. Yet if history cannot produce real explanations, neither can its ally, evolutionary biology. Both history and evolutionary biology must have a common logical fate, the thread of which even today the weird sisters within the community of philosophers of science and physical scientists will snip exceeding small. If you doubt that, consider the passing remarks of a well-known philosopher of science. In his recent book *Representing and Intervening*, Ian Hacking offers:

> The phenomena about the species – say the one that a pride of lions hunts by having the male roar and sit at home base while the females chase after and kill scared gazelle – are anecdotes. But the phenomena of physics – the Faraday effect, the Hall effect, the Josephson effect – are the keys that unlock the universe. (1983:228)

The razor edge of remarks such as this threatens biologists and historians alike with great conceptual damage. But the threat, I think, is an irrational fantasy, which can be dissolved by bringing to the surface some underlying presuppositions. First, consider the way in which the claim can be justified that a given logical pattern is *the* pattern for scientific explanation. The way in which it is done, according to Imre Lakatos (1978), and I believe he is right, is that we take the best examples of knowing and determine the logical patterns they exhibit. For Lakatos, a Popperian, the best examples we have of explanation come from physics, and so the covering law model becomes justified in light of examples culled from Copernicus, Galileo, Newton, and Maxwell. Examples such as this, however, do exhibit one small defect. We no longer believe Copernicus, Galileo, Newton, and Maxwell to have been correct; we do not look to them any longer for good explanations of the natural world. Their science has been superseded, just as Aristotle's physics was replaced by theirs. However, while we certainly no longer expect Aristotle's science to provide sound accounts of the world, we still open the book of another scientist of classical Greece with exactly that expectation. The author begins his book in the third person:

> Thucydides the Athenian wrote the history of the war fought between Athens and Sparta, beginning the account at the very outbreak of the war, in the belief that it was going to be a great war and more worth writing about than any of those which had taken place in the past.[2] (1972:35)

Thucydides' aim in writing his *History of the Peloponnesian War* largely coincides with that of most great historians writing thereafter. He says:

> It will be enough for me . . . if these words of mine are judged useful by those who want to understand clearly the events which happened in the past and which (human nature being what it is) will at some time or other and in much the same ways, be repeated in the future. My work is not a piece of writing designed to meet the taste of an immediate public, but was done to last forever. (1972:48)

Thucydides' history provides sound explanations and understanding of past events. Hence the logical pattern that it exhibits becomes justified and can thus serve as a model for other explanatory efforts in science. Thucydides' history is a narrative, and it is the narrative pattern of explanation that I wish to investigate. My delineation of the structure of narrative explanation will ground two claims I will attempt to stake down. First, that if narrative is the fundamental method of history, then, insofar as evolutionary biology is historical, it must also be the general method of evolutionary biology. This means, of course, that, despite appearances to the contrary, even Darwin's *Origin of Species* must be a narrative, though, I grant, an opaque narrative. I will support this first claim by drawing on examples from literature, history especially, and the *Origin of Species* to illustrate the structure of narrative explanation. My second claim goes further: it is that all explanations of events in time are ultimately narrative in structure. This means that Hempel got it just backwards: it is not that history can offer only explanation sketches, but that nomological-deductive accounts – insofar as they can be detected in such sciences as geology, paleontology, astrophysics, anthropology, and evolutionary biology – provide only narrative sketches; the covering law model yields sound explanations only insofar as that skeleton can be fleshed out imaginatively with the sinew and muscle of the corresponding narrative. Let me first concentrate on depicting the structure of narrative, and then turn to argue the second claim about the ubiquity of narrative explanations in science. My discussion of the structure of narrative will focus on five aspects of narrative accounts: the events narrated, the perspective and authority of the narrator, the temporal dimensions of narrative, its causal bindings, and its explanatory force.

Narratives and Events Narrated

Narratives fix events along a temporal dimension, so that prior events are understood to have given rise to subsequent events and thereby to explain them – that, in brief, is what narratives do. The events related may be designedly fictional, historical, or indeterminate as to their real occurrence in the past. Now let me suggest a first important distinction. We may distinguish between the events, imagined or real, which are narrated and the vehicle expressing them, the narration itself. We might go further and distinguish between the events immediately narrated, and those more remotely indicated, built up, as it were by implication from the events more proximately related; we may call these the immediate and remote events. So, for example, Thucydides describes in detail the immediate events of the civil war on the island of Corcyra, but simultaneously, through allusion and synecdoche, depicts the more remote events of civil wars taking place throughout

Greece and, again even more remotely, the universal character of civil war. Or, take an example from literature. By the time you reach the end of Rachel Ingalls's wonderful novel *Mrs. Calaban*, in which a frustrated British housewife falls in love with a large green froglike monster who happens to walk into her kitchen one summer evening, you realize that the numerous immediate events narrated are building up the remote account of a woman losing her mind (or, as a student of mine more sensitively suggested, of the possibilities of a relationship more real than that with a jerky husband). So Darwin, in the first chapter of the *Origin of Species*, describes the immediate events constituting the practices of Sir John Sebright, Darwin's pigeon-breeding friend, who, as Darwin relates, "used to say that 'he would produce any given feather in three years, but it would take him six years to obtain head and beak'" (1859:31). This and other narrated practices of breeders, as well as the many subsequent elements directly described, are meant to convey a more remote history – that is, the evolution from the first few forms breathed into life on the globe to the multitude of species presently inhabiting it.

Events narrated within a history, whether immediate or remote, have their existence only in the narrative; they are not identical with real events of the past. However, the techniques of the narrative genre – in history texts, for example, such devices as footnotes, bibliography, vividness of expression, logical development, coherence with the reader's other knowledge, and so on – establish an index of reality. The higher the index, the more will the events narrated be regarded as representing past reality. The mercury for this measure climbs as the historian labors to engage those different devices just mentioned. It will fall when the historian makes little use of such instruments, or when he or she constructs events that run against the grain of the reader's firm knowledge, especially concerning what sorts of things the historian could possibly know: thus readers rightly grow restive when the historian ascribes specific thought-acts to subjects without such sentential modifiers as "He must have thought that . . ." or "She likely said to herself something like . . ." The index of reality will give different readings at different times. So, the index of reality for the *Origin of Species* would have been middling when first published, quite high at the time of Darwin's death, and for us, it will have sunk back a bit – after all, we are neo-

Darwinians, which Darwin, needless to say, was not.

The higher the index of reality, the more the readers are invited to step beyond the particular history text to test the adequacy of its claims. Though, paradoxically, the higher the index the more the text suggests that readers need not accept the invitation, for a high index also brings greater authority and confidence in the truth of the narrative. This does not mean, however, that the text hermeneutically seals off readers from real past events and keeps them closeted within the suffocating constructions of the historian's creation. Some (like Derrida and Berkhofer) do argue, of course, that "the only meaning for history is not the past as such but its representation in (and as) a text" (Berkhofer 1989). But these textual constructivists fail to appreciate the power of historical triangulation. The structure of real events in the past comes into relief and is recognized insofar as multiple, independent pieces of evidence stand apart from a particular text that uses them. And to the extent that these fragmental remnants of the past resist interpretations contrary to those which the historian has given them but rather form the tessellated structure of a coherent story, the triangulation *recovers* rather than simply *creates*. The possibility of triangulation and the ready invitation of a text to "examine for oneself the evidence" confirms our ordinary professional-historical judgment that some histories about a topic are better than others – a judgment in which "better" means, not more literate, not more discursive, not more French, but rather having more adequately recaptured the past.

While a work such as the *Origin* will have an overall index of reality, its components will also have indices, which, of course, contribute to the general evaluation. We may designate the particular smaller narrative units that constitute a larger whole "narrites." In Darwin's book, the individual narrites will vary in their index of reality from obviously imaginative stories to narrites of greater reality, to those that tell of events whose historical reality seems completely secure. As an anchor at the high end of the reality scale are the large number of experiments Darwin performed to demonstrate his two chief claims: namely, descent with modification, and natural selection as the principle instrument thereof. So, for instance, in chapter two he tells of his mathematical experiments designed to demonstrate that what in the past were varieties of some species have themselves in the present become species. In chapter three, he relates a large number of experiments: he calculates the tremendous fecundity of even slow-breeding elephants; he plants a plot of ground to determine the severity of struggle for existence among plants; he estimates the number of birds destroyed on his property by the severe winter of 1854-55; he reckons the number and sorts of destruction suffered by a grove of Scotch firs on a relative's estate; and he does experiments on the fertilization of red clover by humblebees. Subsequent chapters find him making experimental observations on slave-making ants, beehive construction, hybrid fertility in the hollyhock, the effects of long sea-water immersion on some eighty-seven kinds of seeds, and the measurable differences between neonates and adults in several varieties of dogs, horses, and pigeons. From beginning to end, the *Origin of Species* is ripe with experiments, all of which carry a high index of reality. At the other extreme, however, are richly imaginative and, in themselves, rather implausible narrites – for instance, Darwin's tale of how whales might have evolved from bears that began swimming and catching insects in their open mouths (1859:184) – a story he quickly purged from the second edition of the *Origin*.

Darwin's implicit strategy, though, was to blur the distinction between narrites of an imaginative character that expressly made the case he wanted to advance but having a very low index of reality, with those of higher index. So, in chapter four, Darwin relates experiments he performed on the fertilization of holly trees and then immediately turns to what he calls an "imaginative case" of how the separation of sexes in plants might have evolved (1859:91-92). Most often, however, the slide from narrites of higher index to those of lower is accomplished silently and invisibly. So, for example, in the third chapter of the *Origin*, where he wishes to portray the "struggle for existence" in nature, Darwin imperceptibly moves down the scale. He first cites respected authorities on the fact of competition within nature, saying: "The elder De Candolle and Lyell have largely and philosophically shown that all organic beings are exposed to severe competition" (1859:62). He next tells of exacting observations of this: "In regard to plants, no one has treated this subject with more spirit and ability than W. Herbert, Dean of Manchester, evidently the result of his great horticultural knowledge" (1859:62). This citational narrite is then followed by a bridge sentence that suggests the struggle in nature is difficult to keep in mind. Then, with wonderful literary immediacy, Darwin begins another narrite, a concrete but imaginative instance:

> We behold the face of nature bright with gladness, we often see superabundance of food; we do not see, or we forget, that birds which are idly singing round us mostly live on insects or seeds, and are thus constantly destroying life; or we forget how largely these songsters, or their eggs, or their nestlings, are destroyed by birds and beasts of prey. (1859:62)

This is a narrite of intermediate reality. Finally, with the next sentence, Darwin moves to narrites that carry the theoretical burden of an important condition for natural selection, but which, if taken by themselves, would have a low index of historical reality:

> I should premise that I use the term Struggle for Existence in a large and metaphorical sense, including dependence of one being on another, and including (which is more important) not only the life of the individual, but success in leaving progeny. Two canine animals in a time of dearth, may be truly said to struggle with each other which shall get food and live. But a plant on the edge of a desert is said to struggle for life against the drought, though more properly it should be said to be dependent on the moisture. (1859:62)

Darwin continues this narrite with the story of the mistletoe whose seedlings may be said to struggle with other seedlings on the same branch of the tree on which they dwell, as well as with those of other plants; the seedlings, he urges, also compete to have birds disseminate their fruit. These derived senses of struggle – does mistletoe struggle, after all? – move up the index of reality because of their association with the earlier narrites of higher index.

Narrative Perspective and Authority

The narrator may make his or her presence felt by an explicit use of the first person personal pronoun, "I," as in "I think," "I believe," "I am well aware," and so on. Darwin's own "I" hovers around almost every page of his text, thus making us conscious of his presence, telling us of the experiments he conducted, the objections he encountered, and the many puzzles his theory solved for him. The explicit use of the first person pronoun suggests, however, that we have the view of a particular person, a given individual who may have a certain authority, but whose perspective is not absolute. Darwin seems to have realized this, especially as the objections to his theory became acute. Through the several later editions of the *Origin*, and particularly in the fifth (1869), he began eliminating the "I" and replacing it with the voice of passive facts. Thus, in the first chapter, phrases such as "I think it must be admitted" and "I think it could be shown that," by the fifth edition become "It must be admitted" and "It can be shown that" (Darwin [1869] 1959:89).[3] Darwin thus understood, at one level, the perspectival character of narrative, but while attempting to smooth over its ego-coarsened edges, he may not have appreciated that narrative still must reflect perspectively.

Whether or not the narrator makes an explicit appearance through the personal pronoun, he or she will yet project a story only sequentially and partially. Events cannot be made present in a narrative in their full character, but only from one perspective at a time. This is vividly illustrated in Akutagawa's story "Rashomon," in which the same events are depicted from the different points of view of several of the characters. Even in the *Origin of Species*, Darwin builds up a more complete picture of the actions of natural selection by describing at different times its several activities and connections: he first fixes one aspect of natural selection obscurely in the first chapter of the *Origin* when he tells of the creative formation of domestic stocks by breeders selecting for the best; he fixes another aspect when he describes the unconscious selection procedures of primitive folk, and thereby reduces the difference between the selections of unreflective nature and unreflective man; but then in chapter four, he contrasts man's selection, which is done to please him, with nature's selection, which is done for the good of the creature selected. And he continues to construct the perspectives on this force called "natural selection" throughout the book. Each new perspective relates a certain aspect of natural selection to yet new events and circumstances, weaving selection throughout the entire complex narrated. Finally, in the last chapter the ultimate perspective is achieved: natural selection is viewed as the creative medium by which God has shaped his world – a view to which I will return in a moment. The architectonic of Darwin's book thus displays an ever widening compass: from selection in respect of fluctuating and self-serving human interest, to selection in respect of normative and altruistic interests – namely, that of the good of each creature – finally to selection in respect of the interest of the universe, selection as a manifestation of Divine Providence. As Darwin's narrative continues to change and widen the perspective on selection, implicating it in an ever larger set of conditions, it becomes more than a currently operating cause in the world: it is a cause with narrative depth, and thus its meaning cannot be captured in a simple definition (such as "change of gene frequencies over time"), but only unravelled in a story, in a narrative of the sort that gave it life originally.

Narratives, as I have suggested, are radically perspectival and, because of that, radically incomplete. Even the omniscient Muse and infinitely fast word-processing Clio could not compose a history that contained all perspectives. This is because of the logic of narrative construction. A history which claimed to offer complete access to some past events because it contained all possible perspectives would have to mention all future events as well, since future events provide a perspective on the past events which produced them: for example, as a historian I study the young Darwin precisely from the perspective of his being the future author of the *Origin of Species*; I examine his early biological ideas with a view to their contribution to his yet-to-be formulated theory. The historian, just as the evolutionary biologist must, logically, investigate past events from the perspective of the future. And even now the reverberating influence of Darwin's early ideas may have diminished but hardly ceased. A history including all reliable perspectives could only be written at the end of time. But not even then, since, as Danto (1965:148-81) observes, it would have to mention itself as one of the future events, and then itself mentioning itself, and so on.

Beyond this imaginative consideration of how Clio might compose history, there are two deeper levels to the logic of narrative construction that require, logically require, the historian – and the evolutionary biologist – to investigate past events from the perspective of the future. First, the historian's and biologist's knowledge, ideas, categories, interests, and techniques are formed in the present; only from the present can one regressively move back in time to narrate past events, but always from the perspective of the knowledge, categories, and so on that stand in the future of those events, namely those learned at the knee of one's major professor. Second, the past contains an infinity of events; but to tell a coherent story, the historian, or evolutionary biologist, must select among them. Typically, he or she will have some central event to explain – chosen because of some present purpose and articulated using present knowledge. The central event, in its turn, will serve as a standard, a guide to pick out from the infinity of antecedent events those that had bearing on the central event, gave rise to it, and caused it. The biologist who wishes to understand the evolution of the mammalian auditory mechanism will use the structures of the incus, malleus, and stapes – that is, our current knowledge of those structures – to trace regressively their evolutionary source to the bones in the jaw of early reptiles. Those three little bones become the central augury that guides the trail into the past. Antecedent events, by their nature, are viewed from the perspective of what they produce, the central events; and central events are chosen in light of the researcher's current knowledge and aims.

This does not mean that the historian must forego the effort to understand the past on its own terms. On the contrary, the historian will attempt to cast a net of antecedent causes to fix some central event. The net must actually grasp the central event, capturing its distinctive features, before the historian can pull its significance into the future. On the other hand, it is well to remember that the precept to fly Whiggishness is one presently preached. The historian is inextricably part of his or her culture, not a creature that can freely transmigrate into the past.

Narrative authority might be regarded as one aspect of narrative perspective. Narratives derive their authority from two different sources: from the text and from the author. The authority of the text is simply a function of the index of reality that it manifests. The higher the index, the more authority we grant it. But texts with a low index might yet be given greater authority because of the author. The distinguished historian E. H. Carr exaggerated when, in his little book *What is History*, he admonished: "Study the historian before you begin to study the facts" (1961:26). But he had a point. Thus, for instance, immediately after publication, the *Origin of Species* already had authority by reason of Darwin's established reputation as a naturalist. Even those who were not completely convinced of the book's argument, yet took the book seriously, regarded it as having authority, because so accomplished a naturalist as Darwin had written it in his mature years.

The Temporal Dimensions of Narrative

Time sinks into narratives in four different ways. We need to distinguish the time of events, the time of narrated events, the time of narration, and the time of narrative construction.

The time of events and the time of narrated events. Implicitly coded in narrative is the duration of events in Newtonian time. We assume that events *in nature* exist in an ever-flowing, equitable time, with each unit comparable to every other. However, the temporal structuring of *narrated* events might be the very opposite of Newtonian. For instance, Harold Pinter's play "Betrayal" begins temporally at the end, the last few days of the time sequence. The next scene goes in the right temporal direction, taking place a few days later; but the third scene falls back to two years before, the fourth a year before that, scene five yet a year earlier, scenes six and seven jump forward a few days, and finally the last scene takes us to a period six years before the final days with which the play began. The audience, though carried back in time and then jolted a few days forward by the structure of the narrated events, yet never loses its temporal bearings, never comes to believe that the actual time of events moves backward or zigzags in the way the narrated events do. On the contrary, Pinter's temporal structuring achieves its purpose because the audience recognizes that events *really* trudge into the future at the same Newtonian pace.

For literature, the more familiar devices of altering the time of narrated events are the flashback, the recollection, and the time-repeat. Time-repeats occur when the depiction of the experiences of one character retraces the time already represented in the depiction of those of another character. These have their familiar counterparts in history and in historical science, as when, for instance, the paleontologist will first discuss the development of geological formations and then, in another section of the narrative, repeat the time sequence in describing the animals and plants that flourished during those geological periods.

Events run in real, Newtonian time; narrated events run in narrative time. Consider how Darwin uses this temporal disjuncture to dramatic effect in his chapter "On the Imperfections of the Geological Record." In order to grasp the long Newtonian time of evolution, he asks the reader to imagine a process occurring during just one period of geological time, that of the denudation of the Weald, the great sea-erosion of rock cliffs in the Kent-Surrey area. Darwin portrays the 500-foot cliffs being eaten away at the rate of one inch a century, and calculates the whole process to have taken 300 million years (1859:287). Darwin's narrative has reduced incomprehensible real time to graspable narrative time: the inch-by-inch destruction of rock walls squeezes real time into a narrative time that we can imagine. By the fifth edition (1869) of the *Origin*, however, Darwin had dramatically reversed this process of temporal compression. In the intervening period Lord Kelvin had calculated that the earth could be no more than about 200 million years old, apparently too small a period for evolution to have taken place. Wily Darwin in response employed a wonderful narrative device, now to expand time. He catches the reader with the observation that "Few of us, however, know what a million really means." He then, in that fifth edition, offers an illustration: "Take a narrow strip of paper," he says, "83 feet 4 inches in length, and stretch it along the wall of a large hall; then mark off at one end the tenth of an inch. This tenth of an inch will represent one hundred years, and the entire strip a million years." But in that tenth of an inch, "a measure utterly insignificant in a hall of the above dimensions," breeders will have introduced several new strains of animals (Darwin [1869] 1959:485-86). Natural selection, Darwin suggests, might be able to accomplish a great deal of work in a hall of 83 feet long. Darwin's narrative has expanded the time for events to occur while shrinking the objections of the physicists.

The time of narration. The time of narration is a less familiar device by which narratives restructure real time as well as narrated time. Consider two ways in which this can occur. The first is through contraction or expansion of sentence duration. At the beginning of his history, Thucydides economically expends a few paragraphs on events in Greece from the earliest times of Cretan hegemony to just before the outbreak of the war between Athens and Sparta – a period of about two thousand years. But he then devotes several hundred pages to the relatively brief twenty-year period of the war. In histories, centuries may be contracted into the space of a sentence, while moments may be expanded through hundreds of paragraphs.

In a given history, the time in sentences – that is, the duration of the writing and reading devoted to events – will serve as a rough index of importance assigned to those events. So in the *Origin*, for example, Darwin mentions four possible objections to his theory in four very short paragraphs, but spends the next 175 pages in answering them. Darwin's opponent St. George Jackson Mivart, in his book *On the Genesis of Species* (1871), reverses these proportions – the bulk of his pages expand the objections to Darwin's theory, and only a few paragraphs state positively what it is. Sir Charles Lyell, in his *Principles of Geology* (1830-1833), made the strategic mistake of devoting about the same amount of sentence time to the description of Lamarck's evolutionary theory as to his own objections to that theory. The slow dripping of sentences that presented Lamarck's theory wore away the resistance of Darwin, Wallace, and Spencer to the new ideas, hardly a consequence Lyell had intended.

A second less familiar way in which the time of narration alters representations of both Newtonian time and narrated time is through hiatus and juxtaposition. These are the temporal boundaries of the scenic property of narration: narratives are related in scenes, in temporal chunks. As a result Newtonian periods will occupy the break between scenes, in the hiatus. However, in the written text, there will be no hiatus, only the juxtaposition of one scene with another. For example, in Thucydides' *History*, Pericles' funeral oration – an encomium to the glories of Athenian city life, the virtues of its people, and the wonder of its laws – occurs at the beginning of winter of the war's first year. The paragraphs immediately after the oration, however, describe the outbreak of the terrible plague that devastated Athens during the following summer. This juxtaposition, with a hiatus of about six months, serves implicitly to contrast the image the Athenians had of themselves as the "school of Greece" with the reality of the plague, which unleashed their more primitive behavior and deeper instincts, upon which "no fear of god or law of man had a restraining influence" (1972:155).

The time of narrative construction. A fourth temporal dimension of narrative – one that differs from real time, the time of narrated events, and the time of narration – is the time of narrative construction. A narrative will be temporally layered by reason of its construction, displaying, as it were both a temporal horizon and a temporal depth.

First consider how the historian's own mode of research and writing will layer the narrative horizontally. Thucydides wrote the first part of his history toward the end of the war, when the awful, subsequent events allowed him to pick out and describe earlier events, however, now tinged with Athenian folly yet to come. Only the benefits of hindsight, for example, could have allowed him to put into the mouth of the Spartan messenger Melesippus, who was sent on a last desperate peace mission just before the first engagement of the war, the prophetic regret: "This day will be the beginning of great misfortunes to Hellas" (1972:131). By the horizontal ordering of time, in which the future temporally structures descriptions of the past, the historian can describe events in ways that the actors participating in the events could not: Melesippus's prophecy was possible only because Thucydides had already lived through it. Or, to take another example, when as a historian I write "In 1837 Darwin was working on his pre-Malthusian theories of species change," I construct (as Danto has argued) a distinctively narrative sentence that Darwin, in 1837, could not have uttered about himself. Likewise, when I describe Darwin's theory in 1859 as containing "residual Lamarckian features," I immediately contract time by linking an event or object with one long in the past – in this case, with both Lamarck the person and with Darwin's own early theories. With this temporal ordering, the narrative implicates past events with their antecedents in the yet more remote past and with their relational consequents in the future; events are lashed down by bindings to the past and the future. Such temporal disciplining forms a distinctively narrative understanding of the past. For real events, though they might carry the effects of their past with them, cannot bear the marks of their future; narrated events, by contrast, are scarred by the narrative tether that holds them secure to both past and future.

Narrative constructions not only stretch out along a temporal horizon, but their layers descend into the author's past, much like a column of sedimentary deposits. Consider, for example, Darwin's description in the *Origin* of the actions of natural selection in relation to man's selection:

> Man can act only on external and visible characters: nature cares nothing for appearances, except in so far as they may be useful to any being. She can act on every internal organ, on every shade of constitutional difference, on the whole machinery of life. Man selects only for his own good; Nature only for that of the being which she tends . . . It may be said that natural selection is daily and hourly scrutinising, throughout the world, every variation, even the slightest; rejecting that which is bad, preserving and adding up all that is good; silently and insensibly working, whenever and wherever opportunity offers, at the improvement of each organic being in relation to its organic and inorganic conditions of life. (1859:83-84)

Down through this strikingly important passage from chapter four of the *Origin*, finished in late 1858, we can plunge to layers immediately below, down to the draft chapter of his *Natural Selection* begun over a year earlier:

> He [man] selects only by the eye & acts therefore on external characters alone: he cannot perceive slight constitutional differences . . . He selects any peculiarity or quality which pleases or is useful to him, regardless whether it profits the being & whether it is the best possible adaptation to the conditions to which the being is exposed . . . See how differently Nature acts! By nature, I mean the laws ordained by God to govern the Universe. She cares not for mere external appearance; she may be said to scrutinise with a severe eye, every nerve, vessel & muscle; every habit, instinct, shade of constitution, – the whole machinery of the organisation. There will be here no caprice, no favouring: the good will be preserved & the bad rigidly destroyed, for good & bad are all exposed during some period of growth or during some generation, to a severe struggle for life. (1975:223-24)

And through this underlying passage one may yet bore down to the bedrock in the 1844 essay (and the immediately lower layer in the 1842 essay) in which natural selection is obviously modeled on the selections of an infinitely wise being, and then becomes a secondary cause in the divine plan:

> Let us now suppose a Being with penetration sufficient to perceive differences in the outer and innermost organization quite

imperceptible to man, and with forethought extending over
future centuries to watch with unerring care and select for any
object the offspring of an organism produced under the fore-
going circumstances; I can see no conceivable reason why he
could not form a new race . . . In accordance with the plan by
which this universe seems governed by the Creator, let us consider whether there exists any secondary means in the economy
of nature by which the process of selection could go on adapting, nicely and wonderfully, organisms, if in ever so small a
degree plastic, to diverse ends . . . Man selects chiefly by the
eye, and is not able to perceive the course of every vessel and
nerve, or the form of the bones, or whether the internal structure corresponds to the outside shape . . . Very differently does
the natural law of selection act . . . The selecting power is not
deceived by external appearances, it tries the being during its
whole life; and if less well adapted than its congeners, without
fail it is destroyed; every part of its structure is thus scrutinised
and proved good towards the place in nature which it occupies.
(1909:85, 87, 94, 95)

The vertical descent into the formation of the *Origin of Species* reveals an
unexpected genealogical connection. Natural selection, as depicted in the
Origin of Species, was fabricated out of the elements of Paley's Creator; and,
as we might expect, it still manifested divine powers in 1859: the natural
selection of the *Origin* gazes omnisciently into the core of living beings, so no
trait escapes its scrutiny; it acts altruistically, for the good of each creature,
and for the general good of the whole of nature; in Old Testament fashion,
it works over vast ages, slowly, constantly and as insensibly as time itself; and
out of the dark chaos of primitive life, it brings up progressively higher
forms. This is Paley's God in mufti.

Efficient and Final Causality in Narrative Accounts

Causality in nature. Four different levels of causality correspond to the
divisions of time associated with narrative explanations. Depending on your
metaphysical view, events in nature will have more or less necessary, productive ties to one another. Most would admit, I believe, that present events
radiate causally into the future in often incalculable ways. Our confidence in
prediction will fall off in direct logarithmic proportion to the distance pro-

jected, the complexity of the events, and (as a dimension of complexity) their responsiveness to circumstances. That is why the evolutionist cannot make many predictions of consequence. I should add, physicists are logically no better off; their projected systems are usually simpler and, as far as circumstances go, dead. They can no more accurately predict the exact trajectory of a falling leaf on a blustery Chicago day than Darwin could have divined the rise and evolutionary development of the HIV virus.

The causality of narrated events. By contrast to events in nature, events in a narrative display a different causal logic. When in 433 B.C. the Athenians of Thucydides' history interfered in an internal affair of Corinth, a Spartan ally, they could not have predicted that war would result – though they might have suspected; they certainly could not have predicted their ignominious defeat in the Sicilian campaign twenty years later. From inside of the scene that Thucydides has set, the future appears open; all things are possible, or at least unforeseeable. But each of his scenes moves inevitably and inexorably to that climax, which, as he portrayed it, was

> the greatest Hellenic action that took place during this war, and, in my opinion, the greatest action that we know of in Hellenic history – to the victors the most brilliant of successes, to the vanquished the most calamitous of defeats; for they were utterly and entirely defeated; their sufferings were on an enormous scale; their losses were, as they say, total; army, navy, everything was destroyed, and, out of many, only few returned. (1972:536-37)

From the period during which Thucydides actually composed his history, he could sight back and detect the steel tracks of causal necessity. He gazed into the past from the perspective of the central event – that is, the Sicilian campaign. That central event formed the final cause in light of which he regressively traced the antecedent, efficient causes and selected them out of an infinity of possible causes. From the perspective of the future, where the final cause lay, everything in the past was fixed, determined. And that final cause, the central event, became the beacon illuminating those causally efficient chains that led up to it. Now, when we read the story, from front to back, we sense both the freedom within the scenes and the constraint as we are pulled along the scenes to an inevitable future. It is precisely the magnetic strength of future resolution that constitutes a considerable part of the power of explanation.

Depending on the historian's narrative practice, the freedom within the scenes, those temporal chunks of action, will be more or less complete, as a function of the distinctively narrative sentences employed. That is, as the author writes those sentences that overtly anticipate the future – for example, when Thucydides' messenger foretells the sorrow in store for Hellas – a given scene will be more tightly fixed in its causal movement. But the strategy of an author may be to emphasize the possibilities. Martin Rudwick, in his *Great Devonian Controversy*, said he wished to write a history that was rigidly nonretrospective, which at each moment would keep the future open (1985:12-13). Within the scenes of his story he reduced the distinctively narrative sentences to a minimum, and thus at one level kept not only his actors, but his readers in the dark night of possibility. But Rudwick himself held a candle, and so each of his scenes only momentarily flutters without apparent direction: quickly enough it flies toward the preordained conclusion. Narratives, like evolved organisms, are created from chance – and necessity.

The causality of narration. The causality involved in narration, as opposed to narrative events, may take several forms, but I will only mention two. The first reflects those temporal hiatuses and scenic juxtapositions to which I have already referred. Thucydides will place one scene in which an action-motivating speech is made hard against another in which action is taken, even though the events themselves might be at fair temporal distance. This narrative design, or emplotment – as White (1987) uses the term – enforces Thucydides' conceit that the deliberation of the speechmakers caused the ensuing action, though frequently, as the ironic historian portrays it, the ensuing action was not what the speechmakers had anticipated. And then there are the subtler ways the actual text causally operates. Consider, for example, Gibbon's *Decline and Fall of the Roman Empire*. As Gibbon begins to describe those outposts at greater distance from Rome, the center of the empire and Gibbon's concern, his sentences grow longer. Or, as another object lesson, we have the work of the great French historian and stylist,

Jean Fontenelle, who remarked that had the cadences of his sentences demanded it, the Thirty Years War would have turned out differently. Those who write history, evolutionary or otherwise, know that Fontenelle's observations have weight.

The causality of narrative construction. By the causality of narrative construction, I mean those several factors that lead the historian – and historical biologist – to attack a particular problem, to give shape to the history in a particular way, to aim at certain conclusions. David Hume said he wrote for literary fame. Erasmus Darwin, Charles's grandfather, took the higher Scottish road; he didn't write for fame but, as he explained, for money. Some biologists, especially the natural theologians whom Darwin read, wrote to justify God's ways to man. Contemporary sociologists of science have discussed such motivations (and others due to class interests and economic benefit), though they often obscure another motivation and another causal source of the shape of narrative science: the motive simply to describe accurately the workings of nature present and of nature past, and to explain the links between the two. This motivation will often be servant to others – the quest for fame, for instance; but these lower motives might, in fact, be most easily achieved when the realistic motive operates. Acting on this latter motive, the passion to give a precise and truthful account, especially as it requires the gathering of evidence, the attention to argument, the careful pursuit of theory, allows the shaping hand of the past, in the form of evidence and its rational organization, to supply the scenes which the historian, in light of central events, will select and craft into his or her narrative.

Explanation in History and Science

The Hempelian model of explanation, as well as the Popper-Lakatos demand for dramatic corroboration, assumes a symmetry between explanation and prediction. Insofar as history and historical biology can make few predictions of any significance, they are dismissed as sciences because of the explanatory impotency that seems entailed by their predictive failures. Many contemporary philosophers of history (e.g., Hayden White, Paul Ricoeur, and

Hans Georg Gadamer)[4] accede to this dismissal. These postmodern philosophers agree, history is not science; but, they urge, history's explanatory techniques are no less legitimate. They defend against the hubris of science (rather, of unregenerate philosophers of science) by adding their bricks to the wall between science and the historical disciplines, and then declaring a new sovereign power of explanation. But a more careful examination of the supposed failure of history to exhibit the predictive force assumed in science will, I believe, begin to open a breech in this distinction. When the barriers are down, we will see, not that historical narrative fails as a scientific explanation, but that much of science succeeds only as historical narrative.

First, consider the level of narrative detail the historical disciplines require. If I were a historian living in the 1830s and attempted to predict the fate of early evolutionary ideas, a safe forecast would be the Mammet-like "Something will happen in regard to them." But history demands a detailed description of events; nothing so vacuous would be tolerated. A riskier though reasonable guess might be that evolutionary ideas would be entertained only by inexperienced naturalists and would never take hold in the scientific community. Reasonable, but disastrously wrong. The problem is that as a historian, it is not that I do not have at my disposal appropriate laws or causal conditions, but that I neither know which laws are relevant nor what the antecedent causal conditions might be (also the position of the physicist of the Chicago leaf). Human ingenuity presents a huge number of possibly relevant laws and the universe extends an infinity of possibly relevant antecedent causal conditions. Precisely what is missing is a central event described at an exacting level of detail that might serve as the final cause for selecting the relevant antecedent conditions and, as will be discussed in a moment, the narrative principles that may be used to help construct and justify an explanation. Once the central event has occurred and the historian fixes it out in appropriate detail, then, of course not prediction, but narrative explanation can be formed, narratives of peculiar explanatory power.

Central events and antecedent causes together determine for the historian what principles or lawlike generalizations may be available for later justification of an explanation. The nomological-deductive model regards laws as the unproblematic given of scientific explanation. When Hempel describes the necessary and sufficient elements of an explanation, he begins with the assumption that the antecedent conditions and general laws lie ready to hand. But let us consider a typical historical event that awaits explanation, such as Darwin's discovery of natural selection.

To construct an explanation of Darwin's discovery, the historian must first give the principle of natural selection the relevant, historically bound expression – not of course, "change of gene frequencies over time," our current way of putting it, nor even the various descriptions of it in the *Origin of Species*, though they will provide a guide, but the several paragraphs in Darwin's *Notebook D*, where the principle appears first to stand out. Among the sentences that reveal his new insight, the historian finds:

> I do not doubt, every one till he thinks deeply has assumed that increase of animals exactly proportional to the number that can live. – We ought to be far from wondering of changes in number of species, form small changes in nature of locality. Even the energetic language of . . . Decandoelle does not convey the warring of species as inference from Malthus . . . One may say there is a force like a hundred thousand wedges trying force into every kind of adapted structure into the gaps in the oeconomy of Nature, or rather forming gaps by thrusting out weaker ones. The final cause of all this wedging, must be to sort out proper structure & adapt it to change. ([1838] 1987:374-75)

Of course, the historian can recognize this as the event that needs explaining only by having regressively moved from a vaguely similar expressions of natural selection in the *Origin of Species* back to this passage in *Notebook D*. It is precisely this regressive move that is required in order to get to the most proximate event to be explained. The intellectual historian regards the passages in the *Origin* as the final cause that conceptually focuses the regressive selection of earlier stages, in this case, of the "same" idea. Then the passage in the notebook, in turn, also serves as a final cause by which to determine the antecedent causes that could produce such a passage. But this explanandum event, unlike the standard examples – such as to explain why an object conducts electricity – must needs send the historian in several different directions; for such a complex event as the *Notebook* passage will have many causes, which will have to be weighted to distribute their relative importance in causing Darwin's idea of natural selection. This weighing of causes is an absolute requirement for constructing an adequate explanation. If the historian mentioned as a significant cause of Darwin's idea that he was born in 1809, such that he could ship out on the *Beagle*, we would judge this, of course, to be a cause, but one not worth mentioning, nor significant in the production of the theory of natural selection.

But in this example, let us simply focus on the standard account given Darwin's theory – namely, that he read Malthus's *Essay on Population*. And let us grant that the reading of Malthus is a perfectly good explanation, at least for our purposes here. What, then, is the law which binds the reading of Malthus with the discovery of natural selection? Obviously it cannot be any law or lawlike generalization such as: if one reads Malthus, one discovers natural selection. Nor could the principle be even so particular as: if Darwin reads Malthus, he discovers natural selection. Darwin could have perused Malthus at other times – for example, while he was at Edinburgh – and he would not have discovered natural selection. Nor, finally, could it be a principle such as: if Darwin reads Malthus on September 28, 1838, he discovers natural selection. That principle is hardly lawlike – it merely re-describes the event. The shrewd historian, when called on *to justify the account*, can usually formulate a generalization, perhaps to the effect: "When one finds ideas in a person's papers that are similar to those in documents that the person read earlier, those ideas were caused by the earlier reading, *ceteris paribus*." But even this won't exactly do, for Darwin actually read a précis of Malthus in Paley's *Natural Theology* (n.d.:479) – some eight years earlier, while still at university – without the immediate consequence of discovering natural selection (though this would be the sort of remote cause – a softening agent – a historian would wish to include in the explanation). Moreover, the operative phrase "similar to" will cover a multitude of historical discriminations; it simply lacks the precision required for any expression of a law. Finally, in order to invoke such a generalization, the historian must know several things that only a partially constructed narrative can provide – for example, that Darwin read Malthus at the "right time," that he was the sort of individual on whom reading would make an impression, and would make the right impression at a certain stage in his mental development. Thus, the historian must construct, at least in working imagination, a rather full narrative, one with a definite temporal structure – *before* any generalization of the sort here suggested could possibly be invoked. And in the written account, the historian must provide a narrative that situates Darwin as a reader of Malthus: the narrative must reconstruct a Malthus passage to make it "similar to" a Darwin passage; and it must make Darwin the kind of person for whom, at a particular time, such reading could have consequence – that is, the narrative must have brought Darwin to the point where the problem of species-transforming adaptation requires a dynamic of population pressure to complete the idea of natural selection. Without the context of the surrounding narrative – both in the construction of the account and in its expression – no such commonplace generalization, as here suggested, could be appealed to. In short, the selection and employment of justifying generalizations depend on narrative rather than the reverse – and this is exactly contrary to the assumption of the nomological-deductive model. For that model supposes that an antecedent cause or causes *as such* might be joined to an explanandum without the prior shaping of those causes in a narrative mold.

Historians (and biologists) construct narrative explanations and readers accept them usually without explicit invocation of generalizations. To be sure, when challenged, the historian might resort to such generalizations to defend the narrative explanation; but to explain something is altogether a logically different activity than to justify its explanation. Lawlike generalizations usually only play a role in the latter, not the former. Here again, the Hempelian model differs from the narrative model.

It might still be objected, though, that laws and generalizations glue narrated events together. So historians, it will be urged, must antecedently, though silently, utilize them in constructing their narratives and readers must antecedently, albeit implicitly, apply them to appreciate the cogency of the history told. This objection is telling, for there is a sense in which principles of a special sort add their strength to the temporal structure of narrative to hold events together. But these are not usually "laws," in any of the conventional senses of that term. I will discuss these "principles of narrative knowledge," as they may be called, in a moment. I can mention now, though, some simple logical considerations that demonstrate laws to have primacy neither in historical nor in natural scientific explanations. Laws, as commonly understood, of course, will occupy an important place in the narrative strategies of some disciplines (e.g., cosmology) more than in others.

In history, as I have tried to illustrate above, the application of even commonplace generalizations depends on an already established narrative framework. Initially the historian will reconstruct the antecedent events in light of a central event, but will do so in the first instance by simply gathering as much as can be known about the events in closest temporal contiguity to the central event, first sifting them in light of the features of that central event. This sifting will yield antecedent events of two general types: those that are earlier stages of the central event (as when the historian moves from Darwin's expression of natural selection in the *Origin* to its earlier formulation in the *Notebooks*); or those that are not stages of the central event, but possible agents of its production (as the reading of Malthus would be). Earlier stages are isolated by reason of temporal relations and, most importantly, by reason of similarity of pattern. A regressive stage-analysis might well bring the historian to a very early developmental phase that bears little resemblance to its end, in which case the series of alterations would stretch back along a determinate temporal path, with proximate similarities fading into remote differences. No recognizably empirical laws, I believe, would be required for such historical reconstruction.

Now for the other kind of antecedent events, those producing alterations in the central event or in the various stages leading up to it. Such modifying events, again in the first instance, must be recognized by the historian as having three features that only an embryonic narrative can invest them with: (a) the required temporal relation to central events; (b) the right weight (i.e., an inchoate narrative must have already situated the antecedent event among other impinging events and given it priority); and, if they are to be connected to the central event by any general principles, (c) the appropriate level of generality – since laws relate one general kind of event to another and only indirectly one particular instance of a general kind to another (a crucial consideration, which I will develop in a moment). Only after a burgeoning narrative has invested the central event and a potential antecedent modifier with such features can the historian (usually tacitly) invoke a general principle. The reader, for whom the central event is explained, will likewise depend on the narrative up to that point to demonstrate that the antecedent event is temporally, weightily, and generally relevant before any tacit understanding of laws might be engaged to join such antecedent event with a central event. In practice, the historian – and reader – will recognize lawlike generalizations only after events have been laid out in temporal sequence and understood immediately as productive.

What is the character of lawlike generalizations that historians typically employ? They are usually not the sort, of course, found cataloged in science textbooks. Consider, now, another version of the principle that might link, for historian or reader, Darwin's discovery with his reading of Malthus. Having first described, explicitly or implicitly, the passage from *Notebook D*, and then having taken into account the mention of Malthus in that passage, the historian would likely turn to Malthus's first *Essay on Population*. What urges such recourse (aside from Darwin's own indication of Malthus as the cause) is indeed knowledge, but not what one would ordinarily call a law. It is the knowledge that in the past, great (and not so great) thinkers have had their important ideas immediately formed by reading predecessors. Not every great theory has this source; nor does a scientist's reading always lead to significant discovery; nor could the historian or reader even begin to offer any statistical expression of the relation of a scientist's reading to the formulation of a significant theory. But the historian knows of cases – that is, has narrative knowledge – that this has happened, and so considers that Darwin might be another like instance. Formation of an historiographic hypothesis of this sort thus arises from previous "narrative" knowledge – that is, awareness of particular episodes in which the causal relationship in question has obtained (e.g., Aquinas's reading of Aristotle, Descartes' reading of Galen, or Spencer's reading of Lyell's reading of Lamarck). The reader of the Darwinian history being constructed will also have at his or her disposal comparable narrative knowledge, and so will be persuaded, if the narrative is tight, that Darwin's reading of Malthus had analogous consequences. Thus the principle that might confirm the tie between the antecedent event and the central event is not a law, not even a lawlike generalization. It is knowledge of previous narrative episodes that parade through imagination in their numbers.

The chief reason for demoting the importance of laws in narrative accounts is the particularity of events. Only Darwin discovered natural selection and only once – if by natural selection we mean those particular ideas recorded on 28 September 1838 in his *Notebook D*. Particular events always outstrip laws and commonplace generalizations, which, therefore, cannot give an account of such events in their narrative immediacy. Any invocation of laws requires a redescription of events, so as to make them repeatable, universal phenomena – exactly the sort of things historians usually only subsequently construct. That is why no law (or set of laws) could logically or convincingly derive, say, Darwin's notebook passage from his particular reading of Malthus. However, the temporalized narrative (rather than the legalized deduction) does relate particular antecedent events to particular central events; the grammar of narrative makes the several, time-bound antecedent events productive of the particularized central event. If challenged about whether the reading of Malthus had any effect on Darwin, the historian might repair to the principle of narrative knowledge that I have mentioned in order to justify the narrative (and he or she would certainly offer as well a number of other reasons – e.g., that Darwin was the sort of person who would be susceptible to such reading, that he himself isolated Malthus as the key, etc.).

At each stage in the construction of a narrative explanation (and in the reader's appreciation of its potency), the already established story serves as the context for arranging the further causes and implicitly securing any generalizations or previous narrative cases – which themselves must be chosen from a myriad. The several temporal and causal dimensions that I have briefly described above provide the structural frame upon which further elements of the story are arranged. And as the narrative builds, it squeezes time in a variety of ways, so that antecedent causes, though perhaps really remote, are drawn close to the central events whose explanation they provide. The varieties of narrative time shrink the proximity until the logical relation of *post hoc ergo propter hoc* is no longer a fallacy but virtually the very principle of narrative explanation. For the reader discovers the simple generalizations or narrative analogues implicated in the story only after the grammar of narrative performs its task, that is, only after prior events are perceived to lead up to the central events. Narratives enmesh central events in causal networks that fix them with inevitability. It is the mesh that explains the event, and thus traps the reader's assent. Only later might the historian or reflective reader spin out the huge number of simple generalizations or analogous cases in justification of the narrative explanation, if need be. The events themselves are justified, that is, explained, by the entangling skein of antecedents and consequences drawn tight by the shrinking of time. A successful narrative makes us first understand that the central events fell into time with inescapable necessity. The temporal contraction and causal bindings of narrative, the web of events in light of which generalizations and similar cases could be adduced are precisely what is missing from an anemic nomological-deductive explanation sketch.

One might suppose that though the Hempelian model is inadequate for history and evolutionary science, it yet captures the essence of explanation in other sciences that seek to explain events in time. But I believe it fails even there and at best can only provide narrative sketches. To demonstrate briefly this failure, consider the example that Hempel uses to explain his model of explanation. In his essay "The Function of General Laws in History," he poses the following as an adequate explanation, against which inadequate historical narratives may be judged:

> Let the event to be explained consist in the cracking of an automobile radiator during a cold night. The sentences of group (1) may state the following initial and boundary conditions: The car was left in the street all night. Its radiator, which consists of iron, was completely filled with water, and the lid was screwed on tightly. The temperature during the night dropped from 39^0 F. in the evening to 25^0 F. in the morning; the air pressure was normal. The bursting pressure of the radiator material is so and so much. Group (2) would contain empirical laws such as the following: Below 32^0 F., under normal atmospheric pressure, water freezes. Below 39.2^0 F., the pressure of a mass of water increases with decreasing temperature, if the volume remains constant or decreases ... From statements of these two kinds, the conclusion that the radiator cracked during the night can be deduced by logical reasoning; an explanation of the considered event has been established. ([1942] 1965:232)

Two observations may be made about this explanation. First, the antecedent conditions and the laws are here stipulated. But in real explanations, these explanans-items must be narratively constructed, and their likelihood established thereby. That is, the task of the explanation is principally to establish the narrated events that lead up to the central event to be explained. These antecedent events must then reduce the temporal gaps between themselves and the central event. It is the temporal constriction that does the explaining, not any formal deduction. At most, the formal reconstruction, with isolation of relevant laws, would aid (yet alone be insufficient) in justifying the narrative. Second, Hempel presumes that it is the "deducing" of the explanandum event (the cracked radiator) that *is the explaining*. The "deducing," however, can be shown quite easily not to be "the explaining." Consider what Hempel left out of his example (which is now my example, born of a Chicago existence). He failed to mention that the owner of the car, a nice new Porsche, had owed a debt to his bookie. And further, something the Chicago ambiance makes one sensitive to, that the passenger door had jimmy marks on it, and that the hood release had been pulled; and, with these now directing our attention to other possible trails of antecedent causes, we also find impact marks on the radiator. Now the real explanation stands clear. Right after the car was parked in front of the owner's house, a juice-man walked up, jimmied the car door to release the hood, and while the radiator was still under pressure, he walloped it with his sledgehammer, and a large crack immediately appeared – thus was left a message about prompt repayment of debts. In other words, Hempel's original statements of the boundary or antecedent conditions and the laws could well be true – and hence the statement of the event could be *correctly deduced* – yet the event would *not be correctly explained*. Thus, under the Hempelian conditions, we could have a correct deduction but an incorrect explanation – which is logically impossible if the "deducing" is the "explaining."

For us to be convinced that the explanans makes the explanandum happen we must also be persuaded that some proposed boundary conditions are the relevant ones. In artificial situations – that is, when a Hempelian textbook asks us simply to accept the adequacy of the boundary conditions and laws – we might come to believe that it is the deductive connection between explanans and explanandum that does the trick. Explanations in the Hempelian style must assert the laws and conditions without giving an account either of their relevance or truth. We stand convinced by jejune nomological-deductive explanations only to the degree that we, as readers, are able to pump narrative blood into them by imagining a story that secures both the relevant conditions and appropriate laws – a story that has the essential feature of bringing the antecedent events temporally tight against the event to be explained.

Narrative understanding is causal understanding: we explain, and thus understand, an event in relation to its causes. But narrative understanding flows beyond the causally efficient. To understand an event, as Aristotle knew, requires one to trace its consequences as well: for a thing is what it becomes. Hence, to understand central events, we must not only regressively track down their efficient causes, but we also must follow out their consequences – what they become. In constructing a narrative explanation, we must, willy-nilly, begin in the present; so in sliding back to the event we wish to explain, we simultaneously regress along the path that leads back from the future. Then in telling of the tale, the historian will move beyond the central event to indicate, at least in fading fashion, the consequences that emerge from the occurrence of the central event. The historian will limn the future of that central event, which is really the trail he or she has followed back from the present moment. The narrative traps central events both by its temporally antecedent causes and its temporally consequent effects. The nomological model fails to heed Aristotle's final causes.

By way of summary, let me mention the crucial differences between the nomological-deductive model and the narrative model of explanation.

1. The logic of narrative construction cannot be separated from the logic of narrative explanation: the description of the central event guides the historian back along the tracks of the possible antecedent events, so as to secure those that might be pulled up to that central event. The fixing of the antecedent events is the fixing of the explanatory causes, while the path from the future (where the historian writes) lays down the telic causes – what the central events will have become. The narrative sentences employed within scenes and the linkages among scenes enmesh central events, then, in a web whose anchors grapple the past and the future of those central events. The nomological-deductive model begins with a stipulation of antecedents and laws, not their establishment in the work of explanation itself, and it performs an *explicatio interrupta* – no conceptual consequences emerge.

2. As antecedent events are sifted and related to the central events which they explain, a weighting occurs. Historical events, after all, are multi-

ply caused; indeed, in a sense all events prior to the central event could be causally related to the central event. Thus the historian must choose among antecedent events in order to give the most cogent, compelling, and causally tight story possible. Events must be weighed and placed within the narrative, so as to provide differential narrative power. Hempel's model ignores the requirement of such weighting.

3. The Hempelian model begins with antecedent causes and relevant laws. The narrative model establishes the antecedent events, supports them, and, through the guidance of central events and temporal contractions, attempts to fix their relevance. In history, biology, and the natural sciences, explanation must demonstrate, not what *might be* the causes of certain central events, but what *are* the causes.

4. The explanatory burden in narrative rests on the temporal binding of antecedent events to central events. The juxtaposition of those antecedent events, by reason of the grammar of narrative explanation, makes central events understandable, reasonable, even inevitable. In the Hempelian case, it is the logical derivation, not the temporal derivation, that carries the power. However, for a formal, logical derivation, lawlike generalizations must be explicitly employed among the explanans items. In the narrative model, principles that may work within the temporal boundaries of a partially constructed narrative to suggest directions for tracking down relevant antecedent events (and subsequently justify them as the cause of central events) – these are principles of narrative knowledge, not laws as the philosopher of science knows them. And such principles – or other generalizations – will usually be explicitly and formally used, post hoc, to justify the narrative.

The Origin of Species as an Opaque Narrative

I have claimed that Darwin's *Origin of Species* is a narrative, despite appearances to the contrary. My justification is simply that if a work displays the elements and logic of a narrative, then it is one. I believe the features of narrative are just as present in the *Origin* as, say, in James Joyce's *Finnegan's Wake* – we simply take it for granted that a novelist writes a narrative novel.

Darwin is not a novelist, so the presumption of narrative form is not urged upon us. The *Origin of Species* is not, of course, an obvious narrative; it is an opaque narrative. This is because the central event – namely, the origin and proliferation of species in nature, from those first few forms into which life was breathed to the endless forms most beautiful and most wonderful that cover the globe – this central event lies hovering far behind the immediate events, imagined and real, that stand in the foreground of the text. That more remote, central event appears on the horizon of the small narrative episodes – the narrites, as I have called them – and lingers there, coming forward most dramatically only in the closing paragraphs of the book. The more remote the central event, the more opaque thus will be the narrative. In explanation sketches offered by the nomological-deductive pattern, the central events may be focused, but the flesh of the narrative must be supplied through the reader's imagination. With opaque narratives, the flesh is there, often in abundance, but the central event, the organizing principle stands in the distance.

In the concluding chapter of the *Origin of Species*, Darwin reflected briefly on the profound alteration he had introduced into the study of life. "When we no longer look," he mused,

> at an organic being as a savage looks at a ship, as at something wholly beyond his comprehension; when we regard every production of nature as one which has had a history . . . how far more interesting, I speak from experience, will [our] study . . . become! (1859:485-86)

Darwin was surely right.

Acknowledgments

Since the original delivery of this paper at the Field Museum Spring Systematics Symposium, I have attempted to persuade other recalcitrant audiences. In particular I am grateful to the members of the Department of History and Philosophy of Science at Cambridge University, to the University of Chicago's Human Sciences Workshop, and to George Reisch and Lawrence Rothfield for trying to force me to reduce obscurity.

Notes

1. Hempel recognizes two kinds of scientific laws, deterministic and statistical. The form of explanation will be the same when either kind of law serves as part of an explanans.

2. Although Thucydides claimed to have begun his history at the very outbreak of the war, we know from internal evidence that he actually began the composition much later. Undoubtedly he kept notes, though, throughout the period of the war. See Rawlings 1981.

3. Louise Wilkerson (1990) called this to my attention.

4. See Hayden White's (1987) discussion of this issue.

References

Berkhofer, R. 1989. "Narrative and the Structure of History." Lecture delivered to the History of Human Sciences Workshop, November, University of Chicago.

Carr, E. H. 1961. *What is History*. New York: Vintage Books.

Danto, A. 1965. *Analytical Philosophy of History*. New York: Columbia University Press.

Darwin, C. 1859. *On the Origin of Species*. London: Murray.

Darwin, C. [1869] 1959. *The Origin of Species by Charles Darwin: A Variorum Text*. Ed. M. Peckham. Philadelphia: University of Pennsylvania Press.

Darwin, C. 1909. *The Foundations of the Origin of Species: Two Essays Written in 1842 and 1844 by Charles Darwin*. Ed. F. Darwin. Cambridge: Cambridge University Press.

Darwin, C. 1975. *Charles Darwin's Natural Selection: Being the Second Part of his Big Species Book Written from 1856 to 1858*. Ed. R. C. Stauffer. Cambridge: Cambridge University Press.

Darwin, C. 1987. *Charles Darwin's Notebooks, 1836-1844*. Ed. P. Barrett et al. Ithaca: Cornell University Press.

Darwin, C. 1988. Darwin's reading notebooks, appendix 4. In *The Correspondence of Charles Darwin*, vol. 4: *1847-1850*, ed. F. Burkhardt et al. Cambridge: Cambridge University Press.

Hacking, I. 1983. *Representing and Intervening*. Cambridge: Cambridge University Press.

Hempel, C. [1942] 1965. The function of general laws in history. In *Aspects of Scientific Explanation*, C. Hempel. New York: Free Press.

Lakatos, I. 1978. *The Methodology of Scientific Research Programmes: Philosophical Papers of Imre Lakatos*. Vol. 1. Cambridge: Cambridge University Press.

Lyell, C. 1830-1833. *The Principles of Geology*. 3 vols. London: Murray.

Mivart, St. G. J. 1871. *On the Genesis of Species*. New York: Appleton.

Paley, W. N.d. Natural theology. In *Works of William Paley, D.D.* Philadelphia: Woodward.

Popper, K. 1974. Darwinism as a metaphysical research program. In *The Philosophy of Karl Popper*, ed. P. Schilpp. LaSalle, IL: Open Court.

Popper, K. 1978. Natural selection and the emergence of mind. *Dialectica* 32:339-55.

Popper, K. [1944] 1966. *The Poverty of Historicism*. 3d ed. New York: Harper Torchbooks.

Rawlings, H. 1981. *The Structure of Thucydides' History*. Princeton: Princeton University Press.

Rudwick, M. 1985. *The Great Devonian Controversy*. Chicago: University of Chicago Press.

Thucydides. 1972. *History of The Peloponnesian War*. Trans. Rex Warner. New York: Penguin Books.

White, H. 1987. *The Content of the Form*. Baltimore: Johns Hopkins University Press.

Wilkerson, L. 1990. The Shift of Perspectives through the Six Editions of the *Origin of Species*. B.A. thesis, University of Chicago.

What's So Special about the Past?

Rachel Laudan

During the past half-dozen years, a number of biologists have become intrigued by analogies between history and their own discipline. Spurred by the problems of reconstructing phylogenies, they have asked whether biologists might find solutions to these problems in the historical literature (O'Hara 1988a, 1988b). For centuries, after all, historians have been professionally concerned with reconstructing the past and have done so with considerable success. Surely biologists could benefit from this experience, or so the argument goes.

I shall counter by suggesting that the initially plausible program of turning to history to learn how to deal with the biological past is misconceived, resting as it does on a couple of tacit assumptions that on careful examination turn out to be problematic. The program assumes first, that all investigations of the past share certain common features that set them off from other kinds of inquiry, and second, that philosophy of history is the best guide to these features. Because it can be more quickly dealt with I shall start with the second of these assumptions.

Turning to the philosophy of history to find out what has been discovered about ways to reconstruct the past seems only natural. If nothing else, what has been written on the philosophy of history far outweighs what has been written on all the other historical sciences combined. Indeed, apart from history, the only historical science to have received any methodological attention at all has been geology (Kitts 1977; Laudan 1987). But the lessons to be learned from philosophy of history are much more limited than might at first sight appear. To begin with, philosophers of history struggle with a number of problems that are quite irrelevant to biologists. Prominent among these are how to handle human intentions and how to cope with the absence of a good causal theory of human behavior, problems that history shares with the social sciences but not with biology. Biology after all does not deal with intentions and in evolutionary theory it already possesses some rather good causal hypotheses. More important though, philosophers of history are preoccupied with the nature of historical explanation, particularly narrative explanation. Beginning in the 1940s Carl Hempel claimed that historical explanations were sketchy versions of explanations in the natural sciences (Hempel [1942] 1965, 1962). According to his deductive-nomological model, scientific explanations worked by deducing what was to be explained from general laws, and historical explanations differed chiefly in the degree of explicitness of the laws invoked. This sparked an intense debate amongst philosophers of history. Many, perhaps most, cognizant of history's roots in literature and the humanities, and its fierce independence from the social sciences in spite of the reconciliatory moves of social and economic historians, rejected the idea that history was nothing more than embryonic science and insisted that history differed from science in fundamental ways (see papers in Dray 1966). In the years since, philosophers of history have continued to debate whether the structure of explanation in history is or is not the same as the structure of explanation in the natural sciences, frequently identifying narrative explanation as characteristic of history and questioning whether it can be reduced to deductive-nomological or statistical explanation (Danto 1985; White 1965; Richards this volume).

This debate was initiated fifty years ago and since then philosophers of history, with a few honorable exceptions (Mandelbaum 1977; Roth 1988, 1989) have failed to keep pace with change in cognate disciplines. For example, philosophers of history still take recent political and diplomatic history as their prime examples, oblivious of the fact that much of the best and most methodologically sophisticated historical scholarship in the last quarter century has been in other areas such as economic and social history. This would not matter were it not for the fact that, as we shall shortly see, political and diplomatic history are perhaps the branches of history furthest removed from the problems biologists encounter when they try to reconstruct the past. Furthermore, philosophers of history have not incorporated the results of the extensive research on theory of explanation carried out since Hempel's pioneering work, research that might significantly alter their analysis of history (surveyed in Kitcher and Salmon 1989). Nor is that all, for in their enthusiasm for questions of explanation, philosophers of history have neglected other active research areas in the philosophy of science such as realism, theories of scientific change, and validation, that are equally relevant to history. The latter is particularly important because what is driving the biologists' interest in philosophy of history is, I believe, not a question of explanation but of epistemology, not a question of the form their theories take but of whether they are reliable and well-founded, that is to say, questions of validation. Biologists want strategies for reconstructing the past as reliably as possible in situations of incomplete information. Of course, theories of explanation demand that the components of the explanation are well warranted. But most discussions of historical explanation are much more concerned with form and with the differences in form between historical and nonhistorical explanation than they are with warrant. In sum, there are reasons to be suspicious about turning to philosophy of history in its present state for guidance about reconstructing the biological past.

But even if this were not so, and philosophy of history once again became a significant branch of philosophy, I would have qualms about assuming its relevance to biologists interested in the past without further question. This is not because I think history is unscientific. On the contrary I am completely convinced that history is (or should be) scientific. Rather, it is because I doubt that the historical sciences share common features that distinguish them from the other sciences. To explain why I shall broaden the discussion beyond history to include all the sciences that deal with the past – the "historical sciences" as I shall term them since the word "history" is generally restricted to human history. Historical sciences are far commoner than is generally recognized, perhaps because the accidents of the organization of modern universities mask their ubiquity. Cosmogony, for example, has always found its home in departments of physics and astronomy. Large parts of paleontology have been housed in geology departments, not in biology departments, because through most of the nineteenth and twentieth centuries geologists found their results crucial while biologists found them peripheral. Archaeology and anthropology are relatively new disciplines without well-established niches in the university structure. But once we appreciate the range of historical sciences, then it makes sense to ask whether biologists might not learn as much about reconstructing the past from geologists, archaeologists, or cosmogonists as from historians.

To structure my discussion of the historical sciences, I shall borrow a way of analyzing them from the great Victorian philosopher of science, William Whewell, aware that doing so opens me to the charge that my philosophy of the historical sciences is even more outdated than that of the philosophers of history. I believe the choice is justified, however, on a number of grounds. Whewell was the first, and thus far the last, philosopher of science to pay attention to all the historical sciences, not just history itself. As a former President of the Geological Society of London and colleague at Trinity College, Cambridge of the leading historians of the day, he was intimately familiar with the best contemporary practice in the historical sciences. And he was much more interested in validation than in explanation. So while his analysis of the historical sciences (or as Whewell termed them, the palaetiological sciences) will doubtless need to be modified, it provides a good starting point. Among them he numbered geology, paleontology, cosmogony, philology, and what we would term archaeology and history. He took geology as his main example, a move that I shall copy, and distinguished three tasks for such a historical science (1837, 3: 402-3): "the Description of the facts and phenomena; – the general Theory of the causes of change appropriate to the case; – and the Application of the theory to the facts." These he called respectively "descriptive geology," "geological dynamics," and "physical geology."

As any scientist knows, description of a domain is not easy. As I see it, descriptive geology faces two major problems: first, how to identify and individuate its basic units or entities; and second, how to determine the relations between those units. Nineteenth-century stratigraphers, for example, had to establish the existence and significance of their units and devise means of detecting and observing them, particularly in the many cases where the record is imperfectly preserved, even before determining their relationships. Only after long debate did they decide that the "formation" – all the rocks laid down in a given period – was the appropriate unit for reconstructing the past (Laudan 1987). They knew full well that most western European rocks were inaccessible to observation over most of their extent. They recognized that since lithology also reflected environmental conditions, it was not an entirely reliable guide to the period in which a rock was deposited. Identifying and individuating formations thus turned out to be a sophisticated task involving evidence from lithology, paleontology and other disciplines. Similar difficulties were encountered in other historical sciences. Scientists recognized fossils as the remains of living beings only after centuries of arguments and counterarguments. Geophysicists found global geomagnetic reversals so improbable and so dependent on sophisticated instrumentation that they subjected both the concept and the instruments to severe scrutiny before accepting them in the mid-1960s. Scholars regarded chipped stones with skepticism for years before they were prepared to grant that they had been manufactured by prehistoric man. Historians now, as in the past, see as one of their trickiest problems finding appropriate units to periodize the past.

Once geologists had identified their units, developed means of individuating them, and found ways of detecting them in the imperfectly preserved record, they faced their second problem, how to determine the relations between them, in this case relations of earlier and later. They relied on the theory that formations had been deposited sequentially, with younger rocks superimposed on older rocks (the principle of superposition). They recognized the limitations of this principle. Igneous rocks, intruded from below into the sequence of formations, might be under, not over, older rocks; structural disturbances subsequent to deposition could overturn the sequence of formations, again resulting in younger rocks under, not over, older rocks. Consequently, they developed ancillary lines of evidence to supplement the principle of superposition. They argued that fossilized worm casts and ripple marks indicated which side of a stratum had originally faced up even if the rock was now reversed, and they checked which sedimentary rocks were intersected by igneous rocks. Gradually they put together an increasingly fine-grained and reliable chronology of the deposition of rocks on the earth's continents, a chronology that they had every reason to believe had sound warrant. Thus, it is clear that descriptive geology, and other descriptive historical sciences, too, involve tricky epistemic problems, problems that scientists have found strategies for solving in many cases, so that they have good reason to believe their conclusions to be well-founded.

If this is correct, we can return briefly to the philosophy of history to correct what I see as a widespread misconception in that literature. A descriptive historical science is nothing other than what philosophers of history call a chronicle or chronology. They define it as an arrangement of past objects or events in a temporal sequence (White 1965:222) – not just any objects or events, but those that we have reason to believe are the same or similar kinds. Their misconception, I suggest, is their tendency to dismiss chronology as "mere" chronology, just a preparation for the narrative they assume to be the characteristic product of historical inquiry and on which they focus most of their attention. This may be because they take their archetypal examples of history from recent political or diplomatic history where the problems of establishing chronology are minor or nonexistent.

Whewell knew better. He recognized the epistemic difficulties geologists encountered in constructing the stratigraphic column and tracing the history of life. We can see that these difficulties occur in many of the historical sciences. Recently geomagnetists have struggled to track the record of geomagnetic reversals. Paleontologists who have done a magnificent job tracing the sequence of major life forms, nonetheless, still face problems with an imperfectly preserved record. Archaeologists, at least until the advent of the "new archaeology" a couple of decades ago, were almost exclusively preoccupied sorting out prehistoric chronology. Even within history, chronology has not always been easy because many events were either not dated or dated on different time scales in different parts of the world. From the fifteenth through the eighteenth century, historians, including leading scholars such as Isaac Newton, devoted interminable hours to reconciling the records of the Hebrews, Greeks, and Romans with the records of other peoples of the Near East. To this day, demographic, social and economic historians have to determine chronologies in their domains. In sum, we should not be misled by the rich written record of modern political and intellectual history into underestimating the difficulties of constructing chronologies. Except in rare cases of well-preserved records (and even there problems of individuating units can occur), descriptive historical science or chronology faces, and in many cases has overcome, severe epistemic difficulties.

This leads to two further questions. First, can the strategies developed to overcome these problems in one historical domain be successfully exported to another historical domain, in the way that some biologists hope to export solutions from history to biology? The answer is that it all depends on the nature of the domains. The principle of superposition, say, works quite well in other historical sciences that deal with objects deposited in layers, such as paleontology and archeology. In history of language it is not so easily applied: when the distinguished nineteenth-century linguist, Max Muller, struck by the apparent analogies between geology and language, attempted to adopt geological methods, he met with sorry results. In written history, it is inappropriate since documents are not arranged in layers: historians trace anachronisms, references from one text to another, and other clues to establish sequence. And in astronomy, it is quite useless: astronomers establish the relative ages of stars by their colors. In biology, which is the chief concern of this volume, paleontologists can use these methods to reconstruct the outlines of the history of life on earth while finding them absolutely useless when it comes to the details simply because the preservation of the record does not support such a fine-grained analysis. Thus the possibility of using a methodology developed in one historical discipline to resolve problems in another depends on how similar the two domains are. That both deal with the past is not enough.

That leads to the second question. Are the epistemic problems we have discussed and the strategies for overcoming them unique to the historical sciences? The answer must be no. Problems of identifying and individuating units and of determining the relations between them occur in all the sciences, not just in the historical sciences. The chronologies of the historical sciences are simply a special case of the general class of descriptive theories. Scientists develop descriptive theories of their domains, whether or not these domains have a diachronic dimension. Doing so involves more than simply reading off the evidence, if for no other reason than that the evidence is so often imperfect. Constructing descriptive theories in nonhistorical sciences involves difficulties similar to those encountered in the historical sciences and calls for resort to the same kinds of methods to deal with them. When Kepler propounded his theory of planetary motion, for example, he used a unit – the planet – the definition of which had been forged over centuries of astronomical inquiry. He could no more easily read off the description of planetary motion from tables of astronomical observations than could geologists easily read off the stratigraphic column from records of field observations. The same is true of descriptive theories in natural history (most systematics), crystallography (crystal structure), biology (cell theory), and a host of other sciences. The imperfectly preserved traces of past objects and events that historical scientists often bemoan as if they faced special problems do not differ in significant epistemic respects from the imperfect traces of objects that are too large, too small, or too distant to be easily observed. Overcoming observational difficulties is always a challenge to scientists; the fact that in the historical sciences many of these difficulties arise from imperfect preservation of the past does not establish the epistemic unity and uniqueness of the historical sciences. Even the claim that records of the past may be completely destroyed and thus forever inaccessible to observation does not make the historical sciences unique, for it is quite possible to imagine that there are contemporary features of the world that we cannot observe directly or indirectly. Hence if we ask "Do descriptive theories in the historical sciences differ epistemically from descriptive theories in the nonhistorical sciences?", the answer is "No." So far as descriptive theory goes then, the historical sciences look just like any other sciences.

Having spelled out my case for the descriptive historical sciences at some length, I can now briefly deal with geological dynamics and physical geology. It might be argued that it is in "geological dynamics" (or causal theory) that geologists (or historical scientists) really find themselves at an epistemic disadvantage compared to their peers in physics or chemistry. Physicists and chemists routinely perform experiments, systematically varying causes and examining the resultant effects. But historical scientists frequently investigate causes that operate too slowly for their effects to fall within the ken of contemporary observation. The rise and fall of mountains and the movement of plates take place over millions of years. The selective pressures on living beings operate over many generations. Human populations and economic systems change over hundreds of years. Causal processes that act so slowly as to dwarf the human time scale obviously cannot be investigated experimentally.

In this context, though, it is worth remembering that once again historical scientists are not in a unique position: many nonhistorical scientists study phenomena on which they cannot perform experiments. Yet, far from languishing, they have produced some of our proudest causal theories, such as Newtonian mechanics, relativity theory, and the theory of evolution. If this is so, then there seems no reason why historical scientists cannot construct causal theories also. And they have in fact regularly done so. Charles Lyell (1830-33), for example, deftly adapted a methodology established in the nonhistorical sciences to deal with the past (Laudan 1982). This was the so-called *vera causa* method, initially articulated by Newton in his famous rules of philosophizing. By the early nineteenth century, the *vera causa* method was generally assumed to involve two strictures. First, scientists should invoke only causes for which they had evidence independent of the effect they were explaining; second, they should also have independent evidence that these causes were adequate to produce the effect. Modifying these strictures to the geological case, Lyell argued that the only way geologists could obtain independent evidence for the existence of postulated past causes was to observe these causes acting at present, and that the only way they could obtain evidence that the cause was adequate to produce the effect was to assume that the present intensity of the cause was no different from its past intensity. On this basis he constructed a causal theory of long-term climatic change. Not everyone agreed with the theory or with his choice of the *vera causa* method in particular, but nobody questioned the appropriateness of his strategy of modifying a methodology developed in a nonhistorical science to overcome related epistemic difficulties in a historical science.

Yet here again philosophers of both history and geology may mislead us, for they routinely deny that historical scientists construct causal theories, suggesting instead that they rely on theories developed in the nonhistorical sciences. For reasons of their own, historians, at least in public, have usually eschewed the suggestion that they formulate causal theories, insisting that they resort to intuition, common sense, or latterly to the social sciences for their repertoire of causes. The philosopher of history, Maurice Mandelbaum, while distancing himself from the position, could state that it was "a commonplace in the literature of our subject that historians are concerned with particular events that occurred at specific times and places, and not with them only in so far as they represent events of a given type" (1977:4). The philosopher of science, Ernst Nagel, took the same line: ". . . a geologist seeks to ascertain . . . the sequential order of geologic formations, and he is able to do so in part by applying various physical laws to his materials of study" (1961:550). For him, the key difference between the historical and the nonhistorical sciences was that the historical sciences rely on the nonhistorical sciences for their causal theories, ".... it is not the geologist's task, *qua* geologist, to establish the laws of mechanics or of radioactive disintegration which he employs in his investigations." The philosopher of geology, David Kitts, followed Nagel when he claimed that the goal of geology was "the construction of a chronicle of specific events occurring at specific times [and that] with all the emphasis in recent years upon 'earth science' and the theoretical physical-chemical foundation of geology, the primary concern with specific events [not with causes] still dominates our discipline" (1977:5). But, as my brief discussion of causal theory in geology suggests, drawing this sharp distinction between the historical and nonhistorical sciences may be premature, for there is a clear parallel between the two. Both construct causal theories. With the exception of experiment, both have the same battery of tests for their theories. And the limits of the use of experiment do not coincide with the boundary between the historical and nonhistorical science.

Finally we come to "physical geology" which Whewell defined as the pairing of descriptive geology and geological dynamics to produce a causal history of the earth (a sense quite different from the current meaning of physical geology, it should be noted). By this Whewell meant just what many philosophers of history call narrative. While studies of narrative are various and frequently arcane, one widely accepted meaning is the use of causal theory (generally believed to have been constructed by the nonhistorical sciences) to link past events together (White 1965:223). Philosophers of history and literary theorists have made much of narrative, frequently restricting the term "history" to narrative accounts of the past, excluding "mere" chronicle as at best protohistory. Following their example a number of scientists and philosophers of science have explored the concept of narrative and have made interesting use of the concept in dealing with the sciences (Ruse 1971; Hull 1975; O'Hara 1988a, 1988b). I place more emphasis on the role of descriptive and causal theories in the historical sciences. But whether or not narrative is the distinctive form of the historical sciences is irrelevant to my argument, because there is no reason to believe that the warrant for narrative is epistemically of a different kind from that for chronology or causal theory albeit that it involves the additional step of deciding on the appropriateness of using particular causal theories to connect particular parts of chronologies.

Readers may notice that throughout this discussion I have fudged the issue of just what makes a theory well-founded be it descriptive, causal or narrative. This is because we do not have a good account, let alone consensus, about what comprises a reliable, well-founded theory, though most scientists and philosophers of science would agree that at least a part of that warrant comes from the way we use evidence to support the theory. Fortunately for my purposes though, we do not need to settle the vexed question of exactly what constitutes a well-founded theory. All we need is to show, as I have sought to do in this essay, is that evidential support for theories about the past is garnered and tested in ways similar to evidential support for theories about the present. If that can be done, the thesis that investigations into the past are epistemically unique can be dismissed because the problems of the historical sciences, like those of the nonhistorical sciences, boil down to the problems of warranting claims based on partial evidence.

I conclude that, if our aim is to devise means of acquiring reliable knowledge, classifying the sciences into the historical and the nonhistorical is not particularly relevant, a conclusion that others have also argued for (Ereshefsky, this volume). True, past objects and events cannot be directly observed. But neither can many of the objects and events with which the nonhistorical sciences deal. All the sciences have to work out tactics for overcoming these difficulties. Whether or not a particular historical science can learn from some other science depends on the nature of that inaccessibility, not on whether it is past or present. In arguing that there is no significant epistemic difference between the historical and the nonhistorical science, I am not forcing the historical sciences back into the procrustean mold of philosophy of physics. If we have learned anything over the past twenty-five years it is that depending on their subject matter different sciences face different methodological problems and that their theories take different forms. It is simply to say that these differences do not map on to the distinction between historical and nonhistorical. The investigation of the past does not have a set of common features that sets it off from other forms of inquiry and, hence, there is no reason to think that biologists can learn more from the philosophy of history than they can from the philosophies of other sciences with cognate epistemic problems, be the sciences historical or nonhistorical. To return to the question motivating this chapter, "What's so special about the past?", I suggest that the answer, from an epistemic point of view, is "Absolutely nothing."

References

Danto, A. C. 1985. *Narration and Knowledge*. (Includes the integral text of *Analytical Philosophy of History*, first published in 1964). New York: Columbia University Press.

Dray, W., ed. 1966. *Philosophical Analysis and History*. New York: Harper and Row.

Hempel, C. [1942] 1965. The functions of general laws in history, 231-42. Reprinted in *Aspects of Scientific Explanation and Other Essays in Philosophy of Science*. New York: The Free Press.

Hempel, C. 1962. Explanation in science and history. In *Frontiers of Science and Philosophy*, ed. R. G. Colodny. Pittsburgh: University of Pittsburgh Press.

Hull, D. 1975. Central subjects and historical narratives. *History and Theory* 14:253-74.

Kitcher, P., and W. Salmon, eds. 1989. *Scientific Explanations*. Minneapolis: University of Minnesota Press.

Kitts, D. 1977. *The Structure of Geology*. Dallas: Southern Methodist University Press.

Laudan, R. 1982. The role of methodology in Lyell's geology. *Studies in History and Philosophy of Science* 13:215-50.

Laudan, R. 1987. *From Mineralogy to Geology: The Foundations of a Science 1650-1830*. Chicago: University of Chicago Press.

Lyell, C. 1830-1833. *Principles of Geology*. 3 vols. London: Murray.

Mandelbaum, M. 1977. *The Anatomy of Historical Knowledge*. Baltimore: Johns Hopkins University Press.

Nagel, E. 1961. *The Structure of Science. Problems in the Logic of Scientific Explanation*. New York: Harcourt, Brace and World.

O'Hara, R. 1988a. Homage to Clio, or, toward an historical philosophy for evolutionary biology. *Systematic Zoology*. 37:142-55.

O'Hara, R. 1988b. Problems in the narrative presentation of evolutionary history. *American Zoologist* 28:144A.

Roth, P. 1988. Narrative explanations: The case of history. *History and Theory* 27:1-13.

Roth, P. 1989. How narratives explain. *Social Research* 56:449-78.

Ruse, M. 1971. Narrative explanation and the theory of evolution. *Canadian Journal of Philosophy* 1:59-74.

Whewell, W. 1837. *History of the Inductive Sciences*. 3 vols. London: Parker.

White, M. 1965. *Foundations of Historical Knowledge*. New York and London: Harper and Row.

The Particular-Circumstance Model
of Scientific Explanation

David L. Hull

The Covering-Law (or Deductive-Nomological) Model of scientific explanation is one of the two major pillars of the logical empiricist analysis of
science. Carl Hempel (1942) formulated this model in response to problems
posed by historical explanation. According to the Covering-Law Model,
scientific explanations involve the derivation (ideally deduction) of a description of the empirical phenomena to be explained from statements of general
laws and particular circumstances. Logical empiricists have spent considerable effort in attempting to characterize general laws (see Ereshefsky, this
volume). They have spent much less time examining the hodgepodge of
statements that are lumped together under the rubric "particular circumstances." Statements of particular circumstances turn out to include everything in addition to general laws that is needed to carry out the derivation.
One goal of this paper is to redress this imbalance.

The trouble with historians, in Hempel's (1965:231) view, is that they
are "concerned with the description of particular events of the past rather
than with the search for general laws which might govern these events."
According to logical empiricists such as Hempel, covering-laws are necessary
for scientific explanations. That is why they term their model the Covering-
Law Model. Of course, statements of particular circumstances are just as
necessary, but the laws carry all the explanatory weight. An explanation
entirely in terms of general laws could count as a genuine scientific explanation, but no concatenation of statements of particular circumstances could
possibly explain anything. Historical explanations pose a problem for the
logical empiricists because they seem to provide extremely satisfying explanations in the absence of much in the way of general laws. Hempel dismisses
historical explanations as mere sketches and accounts for their apparent ex-

planatory appeal by reference to assumed but unstated general laws.

One possibility is that the logical empiricist analysis of "natural law" is too narrow. For example, although Hempel is willing to treat laws as probabilistic in form, he insists that they must be spatiotemporally unrestricted. Perhaps a broader conception of general laws can account for the apparent explanatory character of historical explanations. In this paper I take just the opposite tack, concentrating on the role of particular circumstances. Robert Richards argues in this volume that instead of historical explanations being mere sketches of covering-law explanations, the deductive-nomological pattern is an "abstracted sketch of a full-bodied narrative." In the same spirit, I argue that explanations in terms of particular circumstances are perfectly legitimate and set out what might be termed a Particular-Circumstance Model of scientific explanation. Of course, there may be some general laws lurking around in the background somewhere, but the particular circumstances carry the explanatory load.

In this paper I examine the relative roles and importance of general laws and statements of particular circumstances in scientific explanations. I argue that a natural phenomenon can be explained by showing that it is part of a theoretically significant historical entity or else a property of such an entity. Historical narratives are descriptions of historical entities as they persist through time (see Ereshefsky, this volume). The explanatory force of historical narratives stems from the coherence and continuous development of the historical entities that they describe. General laws are relevant to historical explanations but not as premises from which the events to be explained are derived. Instead, they provide the theoretical context in which historical entities are individuated. Although the issues that I address arose in the context of human history (Mandelbaum 1963; White 1963; Fain 1970), they apply equally to all historical disciplines, for example, cosmology, geology, and paleontology as well as human history.

Inference from Laws versus Historical Reconstruction

Not all sciences are created equal. Some contain very powerful theories as well as easy access to massive amounts of data. Regardless of the relative importance of laws and statements of particular circumstances, explanations are easy to produce. For example, the laws of motion are straightforward and apply without much need to include *ceteris paribus* clauses. The experimental setup necessary to roll lead balls down inclined planes poses no insuperable difficulties. In contrast, we have a superabundance of data about human beings but little in the way of laws governing our behavior. It is certainly true that Peeping Toms rarely molest, but such statements hardly have the same stature as the law of universal gravitation. Although the regularities in reinforcement discovered by behavioral psychologists are general enough, they do not go very far in explaining human behavior. They certainly are not good enough to serve as covering laws in deductivenomological explanations for the sorts of phenomena that historians purport to explain.

Population biology and meteorology present intermediary cases. We understand the processes under investigation quite well, but so many variables are involved and changes occur so rapidly and erratically that inferences are difficult. In this connection, one often reads that evolutionary theory can be used to explain the past but not to predict the future. One difficulty with making inferences in evolutionary biology, not to mention other areas of science as well, is that too many contingencies are too important (see Allen, this volume), but the problems posed by contingencies affect inferences to the past just as severely as inferences to the future. On the basis of current versions of population genetics, inferences to the past are just as difficult as inferences to the future. The appearance of asymmetry arises from the failure to distinguish between inferring the past on the basis of general laws and reconstructing the past on the basis of records. As Laudan (this volume) points out, "we need to distinguish historical reconstruction in a given domain from causal theories and chronologies."

Although certain examples are clear enough, it is far from easy to make a general distinction between those phenomena that count as records and those that do not. Friday's footprint in the sand obviously implied the prior existence of a human being on the beach. The likelihood that any other natural phenomena could produce such a pattern is extremely small. Thus, a footprint can serve as a record of the past. If physicists were to find a container in which all the hydrogen atoms were on one side and all the atoms of nitrogen on the other, they would infer that in the immediate past a partition separated the two gases. Historians and evolutionists try to piece together the past by scrounging up contemporary evidence. They also reason backwards in time from processes and events occurring in the present to similar processes and events in the past. The former is reconstruction on the basis of records; the latter is simple inference. Reconstruction is asymmetrical because we cannot do anything like "reconstruct" the future.

Geologists use a principle that they term the "law of superposition" to help reconstruct the history of the earth. According to this principle, in any sequence of surface-deposited material, each bed tends to be younger than the one below it and older than the one above. This principle can be expressed only as a tendency statement because the earth's crust can buckle, inverting the order of the strata (see Laudan, this volume). Paleontologists assume that fossils are records of previously existing organisms, and reason back and forth between geological strata ordered according to purely geological criteria and the order of fossils. Ancestors should appear in earlier strata than descendants. The goal is to make the orders as determined by geological and paleontological records coincide. In addition, the time needed for these sequences had better jibe with the age of the earth determined by physicists. Finally, historians reconstruct the course of human history on the basis of such things as texts and artifacts. For instance, if Aristotle mentioned his *History of Animals* in his *Metaphysics*, but not vice versa, then he probably began his *Metaphysics* after completing his *History*.

Records are produced by ordinary lawful processes. They are records because their particular makeup is more a function of the contingencies of their history than anything derivable from the theories governing them. One of the tasks of historians of all sorts is to distinguish those patterns that result from natural regularities and those that result from common history. In biology the distinction is between homoplasies and homologies. For population biologists, historical patterns are noise because they can be confused with regularities of process. The opposite is the case for paleontologists, who are interested in reconstructing the history of life on Earth. For them, historical patterns are the message, while the regularities that can be incorporated in general laws are the noise.

The contrast between pattern and process has recently become especially important in the literature concerning cladistic analysis. Certain cladists, such as Nelson and Platnick (1981) insist that ahistorical patterns are prior to any processes that may have produced them. This position runs contrary to the current received view in philosophy of science according to which pattern and process are intrinsically interconnected (see Kitts, this volume). According to philosophers writing in the logical empiricist tradition, neither pattern nor process is in any sense prior to the other. Be that as it may, advocates of the priority of pattern to process have shown how little paleontologists depend on knowledge of the evolutionary process in their reconstructions. Paleontologists do assume descent with modification. If speciation were always saltative, that might influence how they reconstructed phylogeny, but most issues in evolutionary biology have no relevance to paleontology. For example, no matter how the problems surrounding the cost of meiosis are resolved, these solutions are unlikely to touch phylogeny reconstruction.

A second feature of what has come to be known as "pattern cladism" has an even more direct connection to the topic of this volume. At times, pattern cladists seem to be arguing that the past is "unknowable," that there is no difference between those phenomena that count as "records" and those that do not. Nested patterns are nested patterns, and that is that. All diagnosable units should be treated as terminal taxa regardless of whether they are extinct or extant. No taxon can be recognized as ancestral to any other (Nelson and Platnick 1981). In general, I think that pattern cladists make too sharp a distinction between character nesting and all other sorts of evidence that can be used to reconstruct phylogeny. I also think that they have an unrealistic notion of knowledge in science. Perhaps the fossil record, biogeographic distributions, host-parasite relations, embryological development, etc., are less certain than character distribution, but the contrast is one only of degree.

Although the preceding discussion has concerned the relation between evolutionary theory and phylogeny reconstruction, the distinctions and problems apply to all historical endeavors. For example, cosmologists reconstruct the history of the universe on the basis of some very powerful theories but in the absence of anything like the wealth of records available to paleontologists. The most crucial records available to cosmologists are traces of the energy released by the original big bang – a cosmic microwave background.

Physicists claim to be able to reconstruct the first three minutes in the history of the universe almost nanosecond by nanosecond (Weinberg 1977). Even though evolutionary theory may not be as powerful as relativity theory or quantum theory, it seems strange that physicists can "know" what happened in great detail 10 to 15 thousand million years ago in the farthest reaches of the universe while evolutionary biologists cannot "know" what happened here on Earth just a few million years ago. My guess is that cosmologists and pattern cladists are assuming two very different conceptions of what counts as "knowledge."

Futuyma (this volume) attempts to see what problems reconstructed histories pose for population genetics. Put crudely, scientific theories tell us what can and cannot happen. Within these limits particular facts, including historical records, help us to decide what in point of fact did happen. In some areas of science, the relevant theories constrain the possible states of natural phenomena very narrowly so that only a minimal amount of evidence is needed to specify the state of the system uniquely. In others, the relevant theories do not constrain natural phenomena very much so that a greater reliance on data is needed. For example, by specifying values for only a very few variables, we can infer past and future states of an enclosed gas with extreme accuracy. Solid state physics currently does not allow comparable inferences. As far as inferences of this sort are concerned, we can infer the past and the future with equal ease (or difficulty). Inferring what the temperature of a gas was ten minutes ago is no harder (or easier) to decide than what it will be in ten minutes. Although the inferences with respect to particular populations in population genetics are not all that precise, they are equally symmetrical with respect to time. We cannot infer the future states of particular populations very well, but then we cannot infer their past states with any greater precision.

Most process theories are symmetrical with respect to time. Some, however, have a directionality built into them. They provide an arrow to time. Whether evolutionary theory contains anisotropic laws is still under debate (see Ruse, this volume). But the point I wish to make is that *inferring the past on the basis of process theories* is different in kind from *reconstructing the past on the basis of historical records*. On the basis of process theories, we can infer the future as readily as the past. We can reconstruct only the past. We cannot "preconstruct" the future because nothing like "records" of the future exist.

Historical Entities

Process laws must have something to range over – events, fields, entities, something. One common ontology in science is that of entities, their properties, and the events in which they participate. Stars explode, continents drift, species go extinct, and dictators are assassinated. For those theories that range over entities, the recognition of these entities is as important as the discovery of the regularities in which they function. The contrary position arises from two sources. First, the issue is not the discernment of particular historical entities. Any scientist who discovers a new general law is sure to become famous. In special circumstances discovering yet another historical entity may be considered a major achievement, for example, the discovery of additional solar planets. But in most cases, historical entities are cheaper than a dime a dozen. Finding yet another sample of feldspar is hardly a major achievement.

The issue, however, is not the discovery of additional instances of a particular kind of historical entity but the individuation of these entities themselves. The individuation of appropriate entities tends to be devalued because many of the entities over which general laws range are commonsense individuals. Stars, planets, islands, lakes, whales, moths, and even atoms fit our commonsense conceptions of spatiotemporal particulars. However, many commonsense individuals are of no scientific importance, and conversely, many of the entities forced on us by scientific theories do not seem like "individuals" from the human perspective. For example, a Portuguese man-of-war may seem like a single organism, but according to biologists, it is made up of hundreds of distinct organisms. It may be in some sense a single "individual," but it is not a single organism. Conversely, species may not seem to be spatiotemporal particulars, but according to evolutionary theory, that is precisely how they must be treated – deeply entrenched commonsense intuitions notwithstanding. From the point of view of the man or woman on the street, individual people are the most obvious candidates for subjects in human histories, but not all histories are biographies. Historians also write histories of families, nations, cultures, and even ideas. Anyone who thinks that the individuation of such entities is easy is mistaken.

Historians frequently describe their task as the identification of a significant strand to follow in the fabric of history, regardless of whether that strand is a planet circling a star, a continent drifting, or a species evolving. The metaphor is good enough, as long as one distinguishes the entities that make up the strands from the causal chains in which they participate. This distinction becomes more difficult when a sequence of entities forms a more inclusive entity, what I term an "historical entity." In biology, the distinction is between the genealogical actors and the ecological play (Hull 1987). The genealogical network is formed by organisms giving rise to other organisms, whether sexually or asexually. When reproduction is sexual, more inclusive entities are formed – species. Sexual reproduction integrates organisms into species. As species change through time, split, and on occasion merge, they form higher level chains, trees and networks. Paleontologists attempt to reconstruct these historical entities and their genealogical relations. In addition to forming genealogical hierarchies, these entities also function in ecological processes. They compete with each other for resources, form symbiotic relationships, prey on one another, etc. (Eldredge 1985). All genealogical relations are causal, but not all causal relations are genealogical.

As Mink (1969:556) has observed, the "actions and events of a story comprehended as a whole are connected by a network of overlapping descriptions." These overlapping descriptions are of two sorts: those that describe the continuity and unity of the historical entities involved; the other descriptions of the events in which they participate. For example, in biographies the physical continuity of the person through time forms the primary continuity for any historical narrative concerning him. A biography of Benjamin Franklin follows him from birth until death. The events in which he participated are secondary. Similarly, in paleontology, the genealogical continuity of biological taxa through time forms the primary continuity for any historical narrative about their development. Sequences of ecological interactions are of secondary importance. But in all cases, the two together – the genealogical sequences of entities and the causal sequences of events – are responsible for the unity and continuity of historical narratives.

The crucial distinction in this connection is not between biology, on the one hand, and physics and chemistry, on the other hand, but between selection processes and other sorts of processes. Selection processes require replication – sequences of entities connected by some sort of descent. In biological evolution, genes give rise to genes, organisms give rise to organisms, and species give rise to species, but selection processes operate at other levels and in different contexts as well. For example, the reaction of immune systems to antigens (Darden and Cain 1989) and the development of the central nervous system (Edelman 1987) are examples of selection processes that occur within the life-span of a single organism. Conceptual development in general might well be interpreted as a selection process (Hull 1988).

Historical Entities and Historical Explanations

Covering-Law Model explanations explain an event by subsuming it to a kind of event that functions in a general law. We are all aware of the psychological satisfaction that we feel when we discover that the falling of an apple and the movement of the moon around the earth are both instances of the same sort of regularity. But we are also aware of the satisfaction that we feel when we succeed in seeing as a single cohesive whole what at first appeared to be a hodgepodge, or when we fit an isolated element into an already recognized pattern. In historical explanations, an event is not explained by subsuming it under a generalization. Instead, it is explained by integrating it into an organized whole.

The main message of this paper is that subsuming a particular under a general law and individuating the particulars being subsumed are explanatory activities. However, an asymmetry does exist with respect to general laws and the entities over which they range. The theories in which laws function determine which entities are theoretically significant, and theoretically significant theoretical entities take precedence to commonsense entities. Ideally we would like to possess both general laws and theoretically significant historical entities, but sometimes we have to be content just with tracing historical entities through time. When these commonsense historical entities

turn out to coincide with theoretically significant historical entities, the corresponding historical narratives retain their explanatory force. However,
when our theories entail quite different historical entities, then we must
admit that what we took to be explanations were not. Thus, although some
historical explanations may turn out to be spurious as we come to understand
more completely the processes in which they participate, some may also turn
out to be genuine.

According to the view of explanation that I am urging, both aspects of
scientific explanations get their just due. Particular events can be explained
by subsuming them under general laws, as long as we have these laws and
have adequately individuated the entities that function in these regularities.
Both sorts of activities are important in science. Galileo's law for the free
fall of bodies near the earth's surface can be deduced from Newton's laws of
motion (once both are fixed up a bit) and some statements of particular
circumstances. Among these statements must be the specification of how
these bodies are to be reduced to mass points or centers of gravity. Waiving
these considerations as not being sufficiently important to mention is as
unjustified as waiving general laws in particular-circumstance explanations.
We certainly can produce historical explanations of commonsense entities
such as people without much in the way of general laws governing their
behavior. However, if and when we do possess such theories, the explanations derivable from these theories must take precedence over our commonsense explanations.

Conclusion

Philosophers are fond of quoting Socrates in Plato's *Phaedrus* (265e) to the
effect that we should "carve nature at her joints." As Socrates himself put
this principle, "division into species" should be "according to the natural
formation, where the joint is, not breaking any part as a bad carver might."
A vertebrate is literally an organized whole. Its joints are real. Cutting up
a chicken or a sheep at these joints is natural. Scientists strive to cut nature
at its metaphorical joints by distinguishing natural classes, for example, lead
and gold. Strangely enough, most philosophers insist that the metaphorical

usage leads to genuine explanations, while they dismiss any purported explanations based on the literal usage as spurious. In this paper I have argued that historical entities are particulars. However, tracing these particulars through time can nevertheless produce genuine explanations in the form of historical narratives.

This thesis is liable to evoke two polar responses. On the one hand, traditional philosophers are likely to insist that the only way to explain anything scientifically is by subsuming it under a law of nature. But these philosophers themselves present explanations in the absence of anything analogous to laws of nature. Perhaps philosophers do not pretend to provide scientific explanations, but they do present what they take to be explanations of some sort. If philosophers can explain in the absence of laws, why not others? On the other hand, opponents of the Covering-Law Model are sure to complain that I give too much weight to laws of nature. Subsumption is neither necessary nor sufficient for explanation, even scientific explanation. In their more bumptious moments, these iconoclasts are led to exclaim that laws have nothing to do with scientific explanation. They are left, however, with the task of presenting some other model of scientific explanation. I have presented here what might be termed the Particular-Circumstance Model of scientific explanation. It exhibits the same form as the traditional model but with its emphasis reversed.

References

Darden, L., and J. A. Cain. 1989. Selection type theories. *Philosophy of Science* 56:106-29.

Edelman, G. 1987. *Neural Darwinism: The Theory of Neuronal Group Selection*. New York: Basic Books.

Eldredge, N. 1985. *Unfinished Synthesis*. New York: Oxford University Press.

Fain, H. 1970. *Between Philosophy and History*. Princeton: Princeton University Press.

Hempel, C. G. 1942. The function of general laws in history. *The Journal of Philosophy* 39:35-48.

Hempel, C. G. 1965. *Aspects of Scientific Explanation*. New York: The Free Press.

Hull, D. L. 1987. Genealogical actors in ecological plays. *Biology and Philosophy* 1:44-60.

Hull, D. L. 1988. *Science as a Process: An Evolutionary Account of the Social and Conceptual Development of Science*. Chicago: The University of Chicago Press.

Mandelbaum, M. 1963. Objectivism in history, 43-56. In *Philosophy of History*, ed. S. Hook. New York: New York University Press.

Mink, L. O. 1969. History and fiction as modes of comprehension. *New Literary History* 1:541-58.

Nelson, G., and N. Platnick. 1981. *Systematics and Biogeography: Cladistics and Vicariance*. New York: Columbia University Press.

Plato. 1953. *The Dialogues of Plato*, trans. by B. Jowett. Oxford: Clarendon Press.

Weinberg, S. 1977. *The First Three Minutes*. New York: Basic Books.

White, M. 1963. The logic of historical narration, 3-31. In *Philosophy of History*, ed. S. Hook. New York: New York University Press.

The Historical Nature of Evolutionary Theory

Marc Ereshefsky

A familiar claim is that evolutionary biology is a different science than physics and chemistry. The division frequently is drawn on the basis of which disciplines conform to Hempel's (1965) fairly simple covering-law model of explanation. An explanation is an argument whose premises consist of initial conditions and scientific laws. The argument's conclusion is the event to be explained. For example, an explanation for the speed of a falling object cites the height from which it was dropped, the current wind speed, and other initial conditions. Furthermore, the explanation cites Newton's law of gravitation plus any other relevant physical laws. Together these initial conditions and laws imply what the object's speed will be. Thus, on the Hempelian model, they explain why the object travels at the speed it does. The example given here is of a nonstatistical or deterministic explanation. Hempel's model allows for statistical explanations as well. Such explanations cite those statistical laws and initial conditions which jointly imply that an explanandum has a greater than fifty percent chance of occurring. For Hempel, citing the appropriate laws and initial conditions is both sufficient and necessary for providing a perfect or ideal explanation. (Both are necessary unless the explanandum is itself a law. In that case no initial conditions need to be cited).

What is important about Hempel's model is the requirement that scientific explanations must cite laws of nature. It is this requirement which many believe divides evolutionary biology from the physical sciences. The physical sciences seem to abound in laws, and it is thought that the explanations within those sciences typically cite laws. Yet a number of authors have suggested that evolutionary theory lacks laws and cannot provide any Hempelian explanations (Goudge 1963; Smart 1963, 1968; Beatty 1980, 1981; Mayr 1988). Moreover they suggest that this lack of evolutionary laws has one of two implications for evolutionary theory and the Hempelian model.

According to some, it shows that evolutionary theory is not a genuine scientific enterprise (Smart 1963, 1968). According to others, it shows that the Hempelian model, at least as it applies to evolutionary theory, should be abandoned (Beatty 1980, 1981; Mayr 1988; Goudge 1963; Gould 1986; O'Hara 1988).

What is the source of this alleged division between evolutionary theory and the Hempelian model? More specifically, why does evolutionary theory appear to fail the Hempelian requirement that a theory contain laws? Many claim that it is due to the historical nature of taxa. Two prominent arguments to that effect are found in the literature. According to the first, the distribution of traits within a taxon is a unique historical event (Goudge 1963; Simpson 1964; Mayr 1982). In fact such distributions are so unique that the only way to explain them is to cite the particular historical sequences which gave rise to these distributions. There simply are no evolutionary laws which will do the trick. The second argument highlights the evolutionary nature of taxa. From a populational view, taxa are identified first and foremost by their particular position on the tree of life, not by their members sharing some unique qualitative property. Consequently, there are no taxon-specific laws within evolutionary theory (Smart 1963, 1968; Beatty 1980, 1981).

I want to consider several questions here. First, numerous features have been suggested as the distinctive historical aspect of evolutionary theory. Which, if any, of these are truly unique historical features of that theory? Second, assuming that such a feature can be located, does that feature drive a wedge between evolutionary theory and the Hempelian model? And third, if it does, should we admit that evolutionary theory is not a scientific theory, or should we simply abandon the Hempelian model as a model for all scientific theories? I will argue that many of the claimed distinctive historical features of evolutionary theory are not unique to that theory, but are features which one finds also in sciences such as chemistry and physics. Nevertheless, there is an aspect of evolutionary theory which is historical and unique to that theory – namely, the central entities of evolutionary theory, taxa, are a special type of historical entity. Finally, I will suggest that this historical aspect of evolutionary theory makes the theory in some sense unscientific, nor should it make the Hempelian model a useless explanatory paradigm. Instead, I will advocate a compromise between these two positions. This path of compromise is well-worn in the philosophical literature. Ruse (1973), Hull (1975, 1976, 1978, 1981, this volume), Levine and Sober (1985), Rosenberg (1985), and Williams (1986) have all suggested such an approach.

The Search for a Distinctive Historical Methodology

Let us begin with the first question: What is the historical feature of evolutionary theory that separates it from the physical sciences? The biological and philosophical literature abounds with such suggestions. I will restrict my discussion to those features which depend on evolutionary theory having its own distinctive methodology. A recent suggestion for such a feature is found in O'Hara (1988). O'Hara argues that with the advent of evolutionary theory came new types of scientific explanations, one of which is "How Possibly Explanations." "Rather than explaining why necessarily a particular evolutionary event occurred, as a covering law explanation might, a how-possibly explanation merely removes the objections the questioner has to the event's occurrence" (O'Hara 1988:148). For example, when Darwin posited the theory of evolution by natural selection he was confronted with numerous objections, among which was the claim that species are invariant and cannot evolve. As O'Hara points out, many passages of Darwin's *Origin* are devoted to removing this and other objections, that is, providing "how possibly explanations" for the occurrence of evolution by natural selection.

It might be wondered if "how possibly explanations" are indeed explanations. Consider the structure of such an explanation. Darwin's hypothesis of evolution by natural selection was thought to imply that the Earth was a certain age, namely, the time it took terrestrial life to evolve to its present form. However, it commonly was held that the age of the Earth was much less. Hence Darwin's hypothesis seemed to be faced with disconfirming evidence. Darwin attempted to overcome this evidence by arguing that the Earth is in fact much older than his protagonists claimed. The question arises, what has Darwin explained here? It seems that no particular biological phenomenon has been explained. So in what sense is this "how possibly explanation" an explanation? Darwin did explain how an objection to his theory could be removed. But this sounds more like an act of confirmation than of explanation: Darwin is not using a hypothesis to explain some phenomenon, instead he is giving reasons for thinking that a hypothesis (the hypothesis of natural selection) might be true. I suggest that "how possibly explanations" are not explanations – they do not explain the occurrence of any natural phenomena. Hempel (1965:334-35) discusses the distinction between "why" questions which ask for explanations and "why" questions which request reasons supporting a hypothesis.

Still, there is the question of whether "how possibly explanations" are unique to evolutionary theory. Consider the acceptance of the hypothesis that the sea floor is spreading (see Giere 1979:130ff). When this hypothesis was introduced it was considered implausible because it depended on the false assumption that the softer material of the continents can push through the harder material of the oceans' floors. In the 1960s, this objection was overcome by the suggestion that the continents sit on pieces of the Earth's hard crust. The problem of soft material plowing through hard material was, in a "how possibly" fashion, eliminated. Notice that such "how possibly" methodology easily applies to laboratory situations in physics as well. When data disconfirm some hypothesis, a worker can either chalk this up as evidence against the theory or attempt to see if the data are inaccurate. If a plausible reason can be given for showing that the data is incorrect, some disconfirming evidence is eliminated in a "how possibly" fashion. So "how possibly explanations" are found in other scientific disciplines besides evolutionary biology, and their use does not emphasize a distinctive historical feature of evolutionary biology.

Nevertheless, a number of authors think that there are other aspects of evolutionary explanation which distinguish evolutionary theory from the physical sciences. Goudge (1961:65ff), for example, presents the following paradigmatic argument for the inadequacy of the Hempelian model and the need for historical narratives: Many evolutionary events such as the origination of vertebrates or the extinction of the dodos are quite complex. In fact such events are so complex, they are not repeatable but are singular or unique. Given that evolutionary events are singular and unrepeatable, there is no way to generalize them. Thus there simply are no laws which apply to such events. As a result evolutionary events cannot be explained by the Hempelian or covering-law model of scientific explanation. Alternatively, Goudge and others suggest that such events are explained by citing the sequence of events which preceded them – that is, they are explained by presenting an appropriate historical narrative. Explanations in chemistry and physics consistently refer to laws in their explanations. Hence, the use of historical narratives rather than laws in evolutionary explanations marks an importantly distinctive feature of evolutionary theory. (See Mayr 1982:71-72 and Simpson 1964:186 for additional versions of this argument.)

The crucial premise of this argument is the claim that the complexity of an event precludes it from falling under some generalization. Both Ruse (1973:62ff, 210) and Hull (1974:98-99) reply to this claim. Hull points out that "events are not unique in and of themselves but only under certain descriptions." For example, that a particular species of dinosaurs consisting of certain members goes extinct is a unique event: *that* species with *those* members cannot go extinct again. Yet if we describe the same event as an instance of a species going extinct because its food supply was drastically diminished, then that type of event is indeed repeatable and generalizable. Any event, whether biological or purely physical, can be described in such detail that it is unrepeatable (or, at least, is extremely unlikely to occur again). Nevertheless, this does not preclude it from being described with so little detail that it falls under some generalization.

This is an important observation. However, the question remains: Does evolutionary theory contain generalizations which are useful for explaining the occurrence of evolutionary events? If there are no such generalizations, all we are left with to explain evolutionary events are historical narratives – mere descriptions of sequences of past events. If that is the case, then there is a real difference between evolutionary theory and such sciences as physics and chemistry: The explanations in those physical sciences typically cite generalizations, while the explanations in evolutionary theory do not.

Both Ruse (1973) and Williams (1986) have responded that evolutionary theory does contain explanatorily useful generalizations. They argue that even Goudge's examples of narrative explanations rely on such biological laws. Ruse (1973:57, 85-86) maintains that those explanations depend on the laws of population genetics, such as the Hardy-Weinberg law. Williams (1986:516-17) contends that such narrative explanations rely on the laws of natural selection. Part of Ruse's and Williams's motivations for arguing that evolutionary theory contains laws is to show that evolutionary explanations are indeed law-based Hempelian explanations, but they also want to show that evolutionary theory is a scientific theory akin to the (alleged) axiomatic theories of physics and chemistry. Thus each argues that a core section of evolutionary theory consists of a set of axioms or laws; in Ruse's case, it is population genetics, for Williams, it is the laws of selection theory.

Such axiomatizations may bring to the fore certain aspects of evolutionary theory which previously have not been considered. However, the legitimacy of evolutionary theory as a scientific enterprise does not depend on showing that it has an axiomatic core. Something less rigorous will suffice. What is important is that a theory emphasizes certain regularities in nature, regularities which can be referred to in explaining a range of phenomena. The descriptions of these regularities can be called "laws," "generalizations" or whatever. Their usefulness in a theory, that is, their ability to explain a domain of phenomena, does not depend on their being nicely situated in an axiomatic schema, nor require their being in the form of nice, neat formulas, explicitly stating all the necessary and sufficient conditions for when such regularities obtain.

Knowledge of such regularities is found within the body of evolutionary theory. Consider Mayr's (1970) assertion that under certain circumstances, speciation occurs only allopatrically. Mayr's law, as Ghiselin (1989) calls it, is quite useful for explaining why speciation has and has not occurred in certain instances. For example, why are there so many related bird species on the Galapagos Archipelago? Lack (1947) answers that an original group of mainland birds arrived in the Archipelago, and subsequently it or its descendants colonized one island after another. These colonies were isolated from each other and from the mainland population. This isolation allowed the colonies to vary genotypically and phenotypically from the other populations and eventually to become distinct species. So why are there so many related bird species on the Galapagos Archipelago? To a large extent because Mayr's condition on speciation was met a number of times in the evolution of this phyletic line.

It might be countered that although Mayr's law is useful for explaining why some instances of speciation occurred, the generalization called "Mayr's law" is not analogous to the laws found in the explanations of physics and chemistry. Mayr's law is not a neatly formulated, exceptionless law; nor does it provide necessary or sufficient conditions for speciation. This observation undoubtedly is correct. I do not think, however, that it highlights a difference between evolutionary laws and the laws in chemistry and physics. Consider Newton's law of gravitation. How many falling objects conform to it? Many objects fail to do so because of such intervening forces as air resistance, counteracting winds, and electromagnetic forces – just think of falling specks of dust. How many real pendulums conform to the classical law of the pendulum? Again, very few – there are interfering gravitational forces, air resistance, and surface friction to contend with (Giere 1988:76-77). (For further examples of exceptions to physical laws see Scriven's [1961] aptly titled piece "The Key Property of Physical Laws – Inaccuracy" or *How the Laws of Physics Lie* [Cartwright 1984].)

The purpose of showing that physical generalizations have exceptions is not to establish that there are no exceptionless regularities in the universe. Instead, I want to suggest that most generalizations – that is, *descriptions* – of regularities are going to be incomplete. It is important to note the difference between a regularity in nature and the generalization used to describe that regularity. I want to stress the problem in getting complete descriptions or generalizations of regularities. All regularities hold only under certain conditions. Therefore, in order for a generalization of a regularity to be exceptionless, that generalization must list each and every relevant condition. In many cases there is no practical reason for listing all those conditions – they are just implicitly assumed. But more important, in most cases the conditions are so numerous that it is impossible or impractical to list them all.

My point here is twofold: First, I want to show that the physical sciences are no worse than evolutionary biology in citing incomplete generalizations in their explanations. So when one argues that the use of incomplete generalizations in evolutionary theory shows that the theory is a different type of theory, one is, in effect, arguing against a straw man. Second, the use of incomplete generalizations does not imply that the Hempelian model of explanation is a useless paradigm. One way to read Hempel (contra Richards, this volume) is to see that he is setting out a model for *ideally complete* explanations (see Sober 1984:144). Hempel himself admits that most explanations do not meet these specifications (1965:235), and calls such explanations "explanation sketches." Indeed most explanations produced by scientists are explanation sketches. This observation should not cause one to think that there are no criteria for determining the adequacy of a scientific explanation. Hempel himself writes of a difference between "a scientifically acceptable explanation sketch and a pseudoexplanation" (1965:238), and even provides criteria for telling the two apart.

The idea that most explanations are explanation sketches touches on another argument for the distinctiveness of evolutionary explanations. It has been observed that many evolutionary explanations cite only particular historical events and make no explicit reference to scientific laws. For instance, Hull writes:

> In the usual examples given of covering-law explanations [i.e., those from physics and chemistry], the laws are the chief explanatory elements. . . But in evolutionary explanations, the emphasis is just the opposite. It is the particular circumstances in the form of an historical narrative that seem to bear the brunt of the explanatory load. (Hull 1974:99; also see Hull 1981, this volume)

Hull (1981:180) gives the following example. One might wonder why there are no indigenous Australian eutherians given that the conditions in Australia are perfect for such mammals. One answer is that no eutherians were able to reach Australia before the land masses separated. This answer suffices as an explanation even though it cites only a particular circumstance.

Hull is correct in pointing out that many successful explanations mention only particular historical facts, and what Hull emphasizes is an important aspect of all explanations. A "why" question usually makes a request for a small portion of a total or ideally complete explanation. Consider the illustrious Willie Sutton example (from Sober 1984:145, after Garfinkel 1981). A priest asked Sutton why he robbed banks. Sutton replied that that was where the money was. Sutton answered the question, "Why rob banks rather than some other business?" The priest, however, wanted an answer to the question, "Why choose bank robbing as a career rather than some other profession?" Both questions ask for information that highlight different aspects of the total (i.e., ideally complete) explanation of why Sutton robbed banks.

Similarly, explanations in evolutionary biology can be given by highlighting just some pertinent law or just some aspect of a particular historical circumstance. In Hull's example, stating a bit about the history of Australian biogeography explains why there are no indigenous Australian eutherians. In other cases, citing only an evolutionary regularity may explain the event under consideration. For instance, Mayr's (1970) Founder Principle may explain why a small, isolated population diverged from the main population of a species. Of course citing all the appropriate historical circumstances and the relevant biological regularities is required for an *ideally complete* Hempelian explanation, but in most cases citing an aspect of one or the other will suffice. The same is true in chemistry and physics as well. The melting of a wax ball can be explained by pointing out that it was located in the Sahara Desert on a very hot day, or by citing laws which say that solids with a certain chemical makeup melt when heated above a particular temperature. Both evolutionary biology and the physical sciences provide explanations which cite only laws, and both provide explanations which cite only particular historical events. This is the pragmatic nature of all scientific explanations. Thus the use of particular circumstance explanations in evolutionary biology does not distinguish that discipline from the physical sciences.

In summary, the biological and philosophical literature abounds with suggestions for the unique historical feature of evolutionary biology. A common suggestion cites the alleged distinctive explanatory methodology employed by that theory. More specifically, variants on that suggestion cite the theory's use of "how possibly explanations," its reliance on particular circumstance explanations, and the complexity of evolutionary events (thus the need for historical narratives). All of these features, I have argued, occur in the physical sciences as well. Thus the results of this section indicate that evolutionary theory's explanatory methodology is not as distinctive as many claim. Still, there is a historical aspect of evolutionary theory which distinguishes that theory from the physical sciences. It is that aspect I will now discuss.

The Historical Nature of Evolutionary Theory

Mayr has pointed out that all biological phenomena are the result of two types of causes – proximate and ultimate causation (Mayr 1982:72-73; 1988:17-18, 27ff; see also O'Hara 1988 and Gould 1986.) However, exceptions to this are living entities which have no biological ancestry, such as the first instances of life on this planet. Such entities have only proximate causes. There are two ways to explain why a trait is prevalent among the current members of a population. One is by citing the proximate cause of a trait's prominence, namely, the genetic and environmental factors which caused the development of that trait in many of the current members of that population. Alternatively, a trait's prominence can be explained by citing its ultimate or evolutionary cause. An ultimate cause includes the evolutionary forces which first gave rise to that trait in some ancestor of the population, and includes the forces which allowed that trait to be passed on and eventually become prominent within the population.

Notice that when one cites the ultimate cause for the prominence of a trait, one, in effect, highlights an extensive causal network. Such networks can be described as follows: The organisms within a generation of a taxon are affected by selection and other evolutionary forces. Hereditary relations connect that generation to the next one. Depending on the evolutionary forces at work, the frequency of the traits within that taxon may change. This process goes on, generation after generation, in every taxon, creating extensive lineages or branching trees. One of Darwin's achievements was the recognition that these kinds of causal networks are responsible for the distribution of traits found among all organisms.

I would like to emphasize one aspect of such networks. A trait may be introduced to an ancestor of a population, and it may prove to be beneficial. However, unless there is a mechanism for transmitting that trait from its first occurrence, all the way to the current members of population, that trait cannot become prominent among those members. Such transmission of a trait requires the different generations of a population to be connected by reproductive ties, and such ties require those generations to be spatiotemporally connected. Hence the prominence of a trait among the members of a population depends on its organisms forming a spatiotemporally continuous entity. The point here can be generalized: Evolution causes the distribution of traits among the organisms of a taxon only if that taxon consists of organisms which are spatiotemporally connected. Thus taxa, whether they are local populations, species or phyla, must be historical entities. This observation is the basis of Ghiselin's (1974) and Hull's (1976, 1978) individuality thesis, and brings to the fore an historical aspect of evolutionary biology which sets it apart from the physical sciences.

Let us consider the following difference. The units of evolutionary theory, taxa, are genealogical sequences of organisms which pass on historically acquired information. The units of chemistry and physics, on the other hand, do not consist of such sequences of objects. This difference affords evolutionary theory with a distinctive form of explanation. Some similarities among the members of a taxon are the result of their independent exposure to similar environments. Other similarities are due to a trait being genetically transmitted from a common ancestor. In evolutionary biology, many (most?) of the similarities among the members of a taxon can be explained by those similarities being homologies. No such explanation is available for the similarities found among the units of physics and chemistry. The members of an element on the periodic table bear a number of similarities to one another. For example, all chunks of gold have the same atomic weight. Yet this similarity does not depend on the transmission of information from one chunk of gold to another, and thus does not depend on those chunks forming a spatiotemporally continuous entity.

This unique feature of evolutionary theory even distinguishes it from such historical disciplines as cosmology and geology. These disciplines are historical because they attempt to reconstruct and explain certain spatiotemporal sequences of events. But there is something peculiar about the sequences in evolutionary biology, which consist of series of the same type of object, namely organisms, and organisms have the ability to transmit information genetically with great fidelity. Historical sequences in the physical sciences, on the other hand, tend to consist of different sorts of entities. For example, a geological sequence may consist of a volcano becoming a mountain, then a hill, then a plateau. Moreover, the transmission of information between those entities far from measures up to the transmission of information between different generations of a taxon. In brief, the historical se-

quences of evolutionary theory are unique in two ways: No historical sequence in the physical sciences parallels the hundreds or thousands of generations of organisms in some taxa. Furthermore, the fidelity of information
transmitted through those different generations is unmatched in the inorganic
world. (These examples are from Mayr 1988:16ff) The only science which
parallels evolutionary theory in these respects is human history. Social
groups such as the Protestants or the Dodgers' baseball team consist of
series of humans. Some of the similarities found among the members of
such groups can be explained as homologies. Why, for example, do all Dodgers wear uniforms with blue stripes? Perhaps because one of the team's
earlier managers made that decision and that decision has been passed on to
this day. For a revealing analysis of science as an evolving social enterprise,
see Hull (1988).

We have come to a truly distinctive historical nature of evolutionary
theory. The units of evolutionary theory, taxa, consist of sequences of objects which can transmit information with great fidelity. There are no comparable sequences of natural objects in the physical sciences. This is no
small difference, for it is the existence of such sequences that makes the
occurrence of evolution a unique feature of biology as well as human history.

The Historical Fallacy

Having located this distinctive historical aspect of evolution, I now address
the question of whether the historical nature of taxa implies that evolutionary theory needs a new scientific methodology. Smart (1963:54, 1968:93ff)
and Beatty (1980:549-550, 1981:407) have argued that the historical nature of
taxa shows that there are no laws within evolutionary theory. Beatty (1981)
offers a further argument against the existence of evolutionary laws which
does not turn on the historical nature of taxa. I will discuss that argument
elsewhere. This suggests that evolutionary theory is once again at odds with
the Hempelian model of science.

Taxa are historical entities simply because they are entities which can
evolve. The notion that taxa are evolving entities is tied to the shift from
typological thinking to population thinking (Mayr 1982; Sober 1980). From

a populational view, taxa are identified first and foremost by their particular position on the tree of life. Moreover, they are considered ever-changing entities which shed old traits and adopt new ones for both random and opportunistic reasons. A biological trait present in all the current members of a particular taxon could, for example, disappear among its next generation's members as the result of mutation or recombination, yet those latter members would still be considered members of that taxon. Thus from an evolutionary perspective, there is no biological trait which each member of a taxon must have. Hence, there are no laws which specifically apply to all the members of a particular taxon.

Beatty (1980, 1981) and Smart (1963, 1968) adopt this conclusion. They even agree that it shows that evolutionary theory lacks laws and subsequently fails to conform to the Hempelian model. However, Smart and Beatty disagree on what inferences to draw from this conclusion. For Smart (1963:57), the lack of such regularities implies that evolutionary theory is not an "exact science" but merely a descriptive enterprise. For Beatty (1980, 1981), the problem is not with evolutionary biology but with the Hempelian model of science. Beatty contends that the lack of exceptionless biological regularities indicates that the Hempelian model should be replaced with a new view of theories, specifically, with a view which does not require that theories contain exceptionless generalizations. As an alternative to the traditional view of scientific theories, Beatty (1980, 1981) suggests the "semantic view" of theories. According to that view, a theory consists of models, and when a model is instantiated by an empirical system, that model can be used to explain the system. Interestingly, such models contain exceptionless generalizations. Moreover, a model can be used to explain a system *only when* that system strictly conforms to the model's generalizations. Thus it seems that the semantic account of explanation, like the traditional account, requires the use of exceptionless generalizations. See Ereshefsky (in prep.) for a further discussion of this point.

I want to suggest a flaw in Smart and Beatty's argument against the existence of exceptionless biological regularities. Their argument confuses some of the particulars of evolutionary theory for natural kinds of that theory. Scientific theories refer to two sorts of entities – kinds and particulars. A particular is a spatiotemporally continuous entity whose parts need

not share a common qualitative property. For example, the parts of a mete-
orite are parts of that entity because of their spatiotemporal continuity; those
parts need not be of the same type of metal nor share some other qualitative
property. Additional examples of particulars are the solar system, the book
you are now reading, and my pet dog. The members of a natural kind, on
the other hand, need not be spatiotemporally connected but must share some
qualitative property. For example, two chunks of gold are chunks of gold
provided they share a certain atomic weight. Their being chunks of gold
does not depend on their being spatiotemporally connected to each other or
any other chunk of gold.

These considerations have bearing on where one will find exceptionless regularities within a theory, if indeed there are such regularities. The
parts of a particular need not share some common qualitative property; one
should neither expect nor look for exceptionless regularities among all the
parts of a particular. In a search for geological regularities, it would be
wrong to pick up a particular rock and expect to find some qualitative property which each part of the rock must have for the entire existence of that
rock. The parts can change indefinitely so long as they maintain the appropriate spatiotemporal relation. Nevertheless this lack of exceptionless regularities among the parts of a particular rock does not imply that there are no
geological laws. Before reaching that conclusion, we need to see if there are
exceptionless regularities among the kinds of that theory. We should look
for laws concerning all rocks of a certain kind, for example, all granitic rocks,
or for all rock parts of a certain kind, for example, all chunks of iron.

Similar considerations apply to evolutionary biology. In the previous
section we saw that taxa, whether they be local populations, species or higher
taxa, are particulars in evolutionary theory. That is, they are entities whose
members need not share a common qualitative trait but whose members
must be spatiotemporally connected. Taxa play the same role in evolutionary theory as rocks do in geology; they are not the sort of entities whose
members are amenable to exceptionless generalization. Recall Smart's and
Beatty's argument that there are no laws within evolutionary theory because
there are no laws concerning all the members of a particular taxon. Smart
and Beatty certainly are correct in pointing out that there are no biological
laws concerning all the members of a particular taxon, but that does not

imply that there are *no* laws within evolutionary theory. We must look at other ontological levels within evolutionary theory before reaching that conclusion. More specifically, we must look among the kinds of that theory. For example, we need to see if there are any generalizations which range over all taxa of a particular kind, or any generalizations which apply to all organisms of a certain kind independent of their taxonomic membership.

Instances of both sorts of generalizations can be found within evolutionary biology. Mayr's founder principle says that all founder populations which give rise to new species must have the property of being reproductively isolated from the rest of their parental species (see Ghiselin 1989; Hull 1987:173-74). Similarly, Fisher's fundamental theorem of natural selection asserts that all populations in reasonably constant environments increase in fitness in proportion to the genetic variance found within those populations (see Sober 1984:178; Levine and Sober 1985:307-8). Notice that these generalizations do not attribute a property to all the members of a particular taxon, but to all taxa of a certain kind.

Generalizations concerning the different kinds of organisms that occur in various taxa can be found as well. The optimality models of ecology assert that if certain kinds of organisms are found in particular situations, then those organisms have particular optimal strategies. If a predator is in a situation where there is more than one type of prey and the most profitable prey is abundant, then the predator's most efficient foraging strategy is to specialize on that most profitable prey (Krebs and Davies 1981:54). Similarly, Fisher's sex ratio argument provides an optimality property for all sexual females: The best strategy for a female parent to use in producing grandoffspring is to produce offspring who are all of the minority sex (see Sober 1984:51ff). Also a number of authors object to the idea that optimality models contain scientific laws (see Gould 1986 and Beatty 1980). A typical objection points out that an optimal property highlighted by a model is not always the optimal property of a real population. This is certainly correct, but to assert that this shows that the corresponding optimality model does not contain a law is to misconstrue the role of scientific laws. As we saw above, laws assert what will happen to certain kinds of objects *if* certain circumstances obtain. For example, it might be the case that in many situations producing offspring in the minority sex is not optimal. Still, this does not nullify the law that *if* certain circumstances obtained, that would be the optimal strategy. Notice that these generalizations do not attribute a property to all the members of a particular taxon, but instead to certain kinds of organisms in certain types of situations independent of those organisms' taxonomic membership.

These considerations have the following implication for the historical nature of evolutionary theory. I have suggested that the distinctive nature of that theory lies in its main units, taxa, consisting of evolving sequences of organisms. Some authors maintain that the historical/evolutionary nature of taxa implies that there are no exceptionless regularities in evolutionary theory. Indeed, they take this result to imply that evolutionary theory and the Hempelian model are at odds. The point of this section has been to suggest that evolutionary theory and the Hempelian model are not at odds. More specifically, evolutionary theory should not be dismissed as lacking laws because there are no laws concerning all the members of a particular taxon. Evolutionary theory does contain laws. They just exist at a different ontological level than taxa. Finally, it should be noted that evolutionary theory is no different from any other scientific theory in its lack of taxon-specific laws: all theories consist of particulars whose parts are not amenable to exceptionless regularities.

Summary

The major objective of this paper has been to locate the truly distinctive historical nature of evolutionary theory. The most prevalent suggestion for that feature highlights evolutionary theory's inability to conform to the traditional notion of scientific explanation. For example, Goudge and others argue that the complexity of evolutionary events renders such events singular and ungeneralizable. Thus no evolutionary events can be explained by reference to evolutionary laws. This is contrasted with the use of laws and law-based explanations one finds in the physical sciences. In first half of this paper I suggested that this argument turns on an overly idealistic view of the physical sciences and an overly strict view of the traditional model of science. A strict version of that model holds that each scientific explanation must list all the relevant laws and initial conditions needed for inferring an explanandum under consideration. Needless to say, it seems rather moot whether any scientific theories conform to these standards, or whether they should. Both biological and physical events are complex, and generalizations concerning both types of events must be conditionalized. Most of the time it is either impossible or impractical to list all the conditional clauses needed to make those generalizations exceptionless. So neither evolutionary theory nor any scientific theory meets the demands of the strict traditional view of science. Indeed, both evolutionary theory and the physical sciences contain "how-possibly explanations," complex events (thus the need for historical narratives), and particular-circumstance explanations.

Still, there is a historical aspect of evolutionary theory which distinguishes that theory from the physical sciences – even those physical sciences which are taken to be historical disciplines. That feature lies in the ontological nature of taxa. Taxa consist of extensive sequences of objects which can transmit information with great fidelity. There are no comparable sequences of natural objects in the physical sciences. The only sequences which parallel taxa in this way are the social groups studied by historians. Evolutionary theory *is* a unique historical discipline when compared to the physical sciences, but its uniqueness lies in the theory's ontology, not in its methodology.

Acknowledgments

Support for this work was provided by Northwestern University in the form of a Post-Doctorate Fellowship. I thank David Hull and Elliott Sober for their comments on earlier drafts of this paper.

References

Beatty, J. 1980. Optimal-design models and the strategy of model building in evolutionary biology. *Philosophy of Science* 47:532-61.

Beatty, J. 1981. What's wrong with the received view of evolutionary theory? 397-426. In *PSA 1980*, vol. 2, ed. P. Asquith and R. Giere. East Lansing, MI: Philosophy of Science Association.

Cartwright, N. 1983. *How the Laws of Physics Lie*. Oxford: Oxford University Press.

Ereshefsky, M. (In preparation). The Semantic Approach to Evolutionary Theory.

Garfinkel, A. 1981. *Forms of Explanation*. New Haven: Yale University Press.

Ghiselin, M. 1974. A radical solution to the species problem. *Systematic Zoology* 23:536-44.

Ghiselin, M. 1989. Individuality, history, and laws of nature in biology. In *The Philosophy of David Hull*, ed. M. Ruse. Dordrecht: Reidel.

Giere, R. 1979. *Understanding Scientific Reasoning*. New York: Holt, Rinehart and Wilson.

Giere, R. 1988. *Explaining Science*. Chicago: University of Chicago Press.

Goudge, T. A. 1961. *The Ascent of Life*. Toronto: University of Toronto Press.

Gould, S. 1986. Evolution and the triumph of homology, or why history matters. *American Scientist* 74:60-69.

Hempel, C. 1965. *The Aspects of Scientific Explanation and Other Essays in the Philosophy of Science*. New York: The Free Press.

Hull, D. 1974. *The Philosophy of Biological Science*. Englewood Cliffs, NJ: Prentice-Hall.

Hull, D. 1975. Central subjects and historical narratives. *History and Theory* 14:253-74.

Hull, D. 1976. Are species really individuals? *Systematic Zoology* 25:174-91.

Hull, D. 1978. A matter of individuality. *Philosophy of Science* 45:335-60.

Hull, D. 1981. Historical narratives and integrating explanations, 172-88. In *Pragmatism and Purpose*, ed. L. Sumner, J. Slater and F. Wilson. Toronto: University of Toronto Press.

Hull, D. 1987. Genealogical actors in ecological plays. *Biology & Philosophy* 2:168-83.

Hull, D. 1988. *Science as a Process*. Chicago: University of Chicago Press.

Krebs, D., and N. Davies. 1981. *An Introduction to Behavioral Ecology*. Oxford: Blackwell Scientific Publications.

Lack, D. 1947. *Darwin's Finches*. Cambridge: Cambridge University Press.

Levine, A., and E. Sober. 1985. What's historical about historical materialism? *Journal of Philosophy* 82:304-26.

Mayr, E. 1970. *Populations, Species and Evolution*. Cambridge: Harvard University Press.

Mayr, E. 1982. *The Growth of Biological Thought*. Cambridge: Harvard University Press.

Mayr, E. 1988. *Toward a New Philosophy of Biology*. Cambridge: Harvard University Press.

O'Hara, R. 1988. Homage to Clio, or, toward an historical philosophy for evolutionary biology. *Systematic Zoology* 37:142-55.

Rosenberg, A. 1985. *The Structure of Biological Science*. Cambridge: Cambridge University Press.

Ruse, M. 1973. *The Philosophy of Biology*. London: Hutchinson and Company.

Scriven, M. 1961. The key property of physical laws – inaccuracy, 91-101. In *Current Issues in the Philosophy of Science*, ed. H. Feigl and G. Maxwell. New York: Holt, Rinehart and Winston.

Simpson, G. G. 1964. *This View of Life*. New York: Harcourt, Brace and World.

Smart, J. 1963. *Philosophy and Scientific Realism*. London: Routledge and Kegan Paul.

Smart, J. 1968. *Between Science and Philosophy*. London: Routledge and Kegan Paul.

Sober, E. 1980. Evolution, population thinking, essentialism. *Philosophy of Science* 47:350-83.

Sober, E. 1984. *The Nature of Selection*. Cambridge: MIT Press.

Williams, M. 1986. The logical skeleton of Darwin's historical methodology, 514-21. In *PSA 1986*, vol. 1, ed. A. Fine and P. Machamer. East Lansing, MI: Philosophy of Science Association.

HISTORICAL EXPLANATIONS

AND

EVOLUTIONARY BIOLOGY

History and Evolutionary Processes

Douglas J. Futuyma

My training in evolutionary theory, as for many organismal biologists of my generation, came from reading the works of the victors in the Evolutionary Synthesis, and through their students and followers. We learned that among the achievements of the Synthesis was the reconciliation between the genetical theory of evolutionary processes and the inferences of evolutionary history that emerge from the work of paleontologists, comparative morphologists, and systematists. That is, microevolutionary processes, suitably extrapolated through time, were sufficient to account for macroevolutionary histories of change. There have always been those who did not accept this conclusion, however, and in recent years the tension between students of evolutionary history and of evolutionary processes has become considerably more palpable.

Part of the reason for this is that by so confidently and (apparently) successfully arguing the sufficiency of neo-Darwinian evolutionary mechanisms, the architects of the Synthesis left the impression that the problems of macroevolution had largely been solved, and that the primary challenges lay in exploring evolutionary mechanisms more deeply at the population level (Futuyma 1987a). Historical evolutionary biology was moved to the periphery, the study of evolutionary processes in contemporary populations achieved the centrality and glamor that it still retains, and there developed a schism of mutual ignorance, misunderstanding, and even disrespect between historical and what I have called synchronic evolutionary studies. Population biologists are often unfamiliar with the systematics, morphology, biogeography, and history of a group of organisms; systematists and paleontologists frequently have only a superficial command of population genetics.

This has had an impact on the way different people think about evolution. In particular, population biologists, although sometimes paying lip service to the impact of history, tend to think in ahistorical terms. Most of population genetics, all of optimization theory, and much of community ecology is framed in terms of equilibria rapidly approached; history plays little role in the theory and is wished away whenever possible in interpreting data. In contrast, a paleontologist or systematist sees the imprint of history everywhere – in morphology, in biogeography, in the deployment of taxa through time. It should not be surprising that the two evolutionary biologies are frequently at odds.

My aim in this chapter is to suggest ways in which an awareness of history might profit population biologists, both in expanding the conceptual framework of studies of evolutionary mechanisms and in providing subjects for research. To a degree, this is already happening: since the spandrels of San Marco (Gould and Lewontin 1979), we assume adaptation without justification only at risk of skepticism; students of comparative biology have learned the importance of correlations arising from phylogeny (Ridley 1983; Felsenstein 1985; Pagel and Harvey 1988); the lively debate over punctuated equilibrium has brought paleontologists and population geneticists into uneasy but profitable contact. I shall therefore touch on only a few areas of possible exploration, especially those in which information from phylogenetic studies might play a role. I believe that the schism in evolutionary biology may be repaired, and the field will be the stronger, if we can articulate questions to which both historical and synchronic studies can make complementary, mutually illuminating, contributions.

Stasis, Speciation, and Anagenesis

As an example of how an awareness of history might alter our theoretical perspective, I offer a hypothesis concerning punctuated equilibrium that makes minimal assumptions about genetic processes (Futuyma 1987b, 1989). Following Mayr's (1954, 1963) hypothesis of peripatric speciation by genetic revolutions in founder populations, Eldredge and Gould (1972 and many later papers) postulated that the supposedly common pattern of rapid morphological shifts in otherwise long-static lineages reflects biological speciation (i.e., bifurcation of a lineage, with acquisition of reproductive isolation). Their argument, that genetic homeostasis prevents evolution except in con-

cert with the acquisition of reproductive isolation in a small founder population, has been vigorously opposed by population geneticists. The geneticists'
arguments – that there is abundant genetic variation which manifestly enables
rapid response to selection, that local populations diverge rapidly by selection
and/or drift – are convincing, at least as applied to many characters. Less
convincing is their argument that stasis and change merely reflect periods of
stabilizing and directional selection: to hold that the environment is stable
for millions of years, even while the species composition of communities is
turning over, must require considerable faith. Several critics of punctuated
equilibrium (e.g., Maynard Smith 1983; Lande 1986; Levinton 1988) have
pointed out that by active habitat selection, a species (especially of animal)
buffers itself against considerable environmental change, but whether this
accounts for all character stasis is perhaps doubtful (Lande 1986).

My thoughts on this subject changed when I realized the possible
implications of a historical fact of which I, like most population biologists,
had been aware but had not assimilated. As we all know, the geographic
distributions of species have changed continually and often drastically at all
times, although most conspicuously during the Pleistocene (Cushing 1965;
Livingstone 1975; Graham and Lundelius 1984). Moreover, many of the
associations among species that we see today are quite recent, the component
species having moved about rather independently during the Pleistocene
(Davis 1976). Two possible consequences result from these observations.
First, a species is confronted with an ever-changing complement of interacting species. Averaged over any considerable time, coevolution is, therefore,
likely to be diffuse rather than entailing long-continued specific associations
that would promote ever more extreme coevolved adaptation (Futuyma 1983,
1986). Because of conflicting selection pressures imposed by different interacting species over the course of time, many characters that affect the interaction are likely not to evolve in any one direction for very long. Although
diffuse coevolution may in some instances lead to "escalation" (Vermeij
1987), numerous examples of conflicting selection pressures imposed by
different species suggest that stasis may be a frequent outcome (cf. Stenseth
and Maynard Smith 1984).

A second implication of the shifts in species' distributions caused by
climatic change is that the population structure of species is broken down.

As long as the spatially varying regime of selection is constant, populations may diverge to limits set by gene flow. With a shift in the species' range, however, some populations become extinct and formerly unoccupied regions are colonized. If a new region is colonized from several genetically differentiated populations, there will be an episode of massive gene flow (Slatkin 1977), the divergent characters of many of the differentiated populations (especially smaller ones) will be lost to hybridization, and the species will be homogenized at a mean character state near that of the formerly more abundant or widespread variant. Local selection pressures may again give rise to geographic variation, but if the process of homogenization occurs frequently, relative to the sampling interval in the fossil record, the record might show apparent stasis. If it continues repeatedly and indefinitely, the lineage may show little anagenetic change in the long term.

If, in contrast, a locally differentiated population has achieved reproductive isolation from its sister populations, it may colonize the same areas as its sister species, but retain its distinctive character because it does not interbreed with the other, possibly more abundant, form. The retention of whatever divergence it had achieved holds not just for single characters, but even more importantly for suites of genetically independent but functionally coadapted characters (including genetically determined habitat and food preferences) that enable it to occupy a distinctive niche, but which would be lost to recombination if hybridization were to occur. Therefore, the acquisition of reproductive isolation enables the indefinitely long retention of character changes that otherwise would be ephemeral. As this character change may be one in a series of steps toward ever greater divergence from the ancestral condition, the same process repeated sequentially (i.e., a series of speciation events) may facilitate substantial anagenetic change that otherwise would be frustrated by episodic gene flow (Futuyma 1987b, 1989). Therefore punctuations of apparently static lineages may be coincident with, and long-term anagenesis may be facilitated by, speciation – not because speciation enables response to selection by an otherwise refractory gene pool (as supposed by Eldredge and Gould 1972), but because it confers on local evolutionary changes a degree of permanence they otherwise would lack (cf. also Eldredge 1989).

I have no direct evidence for, or even a suggestion for a definitive test of, this hypothesis, but some observations are at least consonant with it. For example, Coope (1979) noted that all North Temperate Quaternary fossil beetles are identical in fine detail to living species, although their geographic distributions have changed drastically, and he suggested that evolutionary change is less likely during periods of climatic change than during more stable times, because the movement of species "keep[s] the gene pools well stirred." Bell (1988) provided evidence from fossil and Recent sticklebacks (*Gasterosteus*) that morphologically differentiated freshwater populations have evolved repeatedly but have short life-spans, while the marine form from which they arise has persisted with little change. Avise (1989) has described striking evidence of dynamic population structure from intraspecific phylogenies of mitochondrial DNA haplotypes. Over broad geographic regions, haplotypes of widespread species such as the sunfish *Lepomis punctatus* and the redwing blackbird *Agelaius phoeniceus* are less divergent than expected in an abundant, geographically structured species. This implies that the species has experienced a population bottleneck, and that its current geographic population structure is quite recent. Avise notes that disasters altering the abundance and distribution of a species are not infrequent even within our limited experience.

The evidence implies, then, that differentiation of populations from an ancestral condition must frequently be erased by shifts in population structure. It also suggests that, because much geographic variation is recent in origin, we should be wary of assuming that populations have attained their selective optima. That caution should be a significant lesson from history.

Questions Arising From Systematics

Many, if not most, of our concepts of macroevolution have arisen from study of the systematics of living organisms. Systematists, especially by the study of morphology, established most of the principles of character evolution with which we are familiar. Many of these principles pose questions that geneticists and population biologists have slighted, but which may prove both accessible and profitable.

Among the phenomena with which every systematist is intimately

familiar are (1) homology, (2) parallel and convergent evolution, (3) variation in evolutionary rates among characters and taxa, including evolutionary
conservatism or "stasis," (4) instances of reversal and nonreversal ("irreversibility") in characters, and (5) differences among clades in diversity and
in exuberance of adaptive radiation. Several of these – homology, stasis, irreversibility, and differences in adaptive radiation – are closely related, in
that they pose the question of why some characters and taxa have evolved so
little. As several authors have noted, there is something of a conflict between the two great themes of *The Origin of Species* – adaptation and homology ("unity of type"). Riedl (1978) argued that homology "is the consequence
of epigenetic fixation beyond recent functional requirements"; Wagner (1989)
likewise argues that homology implies the existence of historically acquired
developmental constraints (i.e., biases in the origin of phenotypic variations).
For if species were indefinitely and immediately adaptable in all respects,
their morphology would frequently lose the trace of common ancestry that
makes phylogenetic analysis possible (often) from morphological data. Yet
morphology does provide evidence of phylogeny. For example, in an analysis
of *Ophraella* and closely allied genera of chrysomelid beetles (see below), I
have found complete congruence of the phylogenies inferred from allozyme
data and from morphology, except among several species that are so closely
related that morphology provides little resolution (Futuyma and McCafferty,
in prep.). The evolutionary stability of many characters therefore poses
questions for the evolutionary geneticist. I shall briefly review some of the
fragmentary genetic literature that bears on the phenomena that systematics
calls to our attention. Some of the most interesting work is quite old, dating
from a less specialized age when many geneticists were motivated by and
familiar with the systematics of organisms.

Homology and Parallelism. Does uniformity of phenotype imply uniformity
of genotype? In some instances, as in demonstrated cases of convergent
evolution, it clearly does not. Many people consider parallel evolution to be
merely convergence among closely related species; others (e.g., D. B. Wake,
pers. com.) use parallelism to describe independent evolution based on the
same developmental pathway, and convergence to describe evolution based
on different developmental mechanisms. For example, under this interpreta-

tion Rutledge et al. (1975) induced convergent evolution among different lines of mice selected for increased tail length, some of which responded by elongation of the caudal vertebrae and others by increase in the number of vertebrae. But this distinction, and even the meaning of homology, can be ambiguous (Roth 1988; Wagner 1989). In a mechanistic sense, one thinks of a character in two species as homologous if it has the "same" genetic and developmental basis. In a phylogenetic context, one thinks of it as homologous if both species have inherited the character immediately from a common ancestor. Yet there are examples, ranging from gross morphological features (e.g., the skeletal structure of the vertebrate limb, Hinchliffe and Griffiths 1983) to molecular features (ciliate cytoskeletons, Williams 1984), in which phylogenetically homologous, structurally similar features have very different developmental or molecular bases. There is conservation of form but not of developmental pathway, implying – and herein lies an unresolved question of considerable interest – that either stabilizing selection or overriding properties of developmental systems (Wagner 1989) constrain the phenotype even while its genetic basis turns over.

The question then arises, when in the course of evolution do the genetic bases of characters diverge among populations that retain the same phenotype? Do identical characters in closely related species, or in conspecific populations, have the same genetic basis? We know of many instances (Cohan 1984) in which independent *responses* of conspecific populations to similar pressures of natural or artificial selection have led to similar phenotypes based on nonallelic (or perhaps only partially overlapping sets of) genes. Examples include insecticide resistance, growth form of plant ecotypes, and vestigial eyes in cave-inhabiting fishes (Wilkens 1988). Among the fascinating findings earlier in this century (and only rarely studied recently) is that interspecific hybrids frequently display developmental instability or other forms of variation in characters that are identical in the parent species. For example, hybrids among species in the *Drosophila melanogaster* group have a high incidence of abnormalities in bristle count and in abdominal sclerites, features that do not differ among the species (Sturtevant 1921, 1929; Biddle 1932; Weisbrot 1963; Coyne 1985). Elevated frequencies of fluctuating asymmetry and other evidence of developmental instability have been observed also in other hybrids (Sumner and Huestis 1921; Levin 1970;

Leary et al. 1985). Goldschmidt's (1940) classic description of intersexual hybrids among geographic populations of the gypsy moth *Lymantria dispar* extends the phenomenon to physiology and to intraspecific divergence. These examples, as well as instances of the breakdown of dominance relationships in species crosses (see below), are closely related to the question of the formation of coadapted, epistatically different gene complexes. The question remains largely unanswered as to whether morphological characters in a broadly distributed but uniform species are likewise genetically divergent among populations – a question that Sturtevant posed in 1921. The instances, cited above, of different bases for convergently evolved characters in different conspecific populations do not quite answer this question, for they describe responses of different populations to a novel selection pressure, rather than genetic divergence, under a common regime of stabilizing selection, from an ancestral genetic constitution. We know even less about the number or developmental function of the genes that yield similar phenotypes. As molecular techniques progress, including the use of molecular markers for mapping polygenes (e.g., Paterson et al. 1988; McGill et al. 1988), such questions may be within reach of an answer.

The Genetics of Conserved Characters. Phylogenetic stasis, or the conservation of character states among the species in a clade, is surely among the major challenges to modern evolutionary biology. At this point, the problem is to choose among numerous competing explanations. These include: (1) Stabilizing selection imposed by ecological factors. (2) Stabilizing selection based on habitat fidelity, which creates or reinforces ecological stabilizing selection. (3) Stabilization by functional interactions among characters. For example, if we consider the height of cheek teeth in horses as a character in isolation, it has evolved astonishingly slowly (Lande 1976a), but if we consider the numerous other concerted changes in skeletal and muscular structure that may be necessary to allow a selective advantage to greater hypsodonty (e.g., Radinsky 1984), the stability and episodic evolution of the character may be less surprising. Riedl (1978) uses the concept of "burden" of a character to describe the compensatory changes in other characters that would be required if that character were altered. Functional interactions among characters may imply considerable epistasis for fitness. (4) Nonlinear mapping functions between genotype and phenotype (e.g., Scharloo 1987), often expressed as thresholds. Threshold characters are likely to evolve episodically (Lande 1978), and imply considerable epistasis for phenotype among the contributing loci. (5) Genetic correlations owing to pleiotropy, perhaps the most frequently discussed developmental constraint. In theory, genetic correlations do not impose an absolute constraint unless they equal ± 1 (or, even if of lesser magnitude, integrate numerous characters), but they can retard evolution and affect its trajectory (Via and Lande 1985; Via 1987). This is one reason why a population may not be at gene frequency equilibrium.

These phenomena provide abundant material for genetic study, at least in principle. (1) What is the relationship between intraspecific and interspecific genetic variation? Remarkably, it is not clear whether, even at the phenotypic level, there is a correlation between the variance within populations and the variance among populations or species. Kluge and Kerfoot (1973) claimed a positive correlation, but their analysis has been questioned (Rohlf et al. 1983). There is not enough information to begin to say whether or not conservative characters, compared to evolutionarily more labile features, have lower additive genetic variance, relatively more nonadditive variance, stronger genetic correlations with other characters (see below), or greater canalization.

(2) Felsenstein (1988; see also Lynch and Hill 1986) has argued that because of their responsiveness to selection and drift, additively inherited polygenic characters may be untrustworthy indicators of phylogeny, but that developmental constraints may help to retain phylogenetic information. If so, we might expect conservative characters often to display constraints arising from pleiotropy and from thresholds and other epistatic effects. (Although the variable, e.g., "liability," underlying a threshold character may be additively polygenic, at the phenotypic level the variance in the character will generally have an epistatic component.)

Under some conditions, epistasis can constrain response to selection, because populations are trapped on local adaptive peaks (Wright 1977). Dobzhansky and his coworkers adduced considerable evidence for epistasis for fitness components in *Drosophila* (e.g., Spassky et al. 1965; Brncic 1954, 1961; Wallace and Vetukhiv 1955). Despite these and numerous other demonstrations of epistasis (e.g., Cavener and Clegg 1981; Wilkens 1988; Weller et al. 1988), many current theoretical and empirical studies proceed as if nonadditive variance were unimportant.

However, epistatic effects are often evident in interspecific crosses, which may offer opportunity to explore the genetic and developmental bases of phylogenetically informative characters. For example, dominance, viewed by some as an example of canalization (Rendel 1967), is often altered in hybrids (Sturtevant 1912, cited by Huxley 1942; Harland 1936; Hollingshead 1930; Huxley 1942). From crosses between species of cotton (*Gossypium*), Harland (1936) determined that characters which show clear dominance and Mendelian segregation within species behave like polygenic characters in F2 and backcross hybrids: dominance, he concluded, depends on the background of "modifiers," and homologous characters in related species differ genetically. A dominant allele in the plant *Crepis tectorum* confers normal viability within that species, but is lethal in hybrids with several other species (Hollingshead 1930). Similarly, an allele segregating as a color polymorphism in *Platypoecilus* causes melanotic tumors in backcross hybrids with *Xiphophorus*, the swordtail (Kosswig 1929). Even more striking are instances in which interspecific hybrids express presumably plesiomorphic characters typical not of their parent species but of more remotely related species, as in crosses among snapdragons, *Antirrhinum* (Baur 1932).

These and many other examples suggest that character differences among species often have a strong epistatic component. As many authors have realized, this conclusion may have important implications for mechanisms of speciation (Mayr 1954, 1963; Templeton 1980; Carson and Templeton 1984; Barton and Charlesworth 1984; Bryant et al. 1986), although we do not presently know how to judge whether populations on different adaptive peaks diverged by a peak shift across an adaptive valley, or by selection alone (Maynard Smith 1983; Barton and Charlesworth 1984). The epistasis implied by these observations might also affect characters' responsiveness to selection; they may represent local fitness optima from which departure requires the interaction of selection and drift. However, we know little of the genetic architecture of such traits, of their developmental pathways, or of their responsiveness to selection.

(3) The dependence of gene expression, such as dominance, on ge-

netic background is closely related to the concept of threshold traits, which may be of enormous evolutionary importance. We may suspect that, as in the case of the number of scutellar and dorsocentral setae in *Drosophila* (Rendel 1967; Scharloo 1987), many evolutionarily conservative traits are threshold characters, but the genetics of invariant characters is so seldom studied that this is by no means certain. Unanswered questions about threshold characters abound. Gabriel Moreno, at Stony Brook, has framed several such questions in his dissertation work: How does the manifestation of a threshold depend on genetic background? Are there thresholds in continuously varying traits? (He has obtained evidence for thresholds in several characters in *Drosophila* that are usually considered additively polygenic.) Is the distinction between "major" and "minor" genes, made by authors such as Rendel (1967), a valid one? Is a threshold a product of natural selection, as Waddington (1957) proposed in his theory of canalization, or is it an immanent, nonadaptive property of the epigenetic system? Scharloo (1987) interprets some of his studies on genetic variation in *Drosophila* wing venation as evidence for evolved canalization. Can these results be generalized to other characters? Can a comparative genetics of related species demonstrate that canalization has evolved? What are the effects on fitness of genetic variation in the degree of canalization? Departures from the norm of a virtually invariant threshold trait are likely to be scored as "major" or "drastic" mutations (e.g., *scute* in *Drosophila*, which alters the number of scutellar bristles), and these, we have long since learned, generally reduce fitness. How might we distinguish "drastic" mutations, with little evolutionary effect, from evolutionarily viable threshold effects?

(4) As noted below, many mutations are known that alter a character to a state not found naturally in the species or its close relatives, but which is typical of more distantly related species. Some mutations increase a character, such as carpel number, when the invariable evolutionary trend has been toward decrease (Stebbins 1974). That such mutations have not been fixed in nature is usually attributed to the deleterious effects of major mutations. These effects are instances of pleiotropy, the source of potentially long-lasting genetic correlations among traits. Because of the possibly constraining effects of genetic correlations, their stability has become an issue of considerable debate (Lande 1980; Barton and Turelli 1987; Turelli 1988).

Insofar as genetic correlations are attributable to linkage disequilibrium, we should expect them to be quite labile; the more interesting question is whether the pattern of pleiotropy evolves readily. This may be dissected further: can the pleiotropic effects of individual genes remain conserved, yet the pattern of genetic correlation change? For instance, the drastic effects on phenotype and viability of mutations such as *eyeless* in laboratory stocks of *Drosophila* are frequently reduced by the accumulation of "modifiers" by natural selection (Morgan 1926; Huxley 1942 cites other examples). In a natural population of blowflies, the incidence of developmental instability (fluctuating asymmetry) caused by an allele for insecticide resistance has lessened over time (Clarke and McKenzie 1987; McKenzie and Clarke 1988). In both the laboratory and natural cases, the major gene displays its original suite of pleiotropic effects when crossed into another genetic background. That some pleiotropic syndromes may be evolutionarily conservative is suggested by such observations as those of Sturtevant (1921), who identified some genes as homologous in *Drosophila melanogaster* and *D. simulans* by the similar pleiotropic properties of their mutant alleles.

These observations, as well as alterations in genetic correlations brought about by artificial selection (Davies and Workman 1971; Sheridan and Barker 1974), seem to imply that despite persistent pleiotropic effects of *individual* loci, genetic correlations may readily evolve and be broken, and may therefore contribute little to long-term evolutionary stability. However, there is also evidence that genetic correlations can persist in some cases, even in the face of artificial selection designed to alter them (Lande 1979), so it remains unclear what the common impact of genetic correlations on long-term stability may be. These observations also raise the possibility that, contrary to the orthodox view, mutations of large effect might sometimes be fixed by strong selection, despite substantial deleterious pleiotropy, if the latter can be ameliorated by selection of polygenic "modifiers" (Wright 1982; Lande 1983). Fixation of mutations of large effect would clearly have important implications for macroevolution. Virtually the only evidence on this question comes from the genetics of species hybrids, and there is considerable difference of opinion on the relative importance of polygenic versus oligogenic differences (e.g., Lande 1981; Coyne 1983; Gottlieb 1984). Some interspecific differences in plants, especially in what may be interpreted as threshold traits, may be based on few substitutions of large effect (Gottlieb 1984; but see East 1935; Coyne and Lande 1985; Gottlieb 1985). Most interspecific differences in animals appear to be polygenic (Lande 1981), but it should be noted that quantitative geneticists vary considerably in their estimates of the number of "effective factors" contributing to variation, with some favoring a rather low estimate (Mather 1979; Thompson and Thoday 1979; Shrimpton and Robertson 1988).

It should be borne in mind that diminution of fitness is a common correlate not only of mutations with large phenotypic effects, but of polygenic responses to artificial selection as well; perhaps, then, we should not exclude the possibility that lineages "escape" from local optima by fixation of single alleles with large effect, followed by polygenic "fine tuning." This appears to have been the case in the evolution of some mimicry systems (Clarke and Sheppard 1960; Turner 1981). Stebbins (1974) suggested that the evolution of higher taxa involves such an "evolutionary decanalization" of traits, followed by "recanalization." In this context, the numerous instances of mutations resembling the characters of distantly related taxa are especially interesting, and are worthy of study at the molecular and developmental levels. Although it is unclear whether any of these have played a role in evolution, Stebbins (1974, citing especially Gottschalk 1971) notes many instances. For example, a mutation in pea (*Pisum*) converts the stamens from the fused condition typical of the papilionoid legumes (except one tribe) to the unfused condition typical of the mimosoid and caesalpinioid legumes; another mutation converts the leaves from the pinnate to the bipinnate condition that, again, is typical of Mimosoideae and Caesalpinioideae but not of the advanced Papilionoideae, among which the genus *Pisum* is included. There may well be no homology between these mutations and the genetics of the Mimosoideae, but the possibility may be worth exploring with modern genetic technology.

Characters That Have Not Evolved

A question underlying all the discussion of constraints is, if organisms have not evolved the features we might expect, or as rapidly as we might expect, why not? The Panglossian answer is that selection has not favored what we wrongly suppose it should have. The advocates of internal constraint invoke, in effect, an insufficiency of selectable genetic variation. (Insufficiency of genetic variation may, of course, have reasons other than genetic constraint.) It is probably impossible to test the selectionist hypothesis, for we are seldom able to reconstruct the history of selection. But we can search for genetic variation in characters that have not evolved. For example, the recent adaptation of several species of grasses to soils impregnated with heavy metals is an outstanding example of rapid response to selection. But why have so few of the plant species in the neighborhood achieved this adaptation? It turns out that among species of grasses that grow near copper mines, populations from normal soils display genetic variation for copper tolerance in those species that have become established on copper-laden soil, but no genetic variation was detected in most of those species that have not become adapted (MacNair 1987). Consider some of the phenomena to which a similar research program might be applied.

Adaptive radiations, we believe, sometimes follow the origin of "key adaptations" (Simpson 1953; Liem 1973; Werdelin 1987; Mitter et al. 1988). Morphology frequently reflects this pattern. For example, flea beetles of the subfamily Alticinae (Chrysomelidae, leaf beetles) have evolved from a galerucine stock, and differ from galerucines chiefly by a derived character, a "spring" in the hind femur that enables them to jump (Furth 1980). The form of the hind tibia and tarsus is monotonously uniform among the 4000 species of Galerucinae, but is extremely diverse in the Alticinae, with numerous modifications of the shape and setae of the tibia and the tarsomeres. These modifications perhaps affect purchase on and lift-off from different kinds of plant surfaces, and so were adaptive once the jumping habit had evolved. Such modifications would perhaps not be adaptive in the Galerucinae, which merely crawl, but where did they come from in the flea beetles? Do galerucines harbor genetic variation in tibial and tarsal structure, ready to be mobilized under the new selection brought about by a key adaptation?

Another phenomenon is irreversibility, or, more generally, evolutionary trends, whereby the prevalent direction of evolution is asymmetrical. There exists no general theory of irreversibility, which has drawn little recent attention from population biologists (Bull and Charnov 1985). That nonreversal should be common seems remarkable, for we might expect reversal to an ancestral condition to be more likely than "progress" to a derived state; indeed, many mutations and developmental anomalies, whether natural or experimentally induced, have an "atavistic" character (Babcock 1947; Stebbins 1950; Hampé 1960; Müller 1986). Nevertheless, trends occur, and some are seldom reversed. As in beetles generally, most of the thousands of species of Chrysomelidae have eleven antennal segments, the ancestral number. Among the eighty North American genera of Galerucinae and Alticinae, departures occur in only two genera, and in both (*Phyllecthris* in the Galerucinae and *Psylliodes* in the Alticinae) the number is reduced to ten. Reduction of segment number is common among beetles, but an increase has occurred in very few lineages (Crowson 1981). Do eleven-segmented species harbor genetic variation in segment number? Is the distribution of mutational variation asymmetrical? Is there asymmetry in the severity of deleterious pleiotropic effects? A reduced segment number has become fixed in the rather large genus *Psylliodes*, as it has in many large families of beetles. Do they carry genetic variation embracing the ancestral condition? How much time or genetic divergence is required to reduce substantially the capacity for reversal? Is it lost because of a paucity of genetic variation or because the character assumes a "burden" (manifested, perhaps, by pleiotropic effects)?

A Model System: Host Associations in Chrysomelid Beetles

I have recently embarked on a study of characters that have not evolved. I will only briefly outline the research program, which asks whether or not, from a genetic point of view, realized evolutionary changes were more likely than changes that might have occurred but (apparently) did not. The character of interest (actually a complex of traits) is host association in oligophagous herbivorous insects.

Within most taxa of oligophagous herbivorous insects, the majority of species are specialized, to a greater or lesser degree, in their host association. In some taxa, related species are variously associated with only distantly related plants, but in many taxa, host association is relatively conservative, in that related species feed on related plants. For example, species of *Helico-*

nius butterflies feed as larvae on various members of the Passifloraceae. Ehrlich and Raven (1964) summarized many such patterns, and noted instances in which closely related butterflies feed on plants that, even though not themselves closely related, share certain secondary compounds. This led them to postulate (among other propositions) that in the course of adaptive radiation of an insect lineage, a species is likely to evolve a shift to a plant that is chemically similar to its ancestor's host. Their paper, and earlier papers by Dethier (1954) and Fraenkel (1959), drew attention to the role of plant secondary compounds as toxic barriers to be overcome by physiological adaptation and as repellant and attractant stimuli that may select for changes in behavior.

Among the questions posed by insect/plant associations is this: suppose that one of two sister species of insects has retained an ancestral association with a particular plant, say *A*, and the other has shifted to plant *B*. Can we understand why the latter evolved an association with *B* rather than one of the many other plants in its environment? (The question of why they should have different specialized associations, rather than having evolved a polyphagous habit, is another complex issue: Futuyma 1983; Futuyma and Peterson 1985; Futuyma and Moreno 1988; Thompson 1988; Bernays and Graham 1988, and associated papers.) A "Panglossian" might answer that any of many other plants could have been adopted, but that selection favored association with plant *B*. This hypothesis assumes that genetic variation is seldom limiting, and might be supported by pointing to the almost inevitable response of experimental populations to selection on virtually any character (Lewontin 1974), and to the rapid adaptation of hundreds of species of insects to novel toxic compounds, that is, insecticides (Georghiou and Taylor 1977). In contrast, an advocate of genetic and phylogenetic constraints might suppose that the insect lineage adapted to plant *B* because it possessed the genetic variation necessary for adapting to that plant but not to most others in the environment. Ehrlich and Raven's (1964) postulate can be viewed as a deduction from this way of thinking, which really only embodies a cardinal principle of the Evolutionary Synthesis: that evolution proceeds gradually, by small phenotypic steps.

I do not know how to test the panselectionist hypothesis, because it is difficult if not impossible to know the history of selection. But the hypothesis of genetic constraint can be at least approached, although not rigorously tested, if we are willing to make the uniformitarian assumption that the genetic variance in a character remains fairly constant throughout much of the history of a lineage (Lande 1976b). Under the hypothesis of genetic constraint, we would predict that a contemporary population of the species associated with the (immediately) ancestrally occupied plant (*A*) should have genetic variation in characters necessary for adoption of plant *B* (to which an evolutionary shift has occurred), but *not* in those necessary for adoption of plants that, in fact, have not been occupied during the history of the lineage. Such plants might include those that serve as hosts to more distantly related species of insects.

Such a program of genetic investigation requires that the history of host associations be inferred for a group of related species of insects. This may be done by inferring the group's phylogeny from independent evidence, and then mapping host association onto the cladogram (e.g., Mitter and Brooks 1983; Miller 1987). If the mapping is simple, the host association at each ancestral node may be inferred under the assumption of evolutionary parsimony, that is, that the history of the character has been no more complex than the data imply (fig. 1).

To this end, I have attempted to infer the phylogenetic relationships among the species of *Ophraella*, a North American genus of galerucine chrysomelid beetles that includes thirteen currently recognized species (LeSage 1986). Each of the species feeds, as both larva and adult, on one or a few species of Asteraceae (Compositae), in a single genus or at most three closely related genera. The hosts fall into four tribes of Asteraceae.

The details of the phylogenetic study will be published elsewhere. It is based on the morphology of all the life history stages and on electrophoresis of nineteen enzyme loci. The two data sets affirm the monophyly of the genus, and yield the same phylogenetic structure except among several morphologically very similar species for which only the electrophoretic data provide any resolution. Of the several phylogenetic methods applied, I place greatest reliance on a cladistic parsimony analysis, using Swofford's (1985) PAUP program with unordered character states, polarity of state changes being given by the condition in outgroups. For electrophoretic data, I scored each allele as a presence/absence character, "presence" meaning an allele

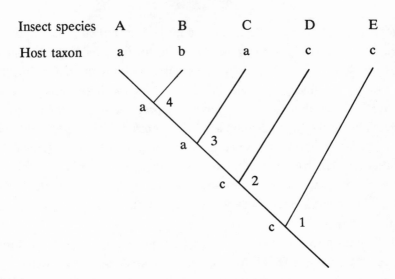

Figure 1. Inference of history of host shifts from an idealized phylogeny of insect taxa distributed over host taxa (lower case letters). By parsimony, the host association at ancestral nodes 1 and 2 was with plant *c*, and at nodes 3 and 4 with plant *a*. Any other hypothesis of host transitions requires extra (e.g., homoplasious) evolutionary changes for which the data provide no evidence. The phylogeny of the insects is assumed to have been inferred from information other than host affiliation.

frequency of $p > 0.05$.

A preliminary estimate of the relationships among the species is provided in figure 2, which also includes the host associations of the taxa. By mapping onto the phylogeny the tribes of Asteraceae with which the beetles are associated, an inference of the history of host shifts is obtained. The ancestral association of the group appears to be with tribe Astereae; from this there have been shifts to Eupatorieae and Heliantheae (subtribe Ambrosiinae). The lineage associated with Ambrosiinae has given rise to species associated with tribe Anthemideae and to one that has reverted to Astereae. This is, perhaps surprisingly, the only instance in which there is evidence of evolutionary reversal (although the species in question, *O. bilineata*, is exclusively associated with a plant genus, *Chrysopsis*, that is not occupied by other Astereae-feeders.)

The inferred history of host shifts provides the basis for genetic studies that are now underway. For example, *Ambrosia artemisiifolia* is a host of

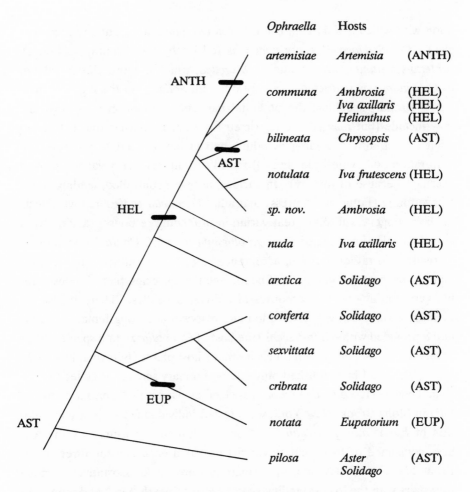

Figure 2. Preliminary estimate of phylogenetic relationships among the species of *Ophraella*, and implied shifts among tribes of asteraceous host plants (upper case abbreviations). The position of *O. bilineata* is ambiguous; it may be more closely related to *O. communa* than to *O. notulata*, but this would not alter the conclusion that there has been reversal to association with Astereae. Associations with tribe Heliantheae are mostly with subtribe Ambrosiinae, although *O. communa* is known to feed also on *Helianthus*, subtribe Helianthinae. Tribal abbreviations: ANTH, Anthemideae; AST, Astereae; EUP, Eupatorieae; HEL, Heliantheae.

Ophraella communa, whereas *Iva frutescens* is occupied exclusively by *O. notulata*. There are some grounds for thinking that *Iva* is an ancestral host, and that association with *Ambrosia* is a derived condition (Futuyma, in prep.). One might then ask if *O. notulata* has the genetic variation necessary for adaptation to *Ambrosia*, but not to, say, *Eupatorium perfoliatum* (association with which is a derived condition in *O. notata*, a distantly related species) or to *Solidago altissima*, which is fed on by the distantly related *O. conferta-sexvittata-cribrata* clade. (*O. arctica*, which is more closely related to *O. notulata*, is restricted to a very different *Solidago* in the high Arctic.)

Broadly speaking, the potential barriers to adoption of a new host may include (but may not be restricted to) plant properties that (1) fail to elicit attraction and feeding by adults and larvae, (2) fail to promote egg maturation and oviposition, and (3) fail to sustain larval survival and growth (perhaps because of toxicity). In various, not well controlled, feeding trials, I have found (Futuyma, in press) that adult *Ophraella* confronted with hosts of their congeners display great variation in feeding response, ranging from complete rejection (e.g., of *Solidago altissima* by >600 *Ophraella communa*) to ready, and rather uniform, acceptance (e.g., of *Iva frutescens* by *O. communa*). In some combinations of beetle and plant species, there is considerable variation among the responses of individual beetles. There is also individual variation in egg maturation and oviposition among female *O. communa* provided with *Iva frutescens* (the host of *O. notulata*), and species differ in larval survival and growth on each other's host plants (Futuyma, in press).

To date I have finished only one preliminary screen for genetic variation. Newly eclosed *O. communa*, collected as pupae on *Ambrosia artemisiifolia* in Stony Brook, New York, were tested individually for their consumption of *Eupatorium perfoliatum*. (Consumption was measured by the leaf area consumed of fresh leaf fragments provided each day for three days.) From 249 such beetles, single-pair matings were made assortatively, among four pairs with the lowest feeding scores (zero or nearly zero) and among 14 pairs with the highest scores. Their progeny were reared on *Ambrosia*, and three to ten progeny of each pair were scored for response to *Eupatorium* for two days, as newly eclosed adults. The correlation among offspring means and midparent values was $r = 0.527$ ($0.01 < p < 0.05$), and the regression of offspring mean on midparent was likewise significant ($F_{1,16} = 6.139$, $y = 47.9 + 1.033x$). The results suggest that the phenotypic variation in feeding response to a congener's host plant has a partly genetic basis. This result happens to tell against the hypothesis that the history of host shifts has been guided primarily by the availability of genetic variation, inasmuch as *Eupatorium perfoliatum* presumably has not figured in the evolutionary history of *O. communa* or any of its closest relatives. It remains to be seen whether this conclusion is general for combinations of species of *Ophraella* and Asteraceae, and whether it holds for characters other than feeding behavior that bear on the likelihood of host shifts.

Conclusions

The study of evolution is fundamentally a study of history. The patterns of diversity that ultimately motivate most of us to study evolution cannot be understood without reference to this history, whether it be glimpsed through paleontology or phylogenetic analysis; and the evolutionary mechanisms that act on any population do so within bounds set by the population's history. Incorporation of a historical evolutionary perspective into the thinking and empirical work of population biologists is likely to increase in the near future, stimulated by the resurgence of interest in macroevolution, by genetic analyses that shed light on population histories, and by improvements in the methods of phylogenetic analysis. Inferences on the recent histories of populations are likely to promote the view that characters are not necessarily at their equilibria. Phylogenetic studies of patterns of character evolution can provide a useful framework for posing and experimentally exploring questions about the genetic architecture of, and genetic variation in, traits of particular interest. Although detailed genetic analysis, comparable to that in *Drosophila melanogaster*, is not possible in most species, the comparative genetic architecture of traits that differ in macroevolutionary pattern may be a profitable realm in which to bridge the gap between studies of evolutionary processes and history.

Acknowledgments

Gabriel Moreno, who has been particularly concerned with many topics of this paper, has contributed importantly to its development. I gratefully acknowledge the National Science Foundation (BSR8516316) for support of my research.

References

Avise, J. C. 1989. Gene trees and organismal histories: A phylogenetic approach to population biology. *Evolution* 43:1192-1208.

Babcock, E. B. 1947. The genus *Crepis*. *University of California Publications in Botany*, Vols. 21, 22. (Cited in Stebbins 1974)

Barton, N. H., and B. Charlesworth. 1984. Genetic revolutions, founder effects, and speciation. *Annual Review of Ecology and Systematics* 15:133-64.

Barton, N. H., and M. Turelli. 1987. Adaptive landscapes, genetic distance and the evolution of quantitative characters. *Genetical Research* 49:157-73.

Baur, E. 1932. Artumgrenzung und Artbildung in der Gattung *Antirrhinum*, Sektion Antirrhinastrum. *Zeitschrift für induktive Abstammungs und Vererbungslehre* 63:256-302. (Cited in Dobzhansky 1937)

Bell, M. A. 1988. Stickleback fishes: Bridging the gap between population biology and paleobiology. *Trends in Ecology and Evolution* 3:320-25.

Bernays, E., and M. Graham. 1988. On the evolution of host specificity in phytophagous arthropods. *Ecology* 69:886-92.

Biddle, R. L. 1932. The bristles of hybrids between *Drosophila melanogaster* and *Drosophila simulans*. *Genetics* 17:153-74.

Brncic, D. 1954. Heterosis and the integration of the genotype in geographic populations of *Drosophila pseudoobscura*. *Genetics* 39:77-88.

Brncic, D. 1961. Integration of the genotype in geographic populations of *Drosophila pavani*. *Evolution* 15:92-97.

Bryant, E. H., S. A. McCommas, and L. M. Combs. 1986. The effect of an experimental bottleneck on quantitative genetic variation in the house fly. *Genetics* 114:1191-1211.

Bull, J. J., and E. L. Charnov. 1985. On irreversible evolution. *Evolution* 395:1149-55.

Carson, H. L., and A. R. Templeton. 1984. Genetic revolutions in relation to speciation phenomena: The founding of new populations. *Annual Review of Ecology and Systematics* 15:97-131.

Cavener, D. R., and M. T. Clegg. 1981. Multigenic response to ethanol in *Drosophila melanogaster*. *Evolution* 35:1-10.

Clarke, C. A., and P. M. Sheppard. 1960. The evolution of mimicry in the butterfly *Papilio dardanus*. *Heredity* 14:163-73.

Clarke, G. M., and J. A. McKenzie. 1987. Developmental stability of insecticide resistant phenotypes in blowfly: A result of canalizing natural selection. *Nature* 325:345-46.

Cohan, F. M. 1984. Can uniform selection retard random genetic divergence between isolated conspecific populations? *Evolution* 38:495-504.

Coope, G. R. 1979. Late Cenozoic fossil Coleoptera: Evolution, biogeography, and ecology. *Annual Review of Ecology and Systematics* 10:247-67.

Coyne, J. A. 1983. Genetic basis of differences in genital morphology among three sibling species of *Drosophila*. *Evolution* 37:1101-18.

Coyne, J. A. 1985. Genetic studies of three sibling species of *Drosophila* with relationship to theories of speciation. *Genetical Research* 46:169-92.

Coyne, J. A., and R. Lande. 1985. The genetic basis of species differences in plants. *American Naturalist* 126:146-50.

Crowson, R. A. 1981. *The Biology of the Coleoptera*. London: Academic Press.

Cushing, E. J. 1965. Problems in the Quaternary phytogeography of the Great Lakes region, 403-16. In *The Quaternary of the United States*, ed. H. E. Wright, Jr., and D. G. Frey. Princeton, NJ: Princeton University Press.

Davies, R. W., and P. L. Workman. 1971. The genetic relationship of two quantitative characters in *Drosophila melanogaster*. I. Responses to selection and whole chromosome analysis. *Genetics* 69:353-61.

Davis, M. B. 1976. Pleistocene biogeography of temperate deciduous forests. *Geoscience and Man* 13:13-26.

Dethier, V. G. 1954. Evolution of feeding preferences in phytophagous insects. *Evolution* 8:33-54.

East, E. M. 1935. Genetic reactions in *Nicotiana*. II. Phenotypic reaction patterns. *Genetics* 20:414-42.

Ehrlich, P. R., and P. H. Raven. 1964. Butterflies and plants: A study in coevolution. *Evolution* 18:586-608.

Eldredge, N. 1989. *Macroevolutionary Dynamics: Species, Niches, and Adaptive Peaks*. New York: McGraw-Hill.

Eldredge, N., and S. J. Gould. 1972. Punctuated equilibria: An alternative to phyletic gradualism, 82-115 In *Models in Paleobiology*, ed. T. J. M. Schopf. San Francisco: Freeman, Cooper.

Felsenstein, J. 1985. Phylogenies and the comparative method. *American Naturalist* 126:1-25.

Felsenstein, J. 1988. Phylogenies and quantitative characters. *Annual Review of Ecology and Systematics* 19:445-71.

Fraenkel, G. 1959. The *raison d'être* of secondary plant substances. *Science* 129:1466-70.

Furth, D. G. 1980. Inter-generic differences in the metafemoral apodeme of flea beetles (Chrysomelidae: Alticinae). *Systematic Entomology* 5:263-71.

Futuyma, D. J. 1983. Evolutionary interactions among herbivorous insects and plants, 209-31. In *Coevolution*, ed. D. J. Futuyma and M. Slatkin. Sunderland, MA: Sinauer.

Futuyma, D. J. 1986. Evolution and coevolution in communities, 369-81. In *Patterns and Processes in the History of Life*, ed. D. M. Raup and D. Jablonski. Dahlem Konferenzen Report 36. Berlin: Springer-Verlag.

Futuyma, D. J. 1987a. *Sturm und Drang* and the evolutionary synthesis. *Evolution* 42:217-26.

Futuyma, D. J. 1987b. On the role of species in anagenesis. *American Naturalist* 130:46573.

Futuyma, D. J. 1989. Macroevolutionary consequences of speciation: Inferences from phytophagous insects, 557-78. In *Speciation and its Consequences*, ed. D. Otte and J. A. Endler. Sunderland, MA: Sinauer.

Futuyma, D. J. In press. The evolution of host specialization in herbivorous insects: Three perspectives. In *Herbivory: Tropical and Temperate Perspectives*, ed. P. W. Price, W. Benson, T. Lewinsohn, and W. Fernandes. New York: Wiley.

Futuyma, D. J., and G. Moreno. 1988. The evolution of ecological specialization. *Annual Review of Ecology and Systematics* 19:207-33.

Futuyma, D. J., and S. C. Peterson. 1985. Genetic variation in the use of resources by insects. *Annual Review of Entomology* 30:217-38.

Georghiou, G. P., and C. E. Taylor. 1977. Pesticide resistance as an evolutionary phenomenon. *Proceedings of the XV International Entomological Congress*, pp. 759-85.

Goldschmidt, R. B. 1940. *The Material Basis of Evolution*. New Haven, CT: Yale University Press.

Gottlieb, L. D. 1984. Genetics and morphological evolution in plants. *American Naturalist* 123:681-709.

Gottlieb, L. D. 1985. Reply to Coyne and Lande. *American Naturalist* 126:146-50.

Gottschalk, W. 1971. *Die Bedeutung der Genmutationen für die Evolution der Pflanzen*. Stuttgart: Fischer.

Gould, S. J., and R. C. Lewontin. 1979. The spandrels of San Marco and the Panglossian paradigm: A critique of the adaptationist programme. *Proceedings of the Royal Society of London B* 205:581-98.

Graham, R. W., and E. L. Lundelius, Jr. 1984. Coevolutionary disequilibrium and Pleistocene extinctions, 223-49. In *Quaternary Extinctions: A Prehistoric Revolution*, ed. P. S. Martin and R. G. Klein. Tucson: University of Arizona Press.

Hampé, A. 1960. La compétition entre des éléments osseux du zeugopode de poulet. *Journal of Embryology and Experimental Morphology* 8:241-45.

Harland, S. C. 1936. The genetical conception of the species. *Biological Reviews* 11:83-112.

Hinchliffe, J. R., and P. J. Griffiths. 1983. The prechondrogenic patterns in tetrapod limb development and their phylogenetic significance, 99-121. In *Development and Evolution*, ed. B. C. Goodwin, N. Holden, and C. C. Wylie. Cambridge: Cambridge University Press.

Hollingshead, L. 1930. A lethal factor in *Crepis* effective only in interspecific hybrid. *Genetics* 15:114-40.

Huxley, J. 1942. *Evolution, the Modern Synthesis*. New York: Wiley.

Kluge, A. G., and W. C. Kerfoot. 1973. The predictability and regularity of character divergence. *American Naturalist* 107:426-42.

Kosswig, G. 1929. Über die veranderte Wirkung von Farbgenen des *Platypoecilus* in der Gattungskreuzung mit *Xiphophorus*. Zeitschrift für induktive Abstammungs- und Vererbungslehre 52:114-20. (Cited in Dobzhansky 1937)

Lande, R. 1976a. Natural selection and random genetic drift in phenotypic evolution. *Evolution* 30:314-34.

Lande, R. 1976b. The maintenance of genetic variability by mutation in a polygenic character with linked loci. *Genetical Research* 26:221-36.

Lande, R. 1978. Evolutionary mechanisms of limb loss in tetrapods. *Evolution* 32:73-92.

Lande, R. 1979. Quantitative genetic analysis of multivariate evolution, applied to brain:body size allometry. *Evolution* 33:402-16.

Lande, R. 1980. The genetic covariance between characters maintained by pleiotropic mutations. *Genetics* 94:203-15.

Lande, R. 1981. The minimum number of genes contributing to quantitative variation between and within populations. *Genetics* 99:541-53.

Lande, R. 1983. The response to selection on major and minor mutations affecting a metrical trait. *Heredity* 50:47-65.

Lande, R. 1986. The dynamics of peak shifts and the pattern of morphological evolution. *Paleobiology* 12:343-54.

Leary, R. F., F. W. Allendorf, and R. L. Knudson. 1985. Developmental instability in high meristic counts in interspecific hybrids of salmonid fishes. *Evolution* 39:1318-26.

LeSage, L. 1986. A taxonomic monograph of the Nearctic galerucine genus *Ophraella* Wilcox (Coleoptera: Chrysomelidae). Memoirs of the Entomological Society of Canada 133:1-75.

Levin, D. A. 1970. Developmental instability in species and hybrids of *Liatris*. *Evolution* 24:613-24.

Levinton, J. S. 1988. *Genetics, Paleontology, and Macroevolution*. Cambridge: Cambridge University Press.

Lewontin, R. C. 1974. *The Genetic Basis of Evolutionary Change*. New York: Columbia University Press.

Liem, K. F. 1973. Evolutionary strategies and morphological innovations: Cichlid pharyngeal jaws. *Systematic Zoology* 22:425-41.

Livingstone, D. A. 1975. Late Quaternary climatic change in Africa. *Annual Review of Ecology and Systematics* 6:249-80.

Lynch, M., and W. G. Hill. 1986. Phenotypic evolution by neutral mutation. *Evolution* 40:915-35.

MacNair, M. R. 1987. Heavy metal tolerance in plants: A model evolutionary system. *Trends in Ecology and Evolution* 2:354-59.

Mather, K. 1979. Historical overview: Quantitative variation and polygenic systems, 5-34. In *Quantitative Genetic Variation*, ed. J. N. Thompson, Jr., and J. M. Thoday. London: Academic Press.

Maynard Smith, J. 1983. The genetics of stasis and punctuation. *Annual Review of Genetics* 17:11-25.

Mayr, E. 1954. Change of genetic environment and evolution, 157-80. In *Evolution as a Process*, ed. J. Huxley, A. C. Hardy, and E. B. Ford. London: Allen and Unwin.

Mayr, E. 1963. *Animal Species and Evolution*. Cambridge: Harvard University Press.

McGill, S., W. Chia, R. Karp, and M. Ashburner. 1988. The molecular analysis of an antimorphic mutation of *Drosophila melanogaster*, *Scutoid*. *Genetics* 119:647-61.

McKenzie, J. A., and G. M. Clarke. 1988. Diazinon resistance, fluctuating asymmetry and fitness in the Australian sheep blowfly, *Lucilia cuprina*. *Genetics* 120:213-20.

Miller, J. S. 1987. Host-plant relationships in the Papilionidae (Lepidoptera): Parallel cladogenesis or colonization? *Cladistics* 3:105-20.

Mitter, C., and D. R. Brooks. 1983. Phylogenetic aspects of coevolution, 65-98. In *Coevolution*, ed. D. J. Futuyma and M. Slatkin. Sunderland, MA: Sinauer.

Mitter, C., B. Farrell, and B. Wiegmann. 1988. The phylogenetic study of adaptive zones: Has phytophagy promoted insect diversification? *American Naturalist* 132:107-28.

Morgan, T. H. 1926. *The Theory of the Gene*. New Haven, CT: Yale University Press.

Müller, G. 1986. Effects of skeletal change on muscle pattern formation. *Bibliotheca Anatomica* 29:91-108.

Pagel, M. D., and P. H. Harvey. 1988. The taxon-level problem in the evolution of mammalian brain size: Facts and artifacts. *American Naturalist* 132:344-59.

Paterson, A. H., E. S. Lauder, J. D. Hewitt, S. Peterson, S. E. Lincoln, and S. D. Tanksley. 1988. Resolution of quantitative traits into Mendelian factors by using a complete linkage map of restriction fragment length polymorphisms. *Nature* 335:721-26.

Radinsky, L. B. 1984. Ontogeny and phylogeny in horse skull evolution. *Evolution* 38:1-15.

Rendel, J. M. 1967. *Canalisation and Gene Control*. London: Logos Press.

Ridley, M. 1983. *The Explanation of Organic Diversity: The Comparative Method and Adaptations for Mating*. Oxford: Clarendon.

Riedl, R. 1978. *Order in Living Organisms: A Systems Approach to Evolution*. New York: Wiley.

Rohlf, F. J., A. J. Gilmartin, and G. Hart. 1983. The Kluge-Kerfoot phenomenon: A statistical artifact. *Evolution* 37:180-202.

Roth, V. L. 1988. The biological basis of homology, 1-26. In *Ontogeny and Systematics*, ed. C. J. Humphries. New York: Columbia University Press.

Rutledge, J. J., E. J. Eisen, and J. E. Legates. 1975. Correlated response in skeletal traits and replicate variation in selected lines of mice. *Theoretical and Applied Genetics* 46:26-31.

Scharloo, W. 1987. Constraints in selection response, 125-49. In *Genetic Constraints on Adaptive Evolution*, ed. V. Loeschcke. Berlin: Springer-Verlag.

Sheridan, A. K., and J. S. F. Barker. 1974. Two-trait selection and the genetic correlation. II. Changes in the genetic correlation during two-trait selection. *Australian Journal of Biological Science* 27:89-101.

Shrimpton, A. E., and A. Robertson. 1988. The isolation of polygenic factors controlling bristle score in *Drosophila melanogaster*. II. Distribution of third chromosome bristle effects within chromosome sections. *Genetics* 118:445-59.

Simpson, G. G. 1953. *The Major Features of Evolution*. New York: Columbia University Press.

Slatkin, M. 1977. Gene flow and genetic drift in a species subject to frequent local extinctions. *Theoretical Population Biology* 12:253-62.

Spassky, B., T. Dobzhansky, and W. W. Anderson. 1965. Genetics of natural populations. XXXVI. Epistatic interactions of the components of the genetic load in *Drosophila pseudoobscura*. *Genetics* 52:653-64.

Stebbins, G. L. 1950. *Variation and Evolution in Plants*. New York: Columbia University Press.

Stebbins, G. L. 1974. *Flowering Plants: Evolution Above the Species Level*. Cambridge: Harvard University Press.

Stenseth, N. C., and J. Maynard Smith. 1984. Coevolution in ecosystems: Red Queen evolution or stasis. *Evolution* 38:870-80.

Sturtevant, A. H. 1912. Federley's breeding experiments with the moth *Pygaera*. *American Naturalist* 46:565-68.

Sturtevant, A. H. 1921. Genetic studies on *Drosophila simulans*. III. Autosomal genes. General discussion. *Genetics* 6:179-207.

Sturtevant, A. H. 1929. The genetics of *Drosophila simulans*. Carnegie Institute of Washington Publication 399:1-62.

Sumner, F. B., and R. R. Huestis. 1921. Bilateral asymmetry and its relation to certain problems of genetics. *Genetics* 6:445-85.

Swofford, D. L. 1985. *PAUP: Phylogenetic Analysis Using Parsimony. User's Manual*. Champaign, IL: Illinois Natural History Survey.

Templeton, A. R. 1980. The theory of speciation by the founder principle. *Genetics* 92:1011-38.

Thompson, J. N. 1988. Evolutionary ecology of the relationship between oviposition preference and performance of offspring in phytophagous insects. *Entomologia Experimentalis et Applicata* 47:3-14.

Thompson, J. N., Jr., and J. M. Thoday, eds. 1979. *Quantitative Genetic Variation*. New York: Academic Press.

Turelli, M. 1988. Phenotypic evolution, constant covariances, and the maintenance of polygenic variation. *Evolution* 42:1342-47.

Turner, J. R. G. 1981. Adaptation and evolution in *Heliconius*: A defense of neoDarwinism. *Annual Review of Ecology and Systematics* 12:99-121.

Vermeij, G. J. 1987. *Evolution and Escalation: An Ecological History of Life*. Princeton, NJ: Princeton University Press.

Via, S. 1987. Genetic constraints in the evolution of phenotypic plasticity, 47-71. In *Genetic Constraints on Adaptive Evolution*, ed. V. Loeschcke. Berlin: Springer-Verlag.

Via, S., and R. Lande. 1985. Genotype-environment interaction and the evolution of phenotypic plasticity. *Evolution* 39:505-23.

Waddington, C. H. 1957. *The Strategy of the Genes*. London: Allen and Unwin.

Wagner, G. P. 1989. The origin of morphological characters and the biological basis of homology. *Evolution* 43:1157-71.

Wallace, B., and M. Vetukhiv. 1955. Adaptive organization of the gene pools of *Drosophila* populations. *Cold Spring Harbor Symposia on Quantitative Biology* 20:303-10.

Weisbrot, D. R. 1963. Studies on differences in the genetic architecture of related species of *Drosophila*. *Genetics* 48:1121-39.

Weller, J. I., M. Soller, and T. Brody. 1988. Linkage analysis of quantitative traits in an interspecific cross of tomato (*Lycopersicon esculentum* X *Lycopersicon pimpinellifolium*) by means of genetic markers. *Genetics* 118:329-39.

Werdelin, L. 1987. Jaw geometry and molar morphology in marsupial carnivores: Analysis of a constraint and its macroevolutionary consequences. *Paleobiology* 13:342-50.

Wilkens, H. 1988. Evolution and genetics of epigean and cave *Astyanax fasciatus* (Characidae, Pisces): Support for the neutral mutation theory. *Evolutionary Biology* 23:271-367.

Williams, N. E. 1984. An apparent disjunction between the evolution of form and substance in the genus *Tetrahymena*. *Evolution* 38:25-33.

Wright, S. 1977. *Evolution and the Genetics of Populations*. Vol. 3. *Experimental Results and Evolutionary Deductions*. Chicago: University of Chicago Press.

Wright, S. 1982. Character change, speciation, and the higher taxa. *Evolution* 36:427-43.

The Conditions for a Nomothetic Paleontology

David B. Kitts

In the *Poetics* Aristotle makes a distinction between poetry and history which, to this day, serves as a starting point for our discussions of the nature of history. He said:

> From what we have said it will be seen that the poet's function is to describe, not the thing that has happened, but a kind of thing that might happen, i.e., what is possible as being probable or necessary. The distinction between historian and poet is not in the one writing prose and the other verse – you might put the work of Herodotus into verse, and it would still be a species of history; it consists really in this, that the one describes the thing that has been, and the other the kind of thing that might be. Hence poetry is something more philosophic and of graver import than history, since its statements are of the nature rather of universals, whereas those of history are singulars. By a universal statement I mean one as to what such or such a kind of man will probably or necessarily say or do – which is the aim of poetry, though it affixes proper names to the characters; by a singular statement, one as to what, say, Alcibiades did or had done to him (*Poetics* 1415b).

Aristotle's disdain for history comes as no surprise. His metaphysics committed him to the position that a study of the past can reveal no knowledge that might not better be revealed in a study of the present, for the past can differ from the present only accidentally. That we suppose there is significant knowledge to be achieved only through a study of the past is one of perhaps half a dozen fundamental ideas which separates us from antiquity. But even if we reject Aristotle's metaphysics we cannot wholly escape the consequences of the distinction he made. History is indeed, unlike poetry and physics, about the thing that has been rather than the thing that might be. The reason for this lies, partly at least, in the very nature of our knowl-

edge of the past. The study of history can be a rational enterprise only if
some restriction is placed upon what we may suppose to have occurred. In
what may be considered the mainstream of historical studies we are not, as
James Hutton put it (1795:547), ". . . to make nature act in violation to that
order which we actually observe. . . ."

Historians have, from time to time, grown impatient with these external restrictions upon our knowledge of the past and have sought a means of
escaping them. Some paleontologists, for example, have lately begun to
envision a science of paleobiology in which theories of macroevolution are
formulated on the basis of historical data. In this chapter I shall consider
what it is that paleontologists hope to achieve in their quest for what some
of them have called a "nomothetic paleontology" and to identify a few methodological difficulties they may encounter in that quest.

Historical Inference: The First Step

Historians often contrast the "facts" of history and their "interpretation", the
facts being the events of the distant past and their interpretation being some
synthesis or explanation that is imposed upon the facts or may even grow out
of them. Paleontologists make much the same distinction, although often in
terms of "facts" and "theories." To say that an event is a fact may simply
mean that it actually occurred. But historians and paleontologists often
mean more than this in their talk of the facts of history. They may be implying, or at least be forgetting to avoid assuming, that the events of the past
not only actually occurred, but that they are the irreducible raw material with
which all higher inferential operations in history begin. But events are not
irreducible nor are they self-evidently distinct. In science the process by
which events are recognized is inseparable from the process by which they
are imbued with significance with respect to some theory. Events of the
distant past and events of the proximate past are no different in this regard,
but the events of the distant past lie at the end of longer and more elaborate
inferential chains. Historical events, however familiar they may become, and
however routine the inferences that support them may seem to be, lie not at
the beginning of our quest for synthesis and historical understanding, but

somewhere well along the way.

Popper considers a preoccupation with the testing of statements about events to be the identifying feature of the historical sciences. Consider his concise contemporary version of the ideographic view of history. He said (1957:143), "The situation is simply this: while the theoretical sciences are mainly interested in finding and testing universal laws, the historical sciences take all kinds of universal laws for granted and are mainly interested in finding and testing singular statements." It is the purpose of this chapter to consider whether such an extreme view is justified, at least for the case of geology and paleontology. It is clear, however, that the finding and testing of singular descriptive statements receives a good deal of attention in those disciplines such as history, archaeology, and paleontology, which are indisputably historical. In the primary historical inference it is supposed that certain states and events in the present are to be explained by linking them with certain states and events in the past. Because events do not point intrinsically beyond themselves to other events, causal connections between past and present must be justified by reference to universal laws or, more commonly, to less comprehensive and formal generalizations. A generalization plainly cannot be tested by the explanatory inference in which it is presupposed, and there is a good reason why attempts are seldom made to test universal laws in any historical context whatever. Physical and biological laws, and even the less rigorous generalizations which are often directly invoked in historical inferences, are tested under the most controlled and circumscribed conditions. The evaluation of theories is problematic enough without compounding the difficulties attending it by performing tests within the complexity of history. Geologists and paleontologists, before they begin their search for the past, are committed to the view that whatever events they may propose as antecedents in explanations of the present, these events will be those that do not violate certain deeply held and widely shared theoretical notions.

Theories not only compel us to suppose that events have something in common, they further maintain their hold upon events by specifying the way and the extent to which they may differ from one another. Historical events are judged to be unique not because each of them can be characterized by some unique property. Properties are shared. Their possession consigns events to classes. A historical event is judged to be unique because it can be assigned as the sole occupant of an intersection of classes each of which is defined by some property. A historical event, although unique in this sense, is not thereby removed from any of the classes whose intersection permitted its uniqueness to be established, nor, what is more significant, from the possibility of being treated in terms of theoretical generalizations which refer to those classes. Not only may we generalize about historical events, in the very act of justifying our knowledge of them we are compelled to do so. There are no theory-free events nor any uninterpreted chronicle composed of them.

The body of scientific theory to which geologists and paleontologists subscribe is not static nor is it a matter for unanimous agreement among contemporaries. It is a hoary maxim that each generation rewrites history. We suppose that those living at different times hold certain characteristic views which condition their perception of the past and which may even result in distortions of history. If events exist independent of our knowledge of them, as most of us suppose that they do, then among different accounts of them there are bound to be contradictions. Some politicians and even historians have been accused of intentionally distorting history for their own nefarious purposes.

Geologists and paleontologists escape almost entirely the suspicion of any intent to distort history. When they rewrite history, as they do from time to time, it is not likely to be seen as the result of a change of opinion, but rather of an advance in knowledge. Scientists, by and large, regard themselves and are regarded by others as people who settle the issues which divide them by an appeal to facts.

At any given moment in the history of geology and paleontology, disputes are less likely to arise out of disagreements about what comprehensive theories are to be presupposed in historical inferences than out of disagreements about what initial and boundary conditions are to be held constant in order that these theories may be effectively employed. Historical scientists are never able to determine values for all of the boundary conditions which their guiding theory has identified as relevant. The response to this difficulty is to suppose, without independent justification for doing so, that some boundary conditions which, according to the theory may vary, have remained constant. This is, in effect, a historical version of "the other things being equal" assumption which is made not in the context of a discussion or experiment where the goal is the elucidation of, or the test of some theory, but in the context of a historical inference where the goal is to test a singular statement about past conditions. Historical inferences, it is clear, are performed against an unproblematic background which includes not only general principles but singular descriptive statements about the kinds of conditions which the inference is meant to discover.

Decisions about whether or not some state or trend is to be assumed to remain constant are usually made on a case by case basis as the circumstances demand. But sometimes a more general methodological commitment may be made as it has been, for example, in the acceptance by some geologists and paleontologists of a principle of parsimony (for example, Anderson [1963] in structural geology, and Gingerich [1976] in paleontology).

When physicists and philosophers have discussed parsimony and simplicity it has nearly always been in connection with theories. The *historical parsimony principle* seems to amount to the claim that, even though an event or process is not theoretically precluded, it does not, as a matter of contingent fact, occur. It might well be true that, though a theory identified some event as possible, the world would be such as to preclude its occurrence. But it is in just the identifying feature of historical disciplines that an attempt is made to avoid assuming that certain possible events occur and to try to find out whether or not they did. To claim, either on metaphysical or methodological grounds, that we should formulate our theories in the most parsimonious way possible does not entail that the events to which the theory refers will be related in the most parsimonious way permitted by the theory. To put it another way, a scientific theory, by itself, does not determine the complexity of the world to which it purports to apply. The laws of classical mechanics specify, in effect, that they will apply to any world containing at least two bodies. Writing history consists of identifying from among all the possible worlds permitted by some presupposed theory, the actual world. This involves describing the actual world in terms of the initial and boundary conditions which some theory identifies as relevant. We would not be writing history if we supposed that every time a heavy body is released just above the earth's surface it takes the most direct, or "parsimonious," path toward the earth's center. Whether or not it does is not something to be assumed. It is something to be found out in the course of historical investigation. A historical scientist may tentatively suppose that the causal sequence leading to the occurrence of some event was parsimonious in the knowledge that it might have been otherwise and even in the expectation that further research would show it to be. G. G. Simpson often said of certain systematic and phylogenetic arrangements that they were permitted by our ignorance rather than sustained by our knowledge. It is plain that the ignorance alluded to by Simpson is not the ignorance of a theory, but the ignorance of historically relevant empirical evidence. Whatever parsimony we may impart to the underlying order of nature which finds its formal expression in scientific theories, it may turn out that, in fact, the temporal expression of that underlying order is overwhelmingly unparsimonious.

Historical Inference: The Second Step

The historical inference that marks our initial step into the past, and which I have called primary historical inference, is, of course, not the end of historical research. If it were then Aristotle's view of history would be justified because, after all, the events generated in primary historical inferences are familiar kinds of events no matter how far removed they may be in time. These events are, moreover, causally linked to other events in the past and in the present in familiar kinds of ways. But in geology and paleontology, and in every genuinely historical discipline, there is some means of moving beyond a chronicle of familiar kinds of events linked to one another in familiar kinds of ways. In each of these disciplines there is some principle which permits events to be temporally ordered without knowing, or supposing, that they are causally related, and consequently makes it possible to find among them previously unrecognized and unsuspected relationships. In geology and paleontology the preeminent noncausal, temporal ordering principle is the law of superposition.

It is important to distinguish between two different kinds of events both of which may be called historical. I have done so by identifying *primary* and *secondary* historical events. A primary historical event is an event with such limited temporal extension that it might be encountered in the lifetime of a single observer. The question of whether or not such an event could occur or has occurred can, in principle, be settled by observation and experiment. Historical events of this kind differ from events we encounter in the present only by virtue of having occurred in the past. They are reached in primary historical inferences.

Secondary historical events are, on the other hand, uniquely historical. They have no counterpart in the present. They are composed of primary events related in a spatial and temporal nexus. Some of the temporal relationships among the primary events composing a secondary event are secured by causal generalizations linking events of certain kinds, but others are related by noncausal ordering principles. Thus, in every secondary event there are some relationships that our knowledge of physics and geology had not led us to expect. We clearly cannot get at these complexes of primary events in the same more or less direct way that we can get at their constituents. If we wish to test the grounds that justify our contention that a secondary event has occurred or could occur, we must test all of the principles used to infer the primary events of which it is composed and all of the principles employed in relating those events to one another. An answer to the question, Did this secondary event occur? or to the question, Have secondary events of this kind occurred? requires that historical inferences be performed.

The New Tectonics As Nomothetic Geology

The "new tectonics" provides a dramatic example of historical inference on a grand scale. Primary events which had been inferred by invoking virtually every principle of physics and geology were related to one another in configurations of immense complexity and great spatial and temporal extension. The temporal order of some of these constituent events rest upon their causal connection, but there are many others which, because of noncausal ordering principles, have been linked in spatial and temporal configurations which had not, perhaps could not, have been anticipated on the basis of some presupposed geological or physical theory. Even more significant was the fact that recurring patterns of these unexpected configurations were recognized.

Earth scientists have taken justifiable pride in the new tectonics, which they consider a revolutionary development, believing, rightly, I think, that it has raised their discipline to a level of prestige in the scientific community that it had not enjoyed since the middle of the nineteenth century. It has been suggested that the earth sciences are, as the result of the revolution, now more rigorous and scientific. The prior external constraint which has been imposed upon historical explanation of secondary events is the same as the one imposed upon the explanation of primary events. No matter how unexpected the relationships among primary events that have been revealed in these elaborate historical inferences, it has been unhesitatingly assumed that contemporary physical theory is a sufficient instrument for their explanation and that, therefore, no new and independent theory is needed to explain the history of the earth. Even if geologists had attempted to formulate new theories for the explanation of secondary events, their latitude would have been severely restricted because the constituent primary events were already deeply imbued with theoretical significance.

Geology is the paradigm historical science. Its goal has been the discovery of events and relationships among events that, being beyond the range of observation, can only be reached in historical inferences, albeit inferences subject to the prior external constraint of physical theory. Even bound by that constraint, our view of the past has been profoundly altered. There has, indeed, been a revolution, a historical revolution appropriate to a historical science. But geology, like every historical science has nomothetic aspects. Some of the generalizations of plate tectonics are plainly meant to be explanatory. The subduction of plates along a continental margin has not only been associated with a certain kind of vulcanism, it explains the occurrence of that kind of vulcanism. To have explanatory efficacy a generalization must at least be projected, that is, its scope must not be exhausted by the instances cited in support of it. The contention that a generalization is projected to unexamined instances cannot be empirically justified, but it can be supported theoretically by showing that the projection is plausible in terms of, or even follows from, a fundamental theory which comprehends it.

The prior, external constraint of physical theory has reduced the scope of geological theorizing but it has not prevented plate tectonics from developing its nomothetic components. It has not even prevented the achievement of some degree of autonomy. Although it is supposed that the explanatory generalizations of plate tectonics could, in principle, be shown to follow from fundamental physical laws, little effort has been made to demonstrate such a relationship. Physical theory does not serve as a set of axioms by which all geological knowledge must be validated. It serves rather as a source of guiding principles for historical research, and a limit permitting us to choose among all the accounts of the past which are consistent with the present state of the earth. And in any quest for a nomothetic geology it would serve as a source of justification for claims that some geological hypotheses are to be accorded theoretical status.

A Nomothetic Paleontology

Paleontologists seem to have expected something even more distinctly nomothetic to emerge from their own historical studies. Beginning with the claim of many that they had proved that evolution had occurred, they have turned to the past with the confidence that it would yield theoretical illumination as well as historical chronicle. The greater expectations of paleontologists do not, it seems to me, arise out of any unique features of the theories that they invoke, for example that evolutionary theory in particular, or even biological theory in general, is historical in some way that physical theory is not (e.g., Grene 1958 and Goudge 1961). But there is a difference between physical historical geology and paleontology which, although it appears to be wholly accidental has, nonetheless, important methodological consequences.

The significant principles of physical theories can be directly instantiated by the objects with which geologists begin their inferences and, consequently, more or less directly by the antecedent events meant to explain them. A body of granite is, for example, characterized by the same properties, for example, mass, density, chemical composition and crystal structure, as are the antecedent events meant to explain it. The situation in paleontology is plainly different. The properties which biology identifies as theoretically significant, such as genetic variability, community structure and energy requirements are simply not to be instantiated *in* fossils nor are they in any direct and straightforward way to be inferred *from* fossils. There is no mystery about this contrast between geology and paleontology. It is the result of the obvious fact that the living bodies and the remains of living bodies, which are the subject matter of biology, do not keep very well.

Not only is this difference between geology and paleontology accidental, it is one of degree only. By ingenious indirect procedures paleontologists may be able, beginning with fossils in their geological setting, to plausibly impart some theoretically significant properties to past biological events. But fossils, by themselves, demand that very little be assumed about the organisms whose remains they are supposed to be. Biological theory has a weaker claim upon fossils than physical theory has upon the objects with which geological inferences began, which makes it easy for the paleontologist to leave the fossil record relatively free of external theoretical constraint. Schindewolf (especially 1950) did not see the Anglo-American's ruling evolutionary theory as an impediment to his formulation of a theory which contradicted it. And when Simpson (especially 1944 and 1953) attributed to organisms of the past all of the properties required of them by synthetic theory, it must have appeared to the saltationists to have been a pretty gratuitous move.

But however weak the hold of biological theories upon fossils seems to be, evolutionists are not quite at liberty to suppose that ancient populations are devoid of any biological properties other than those which appear to be required by the fossil record because, among other things the fossil record becomes a record of evolution only upon one of several possible interpretations. The fossil record is not "raw data." A justification of the hypothesis that populations are related as ancestor to descendant demands a specification of how that relationship is generated. The fact that evolutionary paleontologists and biblical creationists invoke it with equal facility is testimony to the ambiguities surrounding the very notion of a fossil record. Try to imagine a sort of minimal fossil record. Suppose that fossils in their geological setting are interpreted just enough to yield a record of organisms living in populations and communities ordered in space and time which may be imbued with any biological property so long as it does not entail, or even bear upon, modification by descent. Something like it must be at issue in many of the arguments about what the fossil record tells us. But it is only on the basis of an agreed-upon external constraint that we can engage in rational debate about what the fossil record tells us. Of course, there may be perfectly legitimate disagreements about the character and extent of the restriction to be applied, but they are prior to an assessment of the fossil record. The dispute between evolutionists and biblical creationists is only the most incoherent of all of those about the meaning of the fossil record that have arisen outside the boundaries of an agreed-upon external constraint.

Evolutionists have rightly insisted that a distinction be made between the fact that evolution has occurred and a theory meant to explain it. But they have failed to take sufficient account of how intimate the relationship between them is. It is not the case that biologists *discovered* evolution in observable facts and then proceeded to explain it. In his *Origin* Darwin made no distinction between explaining evolution and demonstrating that it had occurred. Just as in the eighteenth century the most compelling reason for supposing that the planets move about the sun in elliptical orbits was the acceptance of a theory purported to entail it, so in the nineteenth and twentieth centuries the most compelling reason for supposing that evolution has occurred was the acceptance of a theory which purported to entail it. If evolution is a fact, it is not a fact that can be established by paleontology, or systematics, or comparative anatomy, or by any combination of these. Theories, in the language of philosophy of science, are underdetermined by the evidence that can be cited in support of them. The fact of evolution, let alone any explanatory theory of evolution, is dramatically underdetermined by fossils and even by the minimal fossil record.

Some prior external constraint must be imposed if only to permit a choice to be made among conflicting accounts of the biological past, all of which are consistent with the minimally interpreted fossil record, for example, among accounts calling for multiple creations, the unfolding of a divine plan of descent, or Darwinian evolution. Most paleontologists have applied an external constraint derived from the biological theory of their day which, while like any theory is underdetermined, is well supported by observation and experiment. But is it reasonable to apply the constraint of theories which have been formulated to explain short-term, local processes to patterns and trends so extended in time and space as to be recognized only in elaborate historical inferences? The answer to this question by those who seek to establish a nomothetic paleontology is that it is not reasonable nor even possible. They claim that the macroevolutionary patterns revealed by paleontology require for their explanation new and independent theories. Gould, the principal exponent of nomothetic paleontology, says (1980:116) "Paleontology is not a pure historical science; it resides in the middle of a continuum stretching from ideographic to nomothetic disciplines" and he envisions that (1980:96) "The formulation by paleobiologists and with paleobiological data, of new macroevolutionary theories should end the subservience of passive transfer and contribute, in turn, to the formulation of a new, general theory of evolution that recognizes hierarchy and permits a set of unifying principles to work differently at various levels." Gould's view that distinct evolutionary processes, unlike the processes of physical geology, operate on different scales of time, that they are hierarchical, plays a central role in his advocacy of a nomothetic paleontology.

Gould (1985) has recognized three levels, or tiers, in the hierarchy of evolutionary processes. The phenomena of the first tier, the immediate adaptations of organisms within populations, can be explained by the principles of contemporary population biology. To put this in terms of historical inference, the first tier is subject to the prior constraints of population biology, the prior constraints within which Simpson supposed (1944 and elsewhere) that all the processes of evolution could be explained. But for Gould the second tier of evolutionary process is subject to explanatory principles emergent with respect to the first tier. He emphasizes (1985:3) that "Emergent principles are additions to, not denials of, well established theories of microevolution." It is on the upper tiers that paleontology, having exclusive access to extended periods of time, comes into its own.

According to Gould (1985:4), "Punctuated equilibrium is a theory for the second tier – it studies the deployment of species and the origin of trends between episodes of mass extinction. . . ." The deployment of species and the origin of trends are secondary events of paleontology which can be reached only in historical inference. Although each side in the notorious dispute between those who subscribe to punctuated equilibrium and those who subscribe to gradualism points to paleontology in support of their position, there are enormous contingent barriers which stand in the way of resolving the issue on evidence provided by the fossil record.

No doubt because of the growing conviction that paleontology has something to contribute to evolutionary theory, there has recently been a concerted effort to overcome these contingent barriers. But the fossil record is not yet permitted to speak wholly for itself. Gould insists, however, that macroevolutionary theories have, or will have, an independent status within evolutionary theory (for example, 1980:98). I am not sure exactly what he intends macroevolutionary theories to be independent of, perhaps only of the theories of the lower tiers. But there is a significant way in which macro-evolutionary theories must be dependent. Paleontology can provide knowledge not only of events, but of patterns and trends among events. It cannot provide justification for the claim that any of its generalizations have explanatory efficacy; that they are, among other things, projected. The justification must come, as it does in geology, from showing that the generalizations are comprehended by theories which, by common consent, have such efficacy. Gould apparently does not suppose that internal justification is possible at the second tier. He and Eldredge, beginning with their first paper on punctuated equilibrium in 1972, have identified many of the prior external restraints imposed on the second tier by contemporary biology.

Because mass extinction is, as Gould puts it (1985:2), ". . . a recurring process now recognized as more frequent, more rapid, more intense, and more different than we have imagined . . ." paleontologists must now cope with yet a third level of evolutionary process. The theories accounting for the survival of individuals and species at the first two levels cannot explain survival in the face of catastrophic events which, as Gould remarks (1985:2), ". . . may undo whatever the lower tiers have accumulated." In the face of those recently recognized circumstances paleobiology is challenged ". . . to construct a general theory for shifting high-order taxonomic pattern in life's history" (Gould 1985:10). The distinction of the second tier from the first is a matter of dispute. It is difficult to imagine that the separation of the third tier from the other two could be. A new theory is demanded.

The third tier is subject to the constraints of the first two tiers and, if there is to be a new theory of the third tier, there must be new constraints suited to that level. Unless we suppose that finally the fossil record will be permitted to speak for itself, then the constraint will be prior and external. Prior constraints limit what we can imagine the past to have been like. But they serve the indispensable function of precluding the chaos that would ensue from admitting any hypothesis that explains the distribution of fossils, and as a source of justification for the claim that what paleontologists formulate in their attempts to explain, are to be accorded the status of theories.

If, as seems likely, evolution is a hierarchical process it does not follow that, for this reason, paleobiology promises to be more nomothetic than other historical sciences. It does entail that there be different theories and different external constraints for each level in the hierarchy which only multiplies the already formidable demands of theory construction. Nor need we suppose that, because biologists have lately come to the view that species are individuals, attempts to formulate a nomothetic human history are doomed to failure (Gould 1980:116). It is enough to recognize that a nomothetic paleobiology is possible and that advances toward rendering it so have already been made, albeit subject to prior external constraints at every level of evolutionary process.

Gould (1985) has set a challenging agenda for paleobiology; to pursue the promising beginning that has been made toward an understanding of the second tier, and to embark upon the task of formulating an entirely new theory for the third tier. To have a reasonable chance of completing this agenda paleobiologists will have to turn their attention to the identification of the prior external constraints to be imposed upon each tier so that they may be able to more clearly distinguish between what they have told the fossils and what the fossils have told them.

References

Anderson, C. A. 1963. Simplicity in structural geology, 175-83. In *The Fabric of Geology*, ed. C. C. Albritton. Reading, MA: Addison-Wesley.

Aristotle. 1984. Poetics, 2316-40. In *The Complete Works of Aristotle, the Revised Oxford Translation*, ed. J. Barnes. Princeton, NJ: Princeton University Press.

Eldredge, N., and S. J. Gould. 1972. Punctuated equilibria: An alternative to phyletic gradualism, 82-115. In *Models in Paleobiology*, ed. T. J. M. Schopf. San Francisco: Freeman, Cooper.

Gingerich, P. D. 1976. Cranial anatomy and evolution of early Tertiary Plesiadapidae (Mammalia, Primates). *University of Michigan Papers in Paleontology* 15:1-140.

Goudge, T. A. 1961. *The Ascent of Life*. Toronto: University of Toronto Press.

Gould, S. J. 1980. The promise of paleontology as a nomothetic evolutionary discipline. *Paleobiology* 6:96-118.

Gould, S. J. 1985. The paradox of the third tier: An agenda for paleobiology. *Paleobiology* 11:2-12.

Grene, M. 1958. Two evolutionary theories. *British Journal for the Philosophy of Science* 9:110-27; 185-93.

Hutton, J. 1795. *Theory of the Earth with Proofs and Illustrations*. Edinburgh: Caddell, Junior, Davies, and Creech.

Popper, K. R. 1957. *The Poverty of Historicism*. Boston: Beacon Press.

Schindewolf, O. H. 1950. *Grundfrazen der Paläontologie*. Stuttgart: E. Schweizerbart.

Simpson, G. G. 1944. *Tempo and Mode in Evolution*. New York: Columbia University Press.

Simpson, G. G. 1953. *The Major Features of Evolution*. New York: Columbia University Press.

HISTORICAL SCIENCE

AND

PHILOSOPHY OF HISTORY

A Threefold Parallelism for Our Time?
Progressive Development in Society, Science,
and the Organic World

Michael Ruse

In the middle of the nineteenth century, the Swiss-American paleoichthy-ologist, Louis Agassiz (1842, 1859), proposed and argued for a threefold parallelism: the order of living beings, the ontogenetic development of individual organisms, and the history of life as seen in the fossil record. Moreover, claimed Agassiz, the unifying thread is that of *progress* – from simple to complex, from the uniform to the highly differentiated, from monad to man. Thus, in the living world – especially the living world of animals – it is possible to order beings along some kind of *scala naturae*, from the invertebrates up through the primates, and eventually to humankind. This mirrors the embryological sequences of a simple organism, which also starts with the primitive and (in one species, at least) culminates in full intelligence. And, although Agassiz was never an evolutionist, he thought that God's creative power unfurls down through time until we reach those organisms made in His image.

I shall not stop here to discuss the intrinsic merits of Agassiz's parallelism or its subsequent fate. Suffice it to say here that, for all its problems – particularly with the thorny question of branching – it had an influence beyond that which Agassiz envisioned, or altogether desired (Bowler 1976, 1984; Ruse 1979). It was to prove a tool without compare in the hands of those whom Agassiz anathematized, the transmutationists! My aim here, rather, is to look at a modern-day possible threefold parallelism, different in many respects but similar in making central the notion of progress. This is a parallelism between the development of society, the development of science, and the development – the evolutionary development – of organisms. I am not sure that there is one prominent enthusiast for this parallelism, mirroring Agassiz as it were, but I do detect varying degrees of advocacy and acceptance. My primary purpose is sympathetic understanding, so I shall stress the disinterested explication of plausible positions. But, as it seems appropriate, particularly towards the end, I shall move into critical comment.

Because the notion of "progress" is so crucial to the discussion, it will be useful to have some idea about this before we start, although part of the need for such an exercise as mine is precisely the fact that most discussions calmly presuppose some sort of preanalytic notion and let matters get worse from there. Following the biologist Francisco J. Ayala (1974, 1982, 1988), one person who has made some effort with the notion, I take it that progress requires change, and that this in some sense involves change in a linear direction. Mere cyclical change could not qualify as progress, even though there is perhaps some flexibility about how directional one must be. One might insist that the change could never falter or double back, particularly at the end. Or one might allow a little backsliding: "There is progress, but we're in a bit of a lull or dip right now."

What is important, whether one be strict or not about reversals, is the recognition that directionality alone is not enough. Progress is a *value* notion (Ayala 1988:76-79). Progress implies that things are in some sense getting better or more desirable – at least, progress in any absolute sense has this implication. "There has been a terrific amount of progress but we're all far worse off" is a contradiction in terms. But, going beyond Ayala, it is useful to distinguish between evaluation and valuing (Nagel 1961). Only the latter is absolute. The former occurs against any arbitrarily specified standard. "To the detriment of us all, humankind has made much progress in its capability for nuclear warfare" is not contradictory – although it may or may not be false.

Talk of the fact of progress (meaning, when used without qualification, the absolute sense) raises questions about causes. These and other matters will have to be kept in mind. For now, however, we can turn to the task in hand and start unpacking the threefold parallelism.

The Development of Society

Suggestions that there might be general laws governing the development of society, "historicism," tend to be treated with (at best) amused contempt (Popper 1974). To quash such thoughts, it is generally thought enough merely to mention the name of Arnold Toynbee, the last great practitioner of this *genre* of historical philosophizing. Yet the fact remains true that there is a tradition in the West, at least since the early part of the eighteenth century, of thinking that the course of society is not entirely random. For all of the admitted backslidings, and few would want to say that there have been none at all, things – generally meaning, things for a goodly proportion of the members of Western society – have gotten better. Material benefits, education, freedom (more or less) have improved. Hence, it is generally thought that there is reasonable expectation of continued progress. We might hope for further improvements. There will be more material benefits, more education for those who want it, and more freedom (more or less).

> As Phlogiston is displaced by Oxygen, and the Epicycles of Ptolemy by the Ellipses of Kepler; so does Paganism give place to Catholicism, Tyranny to Monarchy, and Feudalism to Representative Government, – where also the process does not stop. Perfection of Practice, like completeness of Opinion, is always approaching, never arrived; Truth, in the words of Schiller, *immer wird, nie ist*; never *is*, always is *a-being*. (Carlyle [1831] 1896-1901:38)

The idea of (societal) progress was not espoused by the Ancients, nor indeed was it one which could flourish while Christianity had a dominant hold on the human psyche. There is that in the Biblical story of the fall and of subsequent possibility of salvation through the sacrifice of Jesus which cuts strongly against the notion that there could be any genuine secular improvement of life here on earth (Bury 1920). But, with the coming of the Scientific Revolution, belief in our own abilities to better our lot started to grow, most particularly in the country which spearheaded the Enlightenment and whose intellectuals had the strongest interest in seeing the present order of things overthrown – France. Moreover, as the writings of Condorcet, one of the noblest of all such thinkers, show well, it was these very advances in science and technology which supposedly supply the causal fuel for societal progress.

> As preventative medicine improves, and food and housing becomes healthier, as a way of life is established that develops our physical powers by exercise without ruining them by excess, as the two most virulent causes of deterioration, misery and excessive wealth, are eliminated, the average length of human life will be increased and a better health and stronger physical constitution will be ensured. (Condorcet [1795] 1956:199)

There were national differences in thinking about progress. In Britain, secure in its establishment and plunging headlong into an industrial revolution, progress tended primarily to be thought of in economic terms – forces and benefits. Adam Smith ([1759] 1976, [1776] 1937) and like thinkers argued that progress occurs when the state avoids interference, allowing market forces free play, thus letting the "Invisible Hand" maximize benefits for us all. A major part of this thinking is that there will occur a natural "division of labor" with society growing more complex as tasks are assigned to experts. (Note how complexity might be a mark of progress, even though one may not value complexity in its own right.)

Germany, to the contrary, was the land of idealists – at least in thought. Lacking a unified state and many of the material and political desiderata that the British took for granted, it emphasized a world spirit working its way inevitably up the path of progressive advance. Thus, according to Kant:

> The History of the Human Species as a whole may be regarded as the unravelling of a hidden Plan of Nature for accomplishing a perfect state of Civil Constitution for Society . . . as the sole State of Society in which the tendency of human nature can be all and fully developed. (Quoted by Pollard 1968:86)

Hegel, as is well known, made a full political philosophy out of the upwardly rising world spirit. Thesis leads to antithesis and thus to synthesis. Marx, in turn, although a materialist, never stepped off the transcendentalist escalator of German Idealism. Progressionism was, therefore, built right into his system.

By the middle of the nineteenth century, national ideas of societal progress began to twist and entwine together. This was particularly so, as they were transplanted to North America (Wagar 1972). One often finds a belief in the socioeconomic theories of the British (courtesy particularly of Herbert Spencer) combined with a German-like faith in the upward, God-intended, destiny of the nation. However, it is important to note that progress always had its critics. In Britain, for instance, the idea took a long time to recover its popularity after the horrors of the French Revolution. And, as the nineteenth century drew to a close, the darker side of industrialism, the hollowness of colonialism, and the fear of militarism began to make their marks. People did not necessarily give up on progress, but increasingly they looked for ways to put it back on track. Henry George's (1880) immensely popular proposals for communal land ownership were typical of utopian remedial schemes.

In this century, it seems fair to say that beliefs in progress have never engendered the enthusiasms that they did in previous times (Almond et al. 1982). Two world wars, the rise of Naziism, and the failure of the glorious promise of the Soviet Revolution have seen to that. Moreover, today, given the threats of nuclear and other kinds of warfare, global pollution, an apparently uncontrollable population explosion – not to mention such themes as international terrorism, continued religious strife (North Ireland, Israel, the Punjab), and AIDS – in the view of many it seems almost immoral to talk of progress, let alone to hope for it. The words of Reinhold Niebuhr, written in the dark times of 1940, still seem appropriate.

> History does not move forward without catastrophe, happiness is not guaranteed by the multiplication of physical comforts, social harmony is not easily created by more intelligence, and human nature is not as good or as harmless as had been supposed. (Quoted in Chambers 1958:211)

Yet, humans are optimists, and it would be a bad mistake to end this section by suggesting that the idea of social progress is a spent force, with as little appeal as other obsessions of yesteryear. Whatever may be the gloomy fears of intellectuals and fellow travelers, survey after survey suggests that if recent American presidential elections prove anything, U.S. citizens at least refuse to elect anyone who does not think in a like manner.

Elsewhere in the world also, hopes of progress ride high. After all, what else can leaders offer but such hopes? In these rapidly changing times, one hesitates to make any pronouncements on the official (or unofficial) thoughts on progress in Eastern European countries. What one can say is that, in Russia until very recently, it was still very much part of the state philosophy. Quoting from a recent textbook:

> Marxists are convinced that if the development of morality is approached dialectically, the very dynamics of its contradictions reveal steady progress. Marx noted, with full justice, that the concept of progress is not to be taken in the usual abstract form typical of a metaphysically clumsy mentality. Progress inevitably faces contradictions and the struggle of opposites (in morality, the most common pair of opposites are good and evil), but it does not cease to move towards higher and better ideals. (Bakshtanovskiy et al. 1989:89. Note the name of the publisher!)

Whatever else the present upheavals may spell, it does not seem likely that they will be read as a retreat from progress. If anything, the faith that a better time can come, must come, and will come, seems set fair to flourish.

The Development of Science

Science is Heraclitean, always moving. No one would deny that, although, conversely, no one would deny that science moves irregularly – now leaping forward, now sluggish. Where one branch may be teeming with excitement – major discoveries, eager students, a proliferation of publications – another may be dull and humdrum, polishing up old discoveries and hoping listlessly for major innovations.

But, is there any meaning to the movement? Does the flux of science make sense? Is there any pattern? Is science, not to mince words, progressive, and if it is, what is the nature of this progress and what is the cause? Let me start at the beginning and state about as categorically as one can, that speaking of scientists *qua* scientists – that is, excluding the things, often very silly, that scientists say when being self-reflective – they are strongly committed to the belief that their subject matter does have a pattern and that it does make sense. In particular, scientists believe in progress (of science), and by progress they mean getting closer to the truth (Davis 1986).

Moreover, scientists *qua* scientists are philosophical realists, and by getting closer to the truth they mean getting their theories in better correspondence with the facts of the case. Molecular genetics is better than Mendelian genetics because the unit of inheritance really is the DNA molecule, which in turn really is a double helix. Scientists show their realism-based progressionism by their supreme indifference to history, except as a guide for the very young or a hobby for the very old. And even then they usually care only for history to some Whiggish end. After all, why should one care about the past, if it is not as good as the present?

How far are these views about science well-taken? One might want to look at them with a skeptical eye, if only because the ideology of the progressive nature of science seems so important an element in the successful prosecution of science – externally against rivals for human allegiance, such as religion, and internally to keep people going against all of the daunting obstacles that ignorance and nature seem to throw up. Although it is true that the dispute about whether, independently of our observation, a real world truly exists "out there" is as old as philosophical debate, and although it is true also that this dispute has (and does) reflect itself into thinking about science, it seems true also that the general progressivist view of science is one which has been widely accepted by commentators on science (Losee 1972). At least, this was and is true of those closest to the philosophical end of the spectrum, although recently belief in scientific progress has come under attack from radical thinkers from history, sociology, literary theory, and the like.

Consider, to take an articulate position from the past, the views of William Whewell (1837, 1840), one of the towering figures in the history of the philosophy of science, also one of the great historians of science, and indeed an active scientist in his own right (Butts 1965; Ruse 1976). Whewell was no naïve realist, thinking that what you see is what there is. Rather, he was a sophisticated Kantian (later veering towards Platonism), who saw sci-

ence as a complex fusion of raw experience and mind-given organizing principles – "Fundamental Ideas." But, within this context he saw science as unambiguously, albeit not always smoothly, progressive, as through a series of
"inductive epochs" scientists strive to achieve complete understanding. On
the one hand, the theoretical must be articulated ("explication of conceptions"); on the other hand, the empirical must be collected ("colligation of
facts"); then the two are brought together in an "inductive" leap.

Important for Whewell is the belief that the products of induction can
then themselves serve as facts, for a new round of inductive leaping. This
goes on until finally one reaches the limit of a Fundamental Idea, at which
stage apparently one has established necessary truth. (Although he does not
use this language, this is at least the necessity of the Kantian synthetic *a
priori* – something which Whewell, an ardent Anglican, would have thought
backed by God.) For Whewell, a major mark that one's science is progressing properly, guided by the right Ideas, is when different branches of scientific activity are brought together beneath one hypothesis.

> Accordingly the cases in which inductions from classes
> of facts altogether have thus *jumped together*, belong only to
> the best established theories which the history of science con-
> tains. And as I shall have occasion to refer to this peculiar
> feature in their evidence, I will take the liberty of describing it
> by a particular phrase; and will term it the *Consilience of In-
> ductions*. (Whewell 1840:2, 230)

Whewell remarked that a consilience is *simplicity* by another name, since one
is reducing the required number of explanatory factors.

Let us jump now to the present. The two most influential living commentators on the nature of science are, undoubtedly, Karl Popper (1959,
1962) and Thomas Kuhn (1962). The former's analysis differs in significant
respects from Whewell's, but is no less committed to progressionism. As is
well known, Popper believes that the mark of science – the "criterion of de-
marcation" – is falsifiability, and he believes that science moves forward as
scientists face problems, propose tentative solutions ("bold conjectures"), and
then have others attempt to knock them down. Even in the process of destruction ("refutation"), progress is made, and a body of as-yet-undefeated
knowledge grows (Popper 1972). Unlike Whewell, Popper denies that you

can ever get to the truth (or, if you do, that you can ever know that you have done so), but there does seem to be an asymptotic approach to some sort of absolute (or "objective") knowledge. Popper denies also that one can ever know there is a reality, but he is prepared to assume that there is one. In this sense, he is a "hypothetical realist."

Prima facie, Kuhn's philosophy seems very different, although his constant complaints about misinterpretation should warn one against slick readings. As well known as Popperian falsifiability is the Kuhnian "paradigm," a kind of world picture in which the scientist functions and is generally trapped. (As it happens, later elaboration has shown that the kind of world a paradigm is picturing might be pretty small.) Every now and then, a paradigm seems to come apart, "normal science" is no longer possible, and if you are lucky a new paradigm is produced and there is a "revolutionary" switch. Since paradigms set their own rules, scientific revolutions in some sense stand outside logic – they require rhetoric and emotive persuasion, like political revolutions.

Kuhn is sometimes read as a nonrealist, but it is fairer perhaps to read him in a kind of Kantian way, as seeing reality in an important sense defined and created by the inquiring mind. He is certainly not a Whewellian in seeing the aim and end of science as some kind of finished absolute knowledge. There is always room for another paradigm switch. Yet, in a passage which is often ignored or down-played (or misunderstood), Kuhn, no less than Popper, stakes out a commitment to progress.

> The analogy that relates the evolution of organisms to the evolution of scientific ideas can easily be pushed too far. But with respect to the issues of [this book] it is very nearly perfect. The process described [by me] as the resolution of revolutions is the selection by conflict within the scientific community of the fittest way to practice future science. The net result of a sequence of such revolutionary selections, separated by periods of normal research, is the wonderfully adapted set of instruments we call modern scientific knowledge. Successive stages in that developmental process are marked by an increase in articulation and specialization. And the entire process may have occurred, as we now suppose biological evolution did, without benefit of a set goal, a permanent fixed scientific truth, of which each stage in the development of scientific knowledge is a better exemplar. (Kuhn 1962:172-73)

Admittedly, this is not a comfortable absolute progress, in the sense of travel toward some firm knowledge of objective reality, but it is progress of a kind. Perhaps at the least Kuhn intends a kind of relativistic progress, where the standards by which paradigms are judged involve such virtues as predictive fertility, coherence, consilience, simplicity and more. These virtues are often called "epistemic values" (McMullin 1983); invoking them as standards may perhaps put Kuhn more in the line of one who is evaluating against chosen criteria than valuing against anything absolute.

I confess that I am not absolutely sure about this last point. How arbitrary is the choice of something like predictive fertility? What I am sure of is the relativism of recent commentators who try to "deconstruct" science, using the tools of sociology, literary theory and the like. These people argue that just about any scientific theory is compatible with the facts, whatever these latter may be (Collins 1985). The driving force of scientific change is, therefore, not the real world, but a host of cultural factors – epistemic values, certainly, but also nonepistemic values like politics, sex and gender, religion, status, race, and more.

In the eyes of these critics – Marxists, feminists, gay and civil rights activists, and others – talk of progress towards knowledge of reality is not simply ridiculous, but itself part of the ideology to be ripped away from modern science (Haraway 1989). It is often not easy to decide if there is indeed a reality in the eyes of such critics – at an important level, they do not care. It is equally difficult to decide if there is belief in any kind of progress. Some, at least, seem to think so; but, their kind of progress is to be measured strictly in terms of advance towards greater manifestation of appropriately sought and held standards – more sensitivity to legitimately desired demands of feminism, for instance, or to gay rights. I take it that such progress as this is unambiguously relativistic. Although activists hold their values dear, others – not all of whom are obviously ignorant or incorrigibly corrupt – do not.

This must suffice for a survey of the situation in science. Overall, despite critics and detractors just mentioned, it does seem true to say that beliefs in progress are a lot stronger and more generally held than such beliefs are held about society. I shall return later to more discussion about the question of causes.

The Organic Evolutionary Process

Organic evolution means change. That is a tautology. And, almost as close to the tautological is the fact that, with very minor exceptions, such change does not double back on itself. It is true also that adaptation is a significant mark of the organic – some would say it is *the* significant mark – and that although there may well be other causal factors, natural selection brought on by a struggle for existence is the reason for such adaptation and hence for organic evolution generally.

What of the overall pattern? Almost by definition, in the more than 3.5 billion years since life first appeared on this planet, there has been a rise from the simple to the complex, a process that really caught fire about 600 million years ago at the beginning of the Cambrian. But, does all of this add up to progress of any kind? This is the key question.

It cannot be denied that people have thought that there has been progress. Early evolutionists were progressionist to a person. The French evolutionist Jean Baptiste de Lamarck (1809), for instance, was so keen on progress that he proposed two upward ladders, one for plants and one for animals. Needless to say, we humans come at the peak of the animal ladder, remarkable for a complexity which puts us ahead even of the orangutan.

Other evolutionists of the time were no less progressionist. Listen, for instance, to Dr. Erasmus Darwin:

> Organic Life beneath the shoreless waves
> Was born and nurs'd in Ocean's pearly caves;
> First forms minute, unseen by spheric glass,
> Move on the mud, or pierce the watery mass;
> These, as successive generations bloom,
> New powers acquire, and larger limbs assume;
> Whence countless groups of vegetation spring,
> And breathing realms of fin, and feet, and wing.
>
> Thus the tall Oak, the giant of the wood,
> Which bears Britannia's thunders on the flood;
> The Whale, unmeasured monster of the main,
> The lordly Lion, monarch of the plain,
> The Eagle soaring in the realms of air,
> Whose eye undazzled drinks the solar glare,

> Imperious man, who rules the bestial crowd,
> Of language, reason, and reflection proud,
> With brow erect who scorns this earthy sod,
> And styles himself the image of his God;
> Arose from rudiments of form and sense,
> An embryon point, or microscopic ens!
> (Darwin 1803:1, 295-314)

Until the day of Dr. Darwin's grandson, half a century later, the theme was the same. Then, however, many think that the tune changed, dramatically. Supposedly, Charles Darwin had no time for biological progress and excluded it rigorously from his published writings. After all, what else could he do, given the mechanism of selection? What wins is what wins, and given the right combination of circumstances it could just as easily be the weedy little runt as the magnificent, prancing, prize specimen which has all of the offspring. It could just as easily be the simple as the complex.

As one who used to interpret Darwin this way, let me now rush to say that I think this is all quite wrong (Ospovat 1981). It is true that Darwin recognized that branching is a crucial part of the evolutionary process. It is true also that Darwin denied any simple upwardly progressive force in evolution. It is true, thirdly, that Darwin saw that selection would lead most naturally to a kind of relativistic progress, where one improves particular adaptations, like muscles for speed or teeth for attack ("comparative highness"). But, when this is all said, it remains true that Darwin thought relativistic progress would slide over into absolute progress, where the mark is complexity (Darwin 1859). Unambiguously, Darwin saw humans – primarily white, Anglo-Saxon, male humans – at the top of the list (Darwin 1871; Greene 1977).

With some doubts (to be mentioned later) belief in evolutionary progress has continued down to the present. Only now have formidable critics arisen. Most forceful among these has been George C. Williams, especially in his 1966 classic, *Adaptation and Natural Selection*. He points out that all proposed measures of progress fail, and that they even yield counterintuitive results. If one judges complexity over the whole of ontogeny – and why should one do otherwise? – a good case can be made for saying that the liver fluke is a higher life form than humans!

You may think (I used to think) that this is the end of matters. Biological progress has gone the way of Lamarckism. Certainly, there is no shortage of voices prepared to give this impression. Stephen Jay Gould (1989) is simply the loudest and most persistent. However, matters are not this straightforward. Biological progressionism is a hardy plant (or weed, if you prefer). Relativistic progress of an explicitly Darwinian kind, presupposing evaluation against a standard, rides high. I will return to this point later. For now, I want to remark how endorsement of a fairly absolute kind of progress – monad to man – can be found readily in the biological literature. Listen, for instance, to E. O. Wilson:

> We should first note that social systems have originated repeatedly in one major group of organisms after another, achieving widely different degrees of specialization and complexity. Four groups occupy pinnacles high above the others: the colonial invertebrates, the social insects, the nonhuman mammals, and man. (Wilson 1975:379)

And then:

> The typical vertebrate society . . . favors individual and in-group survival at the expense of societal integrity.
> Man has intensified these vertebrate traits while adding unique qualities of his own. In so doing he has achieved an extraordinary degree of cooperation with little or no sacrifice of personal survival and reproduction. Exactly how he alone has been able to cross to this fourth pinnacle, reversing the downward trend of social evolution in general, is the culminating mystery of all biology. (Wilson 1975:382)

Why should there be this kind of progress? How does one move, especially if one is a Darwinian, from pattern to process? The most articulate explanation has come recently from the pen of John T. Bonner (1987), who argues that there has been and always will be a kind of biological pressure toward increase in bodily size. Bigness has its virtues. So also does smallness, true. But the scale at the top is open-ended in a way that the scale at the bottom is not. For instance, when the mammals went back to the sea, the ecological niches for small animals were crowded. But, there were masses of room for really big animals. Hence, we got the whales.

Continuing this theme, Bonner points out that size requires internal support systems – the greater the size, the greater the needed support. This led to increased complexity, where this can be defined simply in terms of the different number of types of component part – such different parts splitting up the tasks at hand and thus leading to a classic division of labor. Complexity in turn leads to improved adaptations, most importantly sophisticated social skills. Hence, as in traditional accounts, one sees primates – humans, in particular – coming out at the top. The things we value most, by just about any standard, are the winners in life's struggles. Progress reigns!

Comparisons: Society/Science

Let me turn now to similarities and differences between the three developmental processes just discussed: society, science and biology. There are three interfaces, so let us start with that between society and science.

The question is whether there is any similarity of pattern and, if there is, whether this points to any similarity of process, referring now to the causal level. Fairly obviously, many people will answer the first part of the question in the negative, and that will be an end to it. Society is not progressive. Science is. The two processes are clearly different. But, what if one sees some pattern parallelism? This could be because one sees society as progressive, at least in some respects, or because one sees science as less than progressive, at least in some respects.

The strongest way to promote parallelism, perhaps, is to make both of these moves. One might argue that (relativistically) society certainly advances in certain respects, especially with respect to some values one holds dear. Conversely, one might argue that thoughts of an absolute scientific progress to disinterested knowledge of reality are chimerical, but there is still hope of a (relativistic) progress as one incorporates ideologically acceptable values in a better fashion. Society might become more sexually sensitive. Hence, science might become more sexually sensitive. (I am not saying that either does or will.)

What then of causes? There are those, drawn, I suspect, mainly from the scientific community, who see a direct causal connection. Improved science leads to improved technology to improved society. Note, however, that this sequence does not presuppose any parallelism in the processes. One might well – if one takes this sequence seriously, one probably will – think that science is a value-free endeavor, progressing toward knowledge of reality. Society, on the other hand, improves and advances inasmuch as desired values are achieved.

Even the fundamental mechanisms need not be the same. One could think that science requires unreflective creative genius, whereas societal improvement demands uninspired hard grind. (One probably will think this if one holds to the usual parodies of eccentric creative scientists and boring civil servants.) But, suppose one does want to go on to parallelism of causes. On what grounds might one base a case? I think, in the literature, there are hints of at least three.

First, one might highlight some sort of *laissez-faire* causal process, leading to an unrestrained struggle for existence, from which the best will emerge. As we have seen, this was the view accepted by the British political economists of the eighteenth century as that best suited to promote societal progress. It was also a highly popular view in the nineteenth century, and, as is only too well known, has enjoyed a considerable resurgence recently. It is also a view which has had considerable support in the past century as the way that science works, or at least as the way that science works best if it is to advance. Thus, Darwin's great supporter Thomas Henry Huxley wrote:

> Now the essence of the scientific spirit is criticism. It tells us
> that whenever a doctrine claims our assent we should reply,
> Take it if you can compel it. The struggle for existence holds
> as much in the intellectual as in the physical world. A theory
> is a species of thinking, and its right to exist is coextensive with
> its power of resisting extinction by its rivals. (Huxley 1893:229)

Recently, Popper (1974) has been interpreting (or reinterpreting) his position in this light. He argues that the method of bold conjecture and rigorous refutation is *laissez faire* by another name. It is at least a struggle for existence, with the best rising to the top. And, more generally, there is a whole school of "evolutionary epistemology" which believes that science advances by throwing up variants, new ideas, and then letting them fight for survival in the public arena – this latter being the laboratory, the conference, the journal (Ruse 1986).

Central to this vision of progress is the need for struggle, for competition. Pointing to a second way of getting a society/science causal parallel, we find that not all feel that society (at least) advances best through naked aggression. Such people look for different, perhaps softer, methods of change. Methods which, they argue, lead to truer and more lasting advances. Cooperation of one sort or another is usually involved here and various motives for such cooperation are suggested. A recent case of this kind has been proposed by the sociobiologists, who argue that although life may be a struggle, you can often get more out of it if you are prepared to work with your fellows (Ruse 1985).

The same is true in science, argues at least one theorist, David Hull (1988). He sees perpetuation of one's ideas as the driving force behind scientific effort. There is, therefore, the consequent need to cooperate – especially to cite the ideas of others – if one wants to be taken seriously oneself. This perhaps sounds somewhat cynical (this is perhaps somewhat cynical!) but Hull argues that it is not only the way science functions, but also the reason why science functions so very well. There is, for instance, a high premium on honesty, not because scientists are particularly nice people but because fraud spoils the game for everyone and hence is very heavily penalized. One might forgive but one can never forget.

Sociobiological ideas are highly controversial. Many deny them absolutely for society, and Hull's proposals for science also have their critics. This swings me, therefore, to the opposite end of the spectrum, toward the third proposal for promoting the parallelism. What if Marxism is right? Would one not have a similarity of pattern and process in that case? At the societal level this involves the well-known Hegelian dialectic, with thesis going to antithesis, and then the contradiction dissolving into synthesis – advance, and a new, higher point from which to start again.

Recognizing that a Marxian "contradiction" is essentially one of opposition (master and slave are hardly logical contradictories), do we get something similar in the progress of science? Suffice it to say that some have certainly thought so. Richard Lewontin (1974), for instance, sees the development of population genetics as one of position, counterposition, and then resolution – with advance, but with the creation of a whole set of new problems which, in turn, call for renewed application of the dialectic. The classical position in population genetics of Hermann Muller was opposed by the balance position of Theodosius Dobzhansky. The dispute was dissolved by the coming of gel electrophoretic techniques; but, as the controversy over Japanese thoughts on drift shows only too well, the issues have not gone. They have simply been moved to a higher plan. We know more than we did, but there is always more to know.

Here then we have three ways of promoting the parallelism, at the levels of pattern and process. What can be said by way of critical comment? My own oft-expressed feeling is that analogies are a bit like spinach – either you like them, or you don't. One can point out all kinds of health-giving, or life-threatening, properties, but, ultimately, it all comes down to a matter of taste. However, even within these bounds some critical comments can be made. After all, a preference for French cooking over English cooking is a matter of taste, but it is not entirely without some objective foundation.

For myself, the big problem with all purported parallelisms between societal and scientific change is the very much stronger sense of progress one has (I have!) in the case of science over society. I appreciate that there may have been times and places when (absolute) societal progress seemed obvious. But, even if it is true that society progresses, it is not obvious today. Science does, however, seem to progress. Darwinism over Creationism is an advance. Against those who doubt what I am saying, let me make three points. First, like G. E. Moore's proof of external reality, the conviction of scientific progress is so strong that I prefer to think arguments to the contrary must be flawed (Stroud 1984). Which do you relinquish first? The belief that your hand in front of you really exists or the skeptic's argument? The belief that science really progresses or the skeptic's argument? Second, doubters raise questions about the infiltration of values into science, but this (which I fully accept) is far from saying that science does not advance. Perhaps science advances despite, or because of, the values. Third, even if one concludes that science does *not* advance, one is still left with the fact that it *seems* to. None of these points imply that one must endorse an extreme philosophical realism. Indeed, elsewhere I have agreed that such a realism is meaningless (Ruse 1986).

But, assume for a moment that the pattern parallelism is sufficiently strong to go on to ask about process. What then? The first suggested analogy, centering on *laissez-faire* market forces, has all of the problems that lie behind every reference to such forces. At least, it is far from obvious that at the societal level, such forces lead to positive advance. One can say that even the most ardent proponents of *laissez faire*, then and now, usually find reason for all sorts of exceptions. And in any case, the most successful societies around today are precisely those which properly balance individual freedom with government planning – this holds, whether one's criterion of "success" is based on social welfare (as in Scandinavia) or on material gain (as in West Germany or Japan) .

There are difficulties also with the *laissez-faire* idea applied to science. Apart from the problems of working out what, in science, represents a new innovation exactly comparable to a successful innovation in society – is one small successful experiment the equivalent of a new brand of detergent? – it is no more obvious here that unrestrained competition is or would be a good thing. Epistemologically, one might want to shelter an idea for a while (by suspending criticism), if it promises to bear great fruit. Sociologically, it is well known that the "Matthew effect" operates strongly – new ideas from successful scientists get more attention and respect than new ideas from unknown workers (Cole and Cole 1973). Moreover, it is not obvious that this is such a very bad thing. Most scientists would defend it strongly.

Let us move on to the sociobiological analogy. There are so many questions here, especially about the application of sociobiology to society, that I need hardly stop to detail them – although for the record I should say that I am probably more sympathetic to human sociobiology than most. What I do want to state is that Hull's (1989) application of sociobiology to the workings of science probably leads to real insight – he himself is his own best advocate in his analysis of the recent history of systematics. Nevertheless, it must be agreed that, inasmuch as Hull's model works, it does raise questions abut the sort of success that the progress of science achieves. If what counts is the getting of others to take your ideas seriously, then at least in theory it is possible that a false idea (judged against the best evidence) gets accepted and a true idea rejected, simply because the false idea is promoted by the scientist with the superior political skills (Ruse, in press).

To the radical sociologist of science this is probably an acceptable conclusion – although, applying a reflexive argument, why then should we rush to agree with them? Here, I will merely note it as a challenge. One can certainly agree that there is a kind of relativism to the progress of science; but, unless one wants to go all the way over to total relativism, it is necessary to show that the kinds of political factors Hull highlights can be reconciled with rationality and an approach to knowledge of reality.

Finally, there is Marxism. Let me say simply that I for one am not convinced that recent events in Eastern Europe show the total collapse of Marxism as a viable epistemology, and that in the case of both society and science it still offers a powerful tool for penetrating insight. Lewontin's analysis alone shows this. But, speaking now of the latter, to quote Aristotle, one swallow does not a summer make. It is far from obvious that all scientific advance requires "contradiction" – or if it does, "contradiction" is probably being used in such an elastic sense as to be virtually meaningless. At the very least, we need a more extended discussion with more examples.

There are other questions also. A Marxist approach to science is often thought to endorse a holistic philosophy, as opposed to "reductionism," whatever that might mean (Rose 1982). At a minimum, particularly given the successes of such sciences as quantum mechanics and molecular biology, this is a position which needs argument before acceptance. Lewontin the scientist raises serious questions for Lewontin the philosopher. However, I stress that I raise questions such as these as questions and not as definitive refutations. No one can (no one should) deny that Marxist analyses of science and its history have been some of the most fruitful of our generation. One does not have to accept the philosophy to appreciate the results – especially those underlining the extent to which social factors do get into science.

These then are some critical reflections on the society/science purported parallelisms. Overall, I am not a great enthusiast, but in detail there are some stimulating signposts.

Comparisons: Society/Biology

I turn next to compare the development of society with the development –
the evolution – of organisms. What one can say is that, at the level of pattern, there is a long history of seeing close analogies between the development of society and the development of organic life, and often this has been
taken over to discussions about process.

It is indeed not too much of an exaggeration to say that organic evolutionary theorizing was conceived in the eighteenth century out of beliefs in
societal progress. What was seen (or hoped for) in society, was seen (or
hoped for) in organisms. Then the latter was taken as support for the former! Moreover, the distinctive national patterns (and processes) of societal
progress were read into and out of the organic world. In France, societal
progress was something fuelled by the intellect, as ideas were developed and
then (if useful) passed from one to another (Pollard 1968). In crucial respects, this was precisely the biological theory of Lamarck, who was inciden-
tally an enthusiast for views about societal progress. He thought organisms
develop new features in response to needs, and these are then transmitted as
part of heredity. The end result is organic progress.

Erasmus Darwin also blurred together his support for the economic
factors of societal progress with the changes he believed to occur in the
world of organisms (McNeil 1987). Crucial for him were ideas about complexity and the division of labor, and just as supportive of the case was the
example of Germany. Here the metaphysics was idealism, and societal progress was seen as the working of the spirit through time. Likewise, in biology we see German thinkers among those most inclined to developmentalism
and change, as the spirit works its powers. Although, somewhat paradoxically, because for an idealist it is the *idea* which matters, we find that German
thinkers rarely felt the need to endorse full-blown actual material organic
evolutionism. Thus Hegel:

> Nature is to be regarded as a *system of stages*, one arising
> necessarily from the other and being the proximate truth of the
> stage from which it results: but it is not generated *naturally* out
> of the other but only in the inner Idea which constitutes the
> ground of Nature. *Metamorphosis* pertains only to the Notion

as such, since only *its* alteration is development. But in Nature, the Notion is partly only something inward, partly existent only as a living individual: *existent* metamorphosis, therefore, is limited to this individual alone. (Hegel 1970:20)

The point could not be clearer, and it is made again in his students' lecture notes:

It is the necessity of the Idea which causes each sphere to complete itself by passing into another higher one, and the variety of forms must be considered as necessary and determinate. The land animal did not develop *naturally* out of the aquatic animal, nor did it fly into the air on leaving the water, nor did perhaps the bird again fall back to earth. If we want to compare the different stages of Nature, it is quite proper to note that, for example, a certain animal has one ventricle and another has two; but we must not then talk of the fact as if we were dealing with parts which had been put together. (Hegel 1970:21)

Charles Darwin also was a progressionist about society – how could he fail to be, coming from a rich, liberal family, with roots deep in the nonconformist, industrial British Midlands? – and this progressionism was taken explicitly into his biology.

What is interesting is the story of evolutionism after the *Origin*, when, although beliefs in societal progress ran high, doubts were starting to emerge – the already mentioned costs of industrialism, sterility of colonialism, and rise of militarism were making manifest their effects. The worries of intellectuals about these sorts of phenomena found their way right into the theorizing of biologists. Typical in this respect was the work of E. Ray Lankester, follower of Huxley, and professor, first in London and then at Oxford. He saw society, British society in particular, in grave danger of decline, primarily because of its lack of attention to science and engineering. Almost immediately, then, we find Lankester stressing that decline – "degeneration" – is a widespread phenomenon in the organic world also, the implication being that we humans should not sit back complacently. Across the Atlantic, meanwhile, the Cambridge (MA) biologist, Alpheus Hyatt (1893), was making a similar case for much the same reasons.

Let us turn the clock now rapidly forward to today. I think one can find the same connections drawn between the development of society and that of organisms. George Williams is an interesting counterexample who proves the case, for he complements his organic nonprogressionism with a somewhat gloomy view of society (Williams 1988). E. O. Wilson (1978, 1984), to the contrary, is optimistic both about society and about organisms. ("Optimistic" is not quite the right word, for Wilson is desperately concerned about ecological issues. "Hopefully confident that society can stay on course, given good will and effort" would be a better characterization.) Gould, however, runs an interesting twist on this scenario. He believes in societal progress but thinks that one of its greatest obstacles is racist thinking about the superiority of some peoples over others (Gould 1981). Since he takes evolutionary views on progress to be some of the greatest supports of racism, he opposes organic progressionism – precisely to make way for societal progressionism (Gould 1989).

Grant now that at the level of pattern, people see parallelisms. Today, as in the past, there is often a straight transfer across when it comes to process. Again, Wilson's name springs immediately to mind, for he thinks the same sociobiological forces govern the forward movement of society as have governed the upward rise of organisms. Interestingly, although he denies that evolution is progressive, Gould (1979) sees the same dialectical forces driving forward society and lying behind his biological theory of punctuated equilibria – at least, he did. (Which point leads me to wonder just how truly nonprogressionist in biology Gould truly is.)

Asking now the critical questions, let me invoke our original distinction between absolute progress and some kind of relativistic progress. With respect to the former, I have expressed little confidence in its existence in society and I confess now to feeling little more in its existence in evolution. Let me put things this way: I do not see that the enthusiasts for progress (thinking now biologically) adequately answer critics like Williams. Perhaps some functional measure of complexity can be formulated – a measure which confirms our preanalytic intuitions – but none seems yet to have been produced. DNA content of individual cells or in total bodily content looked promising, but failed the test.

Bonner's (1987) attempt is the most recent and one of the most honest to argue for organic progress and to offer a causal explanation. But there are some worrisome gaps in his argument. In the first place, the assumption that there will always be an ecological niche for the larger organism seems questionable. Apart from anything else, one might argue that niches do not exist passively, waiting to be occupied. In dynamic fashion, they are created by their occupiers. (Did the Innuit discover a niche in the Arctic or create one?) In the second place, the link between complexity (as Bonner defines it) and size seems loose. Is the giant whale so much more complex than the tiny mouse? In the third place, there is a big move from structural complexity to developmental and (important to us) social complexity. All of these reasons, at the least, make Bonner's case "not proven."

I see little pattern and less process. The interesting question is why evolutionists (including the very best) do. I believe there are at least two reasons. One is a version of what is now called the "anthropic principle." We humans are part of the evolutionary process, and – inasmuch as we ask "Is there progress in evolution?" – we are necessarily at the end of the process (to date) and are able to ask "Is there progress in evolution?" This distorts our answers, making us think we *must* have emerged progressively from the process. The second reason is that evolutionists are scientists. They see progress in their science. They read this into society, and then read it into their biology. There is a crucial case of biased sampling affecting the very set of people who think most about evolution.

Turn now to the question of relativistic progress. I have been happy to grant that this occurs in society. Of course it does, sometimes for good and sometimes for bad. (Whether once relativistic progress has started it keeps going indefinitely is another question.) It clearly occurs also in biology. This is Darwin's comparative highness, and today is the basis of the trendy notion of a biological arms race. Without inquiring too deeply into process (the developments in society raise question of intention, akin to those which will come up in the next section), there may well be a really useful analogy here. Consider, indeed, how someone like Richard Dawkins – discussing the ends of arms races – mixes together the social and the biological.

How do arms races end? Sometimes they may end with
one side going extinct, in which case the other side presumably
stops evolving in that particular progressive direction, and
indeed it will probably even 'regress' for economic reasons
soon to be discussed. In other cases, economic pressures may
impose a stable halt to an arms race, stable even though one
side in the race is, in a sense, permanently ahead. Take run-
ning speed, for instance. There must be an ultimate limit to
the speed at which a cheetah or a gazelle can run, a limit imposed by the laws of physics. But neither cheetahs nor gazelles
have reached that limit. Both have pushed up against a lower
limit which is, I believe, economic in character. High-speed
technology is not cheap. It demands long leg bones, powerful
muscles, capacious lungs. These things can be had by any
animal that really needs to run fast, but they must be *bought*.
They are bought at a steeply increasing price. The price is
measured as what economists call 'opportunity cost'. The opportunity cost of something is measured as the sum of all the
other things that you have to forego in order to have that
something. The cost of sending a child to a private, fee-paying
school is all the things that you can't afford to buy as a result:
the new car that you can't afford, the holidays in the sun that
you can't afford (if you're so rich that you can afford all these
things easily, the opportunity cost, to you, of sending your child
to a private school may be next to nothing). The price, to a
cheetah, of growing larger leg muscles is all the other things
that the cheetah *could have done* with the materials and energy
used to make the leg muscles, for instance make more milk for
cubs. (Dawkins 1986)

I think there are many more questions to be asked at this point. I am
certainly not pleading for uncritical acceptance of the analogy. But, in concluding this part of the discussion, I do suggest that here our parallelism
might yield interesting insights, of both pattern and process.

Comparisons: Science/Biology

The final putative parallelism is between the development of science and the
development or evolution of biology. It is a very popular analogy today, with
respect both to pattern and cause, with (as we have seen) both Popper and
Kuhn trying to locate themselves beneath it. (I confess to some shock at
Kuhn's gall here, given that his notion of paradigm switches is about as anti-

evolutionary as it is possible to be – although perhaps he could draw on the Eldredge/Gould theory of punctuated equilibria, since it, too, makes abrupt change central.)

Since this kind of "evolutionary epistemology" has been written about extensively, including by myself, I shall be brief. The claim is that the pattern of change in science and life is evolutionary and usually also that the process is a shared one of Darwinian struggle and selection. Stephen Toulmin's account is one of the best.

> Science develops . . . as the outcome of a double process: at each stage, a pool of competing intellectual variants is in circulation, and in each generation a selection process is going on, by which certain of these variants are accepted and incorporated into the science concerned, to be passed on to the next generation of workers as integral elements of the tradition.
>
> Looked at in these terms, a particular scientific discipline – say, atomic physics – needs to be thought of, not as the contents of a textbook bearing any specific date, but rather as a developing subject having a continuing identity through time, and characterized as much by its process of growth as by the content of any one historical cross-section . . . Moving from one historical cross-section to the next, the actual ideas transmitted display neither a complete breach at any point – the idea of absolute 'scientific revolutions' involves an oversimplification – nor perfect replication, either. The change from one cross-section to the next is an *evolutionary* one in this sense too: that later intellectual cross-sections of a tradition reproduce the content of their immediate predecessors, as modified by those particular intellectual novelties which were selected out in the meanwhile – in the light of the professional standards of the science of the time. (Toulmin 1967:465-66)

He emphasizes:

> In talking about the development of natural science as 'evolutionary,' I [am not] employing a mere *façon de parler*, or analogy, or metaphor. The idea that the historical changes by which scientific thought develops frequently follow an 'evolutionary' pattern needs to be taken quite seriously; and the implications of such a pattern of change can be, not merely suggestive, but explanatory. (Toulmin 1967:470)

I have two things to say about this analogy. The first is philosophical. At the level of pattern, I consider the analogy to be weak. Science is progressive in a way that organisms are not. At least, science appears progressive in a way not apparently so (to me) in the organic world. This takes us straight to process, where the reason for the disanalogy is obvious. The variants of science are intensional, and the selection of science is teleological, in ways that the variants and selection of biology are not. Darwin's coming up with his views on evolution was part of a purposeful mental process, and the acceptance of his views by biologists was equally reflective. Conversely, however, there is nothing directed about the arrival of a new biological variant, whatever its success. Moreover, success itself is a function of the needs of the moment, without thought to the long-term future.

This all accounts for the direction of science (whatever Kuhn and the sociologists might say to the contrary) and for the nondirection of biology (whatever Wilson and Bonner might say to the contrary). Moreover, the end points of the two processes show how different they are. Agree that biology promotes complexity. However this might be defined, there seems consensus that this involves a division of labor. Yet as Whewell (1840) shows, brilliantly, scientific advances center on a flight from complexity. The great scientific theory is the truly simple theory. It is the theory where there is no division of labor, because all of the work is done by one hypothesis.

Philosophically, therefore, the parallelism is weak, which brings me to my second point. Notwithstanding the philosophical arguments, some of the best recent history of science uses the parallelism as its historiographic model! I refer, in particular, to the work of David Hull (1989) and even more to that of Robert Richards (1988). The latter in particular has used the model skillfully to tell the tale of the development of evolutionary theories of mind and behavior for the past two hundred years. I could now say that an even better job might have been done without the model. I could now point out that some great works have been written despite, or because of, their author's pretty funny philosophical ideas (Tolstoy and Dostoevsky spring to mind.) But that all sounds like sour grapes. So let me conclude simply by reiterating that I do not like the analogy, but that ultimately it is all a matter of taste. One person's philosophical poison is clearly another person's historical food.

Conclusion

What, if anything, remains to be said? Just this. Agassiz's threefold law had its critics and ultimately was not destined to survive, at least in the form proposed. But it was a powerful factor in the forward movement of the science of his day, and moreover remnants survive in the thinking of our day. Perhaps the same will hold of the threefold law I have been discussing. If so, that is not such a bad fate.

References

Agassiz, L. 1842. On the success and development of organized beings at the surface of the terrestrial globe, being a discourse delivered at the inauguration of the Academy of Neuchatel. *Edinburgh New Philosophical Journal* 23:388-99.

Agassiz, L. 1859. *Essay on Classification*. London: Longman, Brown, Green, Longmans, and Roberts and Trübner.

Almond, G., M. Chodorow, and R. H. Pearce. 1982. *Progress and its Discontents*. Berkeley: University of California Press.

Ayala, F. J. 1974. The concept of biological progress, 339-54. In *Studies in the Philosophy of Biology*, ed. F. J. Ayala and T. Dobzhansky. London: Macmillan.

Ayala, F. J. 1982. The evolutionary concept of progress, 106-24. In *Progress and Its Discontents*, ed. G. Almond, M. Chodorow, and R. H. Pearce. Berkeley: University of California Press.

Ayala, F. J. 1988. Can "progress" be defined as a biological concept?, 75-96. In *Evolutionary Progress*, ed. M. H. Nitecki. Chicago: University of Chicago Press.

Bakshtanovskiy, V. I., et al. 1989. *Ethics*. Moscow: Progress Publishers.

Bonner, J. T. 1987. *The Evolution of Complexity*. Princeton, NJ: Princeton University Press.

Bowler, P. J. 1976. *Fossils and Progress*. New York: Science History Publications.

Bowler, P. J. 1984. *Evolution: The History of an Idea*. Berkeley: University of California Press.

Bury, J. B. 1920. *The Idea of Progress. An Inquiry into Its Origin and Growth*. London: Macmillan.

Butts, R. 1965. Necessary truth in Whewell's theory of science. *American Philosophical Quarterly* 2:1-21.

Carlyle, T. [1831] 1896-1901. Characteristics, 3, 1-43. In *Critical and Miscellaneous Essays*, ed. H. D. Traill. New York: Chapman and Hall.

Chambers, C. A. 1958. The belief in progress in twentieth-century America. *Journal of the History of Ideas* 19:197-224.

Cole, J. R., and S. Cole. 1973. *Social Stratification in Science*. Chicago: University of Chicago Press.

Collins, H. 1985. *Changing Order*. London: Sage.

Condorcet, A. N. [1795] 1956. *Sketch for a Historical Picture of the Progress of the Human Mind*. New York: The Noonday Press.

Darwin, C. 1859. *On the Origin of Species*. London: John Murray.

Darwin, C. 1871. *The Descent of Man*. London: John Murray.

Darwin, E. 1803. *The Temple of Nature*. London: J. Johnson.

Davis, B. D. 1986. *Storm Over Biology: Essays on Science, Sentiment, and Public Policy*. Buffalo, NY: Prometheus.

Dawkins, R. 1986. *The Blind Watchmaker*. London: Longman.

George, H. [1880] 1926. *Progress and Poverty*. Reprint. Garden City, NY: Random House.

Gould, S. J. 1979. Episodic change versus gradualist dogma. *Science and Nature* 2:5-12.

Gould, S. J. 1981. *The Mismeasure of Man*. New York: Norton.

Gould, S. J. 1989. *Wonderful Life*. New York: Norton.

Greene, J. C. 1977. Darwin as a social evolutionist. *Journal of the History of Biology* 10:1-27.

Haraway, D. 1989. *Private Visions*. New York: Routledge.

Hegel, G. F. W. 1970. *Philosophy of Nature*. Oxford: Oxford University Press.

Hull, D. L. 1988. *Science as a Process*. Chicago: University of Chicago Press.

Huxley, T. H. 1893. The coming of age of the origin of species, 227-43. In *Collected Essays: Darwiniana*, vol. II. London: Macmillan.

Hyatt, A. 1893. Phylogeny of an acquired characteristic. *Proceedings of the American Philosophical Society* 32:349-647.

Kuhn, T. S. 1962. *The Structure of Scientific Revolutions*. Chicago: University of Chicago Press.

Lamarck, J. B. [1809] 1963. *Zoological Philosophy*. Translated by H. Elliot. New York: Hafner.

Lewontin, R. C. 1974. *The Genetic Basis of Evolutionary Change*. New York: Columbia University Press.

Losee, J. 1972. *A Historical Introduction to the Philosophy of Science*. Oxford: Oxford University Press.

McMullin, E. 1983. Values in science, 3-28. In *PSA 1982*, vol. 2, ed. P. Asquith and T. Nickles. East Lansing, MI: Philosophy of Science Association.

McNeil, M. 1987. *Under the Banner of Science: Erasmus Darwin and His Age*. Manchester: Manchester University Press.

Nagel, E. 1961. *The Structure of Science*. London: Routledge and Kegan Paul.

Ospovat, D. 1981. *The Development of Darwin's Theory*. Cambridge: Cambridge University Press.

Pollard, S. 1968. *The Idea of Progress*. London: Watts.

Popper, K. 1959. *The Logic of Scientific Discovery*. London: Hutchinson.

Popper, K. 1962. *Conjectures and Refutations*. New York: Basic Books.

Popper, K. 1972. *Objective Knowledge*. Oxford: Oxford University Press.

Popper, K. 1974. Intellectual autobiography. In *The Philosophy of Karl Popper*, ed. P. A. Schilpp. LaSalle, IL: Open Court.

Richards, R. J. 1988. *Darwin and the Emergence of Evolutionary Theories of Mind and Behavior*. Chicago: University of Chicago Press.

Rose, S. 1982. *Against Biological Determinism*. London: Allison and Busby.

Ruse, M. 1976. The scientific methodology of William Whewell. *Centaurus* 20:227-97.

Ruse, M. 1979. *The Darwinian Revolution: Science Red in Tooth and Claw*. Chicago: University of Chicago Press.

Ruse, M. 1985. *Sociobiology: Sense or Nonsense?* 2d ed. Dordrecht: Reidel.

Ruse, M. 1986. *Taking Darwin Seriously*. Oxford: Blackwell.

Ruse, M. In press. Great expectations. *Quarterly Review of Biology* 65.

Smith, A. [1759] 1976. *The Theory of Moral Sentiments*. Ed. D. D. Raphael and A. L. Macfie. Oxford: Oxford University Press.

Smith, A. [1776] 1937. *The Wealth of Nations*. New York: Modern Library.

Stroud, B. 1984. *Scepticism*. Oxford: Oxford University Press.

Toulmin, S. 1967. The evolutionary development of natural science. *American Scientist* 57:456-71.

Wagar, W. 1972. *Good Tidings: The Belief in Progress from Darwin to Marcuse*. Bloomington, IN: Indiana University Press.

Whewell, W. 1837. *The History of the Inductive Sciences*. London: Parker.

Whewell, W. 1840. *Philosophy of the Inductive Sciences*. London: Parker.

Williams, G. C. 1966. *Adaptation and Natural Selection*. Princeton: Princeton University Press.

Williams, G. C. 1988. Huxley's evolution and ethics in sociobiological perspective. *Zygon: Journal of Religion and Science* 23:383-407.

Michael Ruse

Wilson, E. O. 1975. *Sociobiology: The New Synthesis*. Cambridge: Harvard University Press.

Wilson, E. O. 1978. *On Human Nature*. Cambridge: Harvard University Press.

Wilson, E. O. 1984. *Biophilia*. Cambridge: Harvard University Press.

How Microevolutionary Processes
Give Rise to History

Robert Boyd and Peter J. Richerson

Over the last decade a number of authors, including ourselves, have attempted to understand human cultural variation using Darwinian methods. This work is unified by the idea that culture is a system of inheritance: individuals vary in their skills, habits, beliefs, values, and attitudes, and these variations are transmitted to others through time by teaching, imitation, and other forms of social learning. To understand cultural change we must account for the microevolutionary processes that increase the numbers of some cultural variants and reduce the numbers of others.

Social scientists have made a number of objections to this approach to understanding cultural change. Among these is the idea that culture can only be explained historically. Because the history of any given human society is a sequence of unique and contingent events, explanations of human social life, it is argued, are necessarily interpretive and particularistic. Present phenomena are best explained mainly in terms of past contingencies, not ahistorical adaptive processes that would erase the trace of history. Like other scientific (rather than historical) explanations of human cultures, the argument goes, Darwinian models cannot account for the lack of correlation of environmental and cultural variation, nor the long term trends in cultural change.

In this chapter, we defend the Darwinian theories of cultural change against this objection by suggesting that several cultural evolutionary processes can give rise to divergent evolutionary developments, secular trends, and other features that can generate unique historical sequences for particular societies. We also argue that Darwinian theory offers useful tools for those interested in understanding the evolution of particular societies. Essentially similar processes act in the case of organic evolution. Darwinian theory

is both scientific and historical. The history of any evolving lineage or culture is a sequence of unique, contingent events. Similar environments often
give rise to different evolutionary trajectories, even among initially similar
taxa or societies, and some show very long-run trends in features such as size.
Nonetheless, these historical features of organic and cultural evolution can
result from a few simple microevolutionary processes.

A proper understanding of the relationship between the historical and
the scientific is important for progress in the social and biological sciences.
There is (or ought to be) an intimate interplay between the study of the
unique events of given historical sequences and the generalizations about
process constructed by studying many cases in a comparative and synthetic
framework. The study of unique cases furnishes the data from which generalizations are derived, while the generalizations allow us to understand better
the processes that operated on particular historical trajectories. We cannot
neglect the close, critical study of particular cases without putting the data
base for generalization in jeopardy. Besides, we often have legitimate
reasons to be curious about exactly how particular historical sequences, such
as the evolution of *Homo sapiens*, occurred. On the other hand, it is from
the study of many cases that we form a body of theory about evolutionary
processes. No one historical trajectory contains enough information to obtain
a very good grasp of the processes that affected its own evolution. Data are
missing because the record is imperfect. The lineage may be extinct, and so
direct observation is impossible. Even if the lineage is extant, experimenta-
tion may be impossible for practical or ethical reasons. Potential causal
variables may be correlated in particular cases, and so understanding their
behavior may be impossible. The comparative method can often clarify such
cases. "Scientists" need "historians" and vice versa.

Darwinian Models of Cultural Evolution

Over the past two decades, a number of scholars have attempted to understand the processes of cultural evolution in Darwinian terms. Social scientists
(Campbell 1965, 1975; Cloak 1975; Durham 1976; Ruyle 1973) have argued
that the analogy between genetic and cultural transmission is the best basis

for a general theory of culture. Several biologists have considered how culturally transmitted behavior fits into the framework of neo-Darwinism (Pulliam and Dunford 1980; Lumsden and Wilson 1981; Boyd and Richerson 1985; Richerson and Boyd 1989a; Cavalli-Sforza and Feldman 1983; Rogers 1989). Other biologists and psychologists have used the formal similarities between genetic and cultural transmission to develop theories describing the dynamics of cultural transmission (Cavalli-Sforza and Feldman 1973, 1981; Cloninger et al. 1979; Eaves et al. 1978). All of these authors are interested in a synthetic theory of process applying to how culture works in all cultures, including in other species which might have systems with a useful similarity to human culture. Note that this last broadly comparative concern is likely to be useful in dissecting the reasons why the human lineage originally became more cultural than typical mammals.[1]

The idea that unifies the Darwinian approach is that culture constitutes a system of inheritance. People acquire skills, beliefs, attitudes, and values from others by imitation and enculturation (social learning), and these "cultural variants" together with their genotypes and environments, determine their behavior. Since determinants of behavior are communicated from one person to another, individuals sample from and contribute to a collective pool of ideas that changes over time. In other words, cultures have similar population-level properties as gene pools, as different as the two systems of inheritance are in the details of how they work. (In one respect, the Darwinian study of cultural evolution is more Darwinian than the modern theory of organic evolution. Darwin not only used a notion of "inherited habits" that is much like the modern concept of culture, but also thought that organic evolution generally included the property of the inheritance of acquired variation, which culture does and genes do not.)

Because cultural change is a population process, it can be studied using Darwinian methods. To understand why people behave as they do in a particular environment, we must know the nature of the skills, beliefs, attitudes, and values that they have acquired from others by cultural inheritance. To do this we must account for the processes that affect cultural variation as individuals acquire cultural traits, use the acquired information to guide behavior, and act as models for others. What processes increase or decrease the proportion of people in a society who hold particular ideas about how to behave? We thus seek to understand the cultural analogs of the forces of natural selection, mutation, and drift that drive genetic evolution. We divide these forces into three classes: random forces, natural selection, and the decision-making forces.

Random forces are the cultural analogs of mutation and drift in genetic transmission. Intuitively, it seems likely that random errors, individual idiosyncrasies, and chance transmission play a role in behavior and social learning. For example, linguists have documented a good deal of individual variation in speech, some of which is probably random individual variation (Labov 1972). Similarly, small human populations might well lose rare skills or knowledge by chance, for example, due to the premature deaths of the only individuals who acquired them (Diamond 1978).

Natural selection may operate directly on cultural variation. Selection is an extremely general evolutionary process (Campbell 1965). Darwin formulated a clear statement of natural selection without a correct understanding of *genetic* inheritance because it is a force that will operate on *any* system of inheritance with a few key properties. There must be heritable variation, the variants must affect phenotype, and the phenotypic differences must affect individuals' chances of transmitting the variants they carry. That variants are transmitted by imitation rather than sexual or asexual reproduction does not affect the basic argument, nor does the possibility that the source of variation is not random. Darwin imagined that random variation, acquired variation, and natural selection all acted together as forces in organic evolution. In the case of cultural evolution, this seems to be the case. It may well be, however, that behavioral variants favored by natural selection depend on the mode of transmission. The behaviors that maximize numbers of offspring may not be the same as those that maximize cultural influence on future generations (Boyd and Richerson 1985).

Decision-making forces result when individuals evaluate alternative behavioral variants and preferentially adopt some variants relative to others. If many of the individuals in a population make similar decisions about variants, especially if similar decisions are made for a number of generations, the pool of cultural variants can be transformed. Naive individuals may be exposed to a variety of models and preferentially imitate some rather than others. We call this force biased transmission. Alternatively, individuals may modify existing behaviors or invent new ones by individual learning. If the modified behavior is then transmitted, the resulting force is much like the guided, nonrandom variation of "Lamarckian" evolution. Put differently, humans are embedded in a complex social network through which they actively participate in the creation and perpetuation of their culture.

The decision-making forces are derived forces (Campbell 1965). Decisions require rules for making them, and ultimately the rules must derive from the action of other forces. That is, if individual decisions are not to be random, there must be some sense of psychological reward or similar process that causes individual decisions to be predictable, in given environments at least. These decision-making rules may be acquired during an earlier episode of cultural transmission, or they may be genetically transmitted traits that control the neurological machinery for acquisition and retention of cultural traits. The latter possibility is the basis of the socio-biological hypotheses about cultural evolution (Alexander 1979; Lumsden and Wilson 1981). These authors, among others, argue that the course of cultural evolution is determined by natural selection operating indirectly on cultural variation through the decision-making forces.

Like natural selection, the decision-making forces may improve the fit of the population to the environment. The criteria of fit depend on the nature of the underlying decision rules. This is easiest to see when the goals of the decision rules are closely correlated with fitness. If human foraging practices are adopted or rejected according to their energy payoff per unit time (optimal foraging theory's operational proxy for fitness), then the foraging practices used in the population will adapt to changing environments much as if natural selection were responsible. If the adoption of foraging practices is strongly affected by consideration of prestige, say that associated with male success hunting dangerous prey, then the resulting pattern of behavior may be different. However, there will still be a pattern of adaptation to different environments, but now in the sense of increasing prestige rather than calories.

What Makes Change Historical?

It has often been argued that historical and scientific explanations are different in kind. Ingold (1985) gives two important versions of this argument. Some authors (e.g., Collingwood 1946) argue that history is uniquely human because it entails conscious perception of the past. The second view (e.g., Trigger 1978) is quite different, and holds that history involves unique, contingent pathways from the past to the future that are strongly influenced by unpredictable, chance events. We focus on the latter view here. For example, capitalism arose in Europe rather than China, perhaps because Medieval and Early Modern statesmen failed to create a unified empire in the West (McNeill 1980), and marsupials dominate the Australian fauna perhaps because of Australia's isolation from other continents in which placental mammals chanced to arise. In contrast, it is argued, scientific explanations involve universally applicable laws. In evolutionary biology and in anthropology, these often take the form of functional explanations, in which only knowledge of present circumstances and general physical laws (e.g., the principles of mechanics) are necessary to explain present behavior (Mitchell and Valone 1990). For example, long fallow horticulture is associated with tropical forest environments, perhaps because it is the most efficient subsistence technology in such environments (Conklin 1969).

It has been argued, perhaps nearly as often, that this dichotomy is false. Eldredge (1989:9) provides a particularly clear and forceful example of a common objection: all material entities have properties that can change through time. Even simple entities like molecules are characterized by position, momentum, charge, and so on. If we could follow a particular water molecule, we would see that these properties changed through time – even the water molecule has a history, according to Eldredge. Yet, everyone agrees that we can achieve a satisfactory scientific theory of water. Historical explanations, Eldredge argues, are just scientific explanations applied to systems that change through time. We are misled because chemists tend to study the average properties of very large numbers of water molecules.

This argument explains too much. Not all change with time is history in the sense intended by historically oriented biologists and social scientists. To see this consider an electrical circuit composed of a voltage source, a capacitor and a fluorescent light. Under the right conditions, the voltage will oscillate through time, and these changes can be described by simple laws. Are these oscillations historical? In Eldredge's view they are; the circuit has a history, a quite boring one, but a history nonetheless. Yet such a system does not generate unique and contingent trajectories. After the system settles down one oscillation is just like the previous one, and the period and amplitude of the oscillations are not contingent on initial conditions. They are not historical in the sense that "one damn thing after another" (Elton 1967:40) leads to cumulative, but unpredictable change.

What then makes change historical? We think that two requirements capture much of what is meant by "history." These two requirements pose a more interesting and serious challenge for reconciling history with a scientific approach to explanation. Consider a system like a society or a population that changes through time both under the influence of internal dynamics and exogenous shocks. Then we suggest that the pattern of change is historical if:

A. Trajectories are not stationary on the time scales of interest. History is more than just change – it is change that does not repeat itself. On long enough time scales, the oscillations in the circuit become stationary, meaning that the chance of finding the system in any particular state becomes constant. Similarly, random day-to-day fluctuations in the weather do not constitute historical change if one is interested in organic evolution because, on long evolutionary time scales the there will be so many days of rain, so many days of sun, and so on. By choosing a suitably long period of time, we can construct a scientific theory of stationary processes using a statistical rather than strictly deterministic approach. In the case of nonstationary historical trajectories, a society or biotic lineage tends to gradually become more and more different as time goes by. There is no possibility of basing explanation on, say, a long-run mean about which the historical entity fluctuates in some at least statistically predictable way, because the mean calculated over longer and longer runs of data continues to change significantly. One of the most characteristic statistical signatures of nonstationary processes is that the variance they produce grows with time rather than converging on a finite value. Note that a process that is historical in one spatio-temporal frame *may* not be in another. If we are not too interested in a specific species or societies in given time periods, we can often average over longer periods of time or many historical units to extract ahistorical generalizations. Any given water molecule has a history, but it is easy to average over many of them and ignore this fact.

B.   *Similar initial conditions give rise to qualitatively different trajectories.*
Historical change is strongly influenced by happenstance. This requires that the dynamics of the system must be path dependent; isolated populations or societies must tend to diverge even when they start from the same initial condition and evolve in similar environments. Thus, for example, the spread of a favored allele in a series of large populations is not historical. Once the allele becomes sufficiently common it will increase at first exponentially, and then slowly, asymptotically approaching fixation. Small changes in the initial frequencies, population size, or even degree of dominance will not lead to qualitative changes in this pattern. In separate but similar environments, populations will converge on the favored allele. Examples of convergence in similar environments are common – witness the general similarity in tropical forest trees and many of the behaviors of the long fallow cultivators who live among them the world over. On the other hand, there are also striking failures of convergence – witness the many unique features of Australian plants, animals, and human cultures. The peculiar hanging leaves of eucalypts, the bipedal gait of kangaroos, and the gerontocratic structure of Australian Aboriginal societies make them distinctively different from the inhabitants of similar temperate and subtropical dry environments on other continents.

It is important not to blur the distinction between simple trajectories and true historical change; it is easy to see how evolutionary processes like natural selection give rise to simple, regular change like the spread of a favored allele or subsistence practice. However, it is not so easy to see how such processes give rise to unique, contingent pathways. Scientists tout the approach to steady states and convergence in similar situations as evidence for the operation of natural "laws," so it seems natural to conclude that a lack of stationarity and convergence are evidence of processes that cannot be subsumed in the standard conceptions of science. Our argument is that things are not at all that simple. There is every reason to expect that perfectly ordinary scientific processes, ordinary in the sense that they result from natural causes and are easily understood by conventional methods, regularly generate history in the sense defined by these two criteria.

How Do Adaptive Processes Give Rise to History?

Let us begin with the two most straightforward answers to this question. First, it could be that most evolutionary change is random. Much change in organic evolution may be the result of drift and mutation, and much change in cultural evolution may result from analogous processes. The fact that drift is a very slow process would explain long-term evolutionary trends. Raup (1977) and others argue that random-walk models produce phylogenies that are remarkably similar to real ones. The fact that cultural and genetic evolutionary change is random would allow populations in similar environments to diverge from each other. It seems likely that some variation in both cases evolves mainly under the influence of nonadaptive forces – for example, much of the eukaryotic genome does not seem to be expressed and evolves under the influence of drift and mutation (Futuyma 1986:447). Similarly, the arbitrary character of symbolic variation suggests that nonadaptive processes are likely to be important in linguistic change and similar aspects of culture. In both cases, isolated populations diverge at an approximately constant rate on the average. However, to understand why a particular species is characterized by a particular DNA sequence, or why a particular people use a particular word for mother, one must investigate the sequence of historical events that led to the current state.

It also possible that historical change is generated by abiotic environmental factors (Valentine and Moores 1972). Long-term trends in evolution could result from the accurate adaptive tracking of a slowly changing environment. For example, during the last hundred million years there has been a long-term increase in the degree of armoring of many marine invertebrates living on rocky substrates and a parallel increase in the size and strength of feeding organs among their predators (Vermeij 1987; Jackson 1988). It is possible that these biotic trends have been caused by long-run environmental changes over the same period – for example, an increase in the oxygen content of the atmosphere (Holland 1984). Similarly, beginning perhaps as much as 17,000 years ago, humans began a shift from migratory big game hunting to sedentary, broad spectrum, more labor-intensive foraging, finally developing agriculture about 7,000 years ago (Henry 1989). Many authors (e.g., Reed 1977) have argued that the transition from glacial to interglacial climate that occurred during the same period is somehow responsible for this change. Similarly, differences among populations in similar environments may result from the environments actually being different in some subtle but important way. For example, Westoby (1989) has argued that some of the unusual features of the Australian biota result from the continent-wide predominance of highly weathered, impoverished soils on this relatively undisturbed continental platform. Perhaps the failure of agriculture to develop in or diffuse to Aboriginal Australia, despite many favorable preconditions and the presence of cultivators just across the Torres Strait, also reflects poor soils.

It is more difficult to understand how adaptive processes like natural selection can give rise to historical trajectories. There are two hurdles: First, adaptive processes in both organic and cultural evolution appear to work on rather short time scales compared to the time scales of change known from the fossil record, archaeology and history. Theory, observation, and experiment suggest that natural selection can lead to change that is much more rapid than any observed in the fossil record (Levinton 1988:342-47). For example, the African Great Lakes have been the locus of spectacular adaptive radiations of fishes amounting to hundreds of highly divergent forms from a few ancestors in the larger lakes (Lowe-McConnell 1975). The maximum time scales for these radiations, set by the ages of the lakes and not counting that they may have dried up during the Pleistocene, are only a few million years. The radiation in Lake Victoria (about 200 endemic species) seems to have required only a few hundred thousand years. Adaptive cultural change driven by decision-making forces can be very fast indeed as is evidenced by the spread of innovations (Rogers 1983). It is not immediately clear how very short time-scale processes such as these can give rise to longer term change of the kind observed in both fossil and archaeological record unless the pace of change is regulated by environmental change. In the absence of continuing, long-term, nonstationary environmental change, adaptive processes seem quite capable of reaching equilibria in relatively short order. In other words, both cultural and organic evolution seem, at first glance, to be classic scientific processes that produce functional adjustments too rapidly to account for the slow historical trajectories we actually observe.

Second, it is not obvious why adaptive processes should be sensitive to initial conditions. Within anthropology the view that adaptive processes are ahistorical in this sense underpins many critiques of functionalism. Many anthropologists claim that it is self-evident that cultural evolution is historical, and that, therefore, adaptive explanations (being intrinsically equilibrist and ahistorical) must be wrong. For example, Hallpike (1986) presents a variety of data which show that peoples living in similar environments often have quite different social organization, and historically related cultures often retain similar social organizations despite occupying radically different environments. Because functionalist models predict a one-to-one relationship between environment and social organization, he argues, these data falsify the functionalist view. Indeed, functionalists like Cohen (1974:86) expect to see history manifest only in the case of functionally equivalent symbolic forms (see below). Biologists have generally been more aware that a population's response to selection depends on phylogenetic and developmental constraints and, therefore, that evolutionary trajectories are, at least to a degree, path dependent. Nonetheless, lack of convergence is sometimes used to argue to the lack of importance of natural selection. Should selection not cause populations exposed to similar environments to converge on similar adaptations? Certainly, some striking convergences from unlikely ancestors do exist.

Here we argue that path dependence and long-term change are likely to be consequences of any adaptive process analogous to natural selection. Our claims are rather general, and are thus independent of the nature of the transmission process (genetic or cultural), and of the details of development. Let us begin with an especially simple example of genetic evolution. Consider a large population of organisms in which individuals' phenotypes can be represented as a number of quantitative characters. Let us assume that there are no constraints on what can evolve due to properties of the genetic system itself. One model with this property assumes that the distribution of additive genetic values[2] for each character is Gaussian, that there are no genetic

Contours of log $\overline{W}$

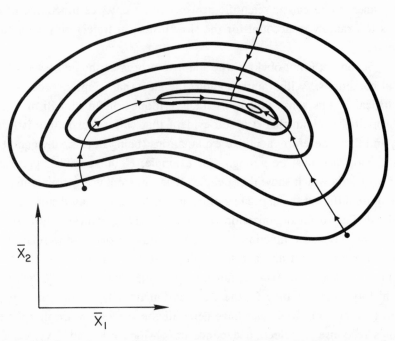

Figure 1. This figure shows two adaptive topographies. The axes are the mean genetic value in a population for two characters. The contour lines give contours of equal mean fitness. Populations beginning at different initial states all achieve the same equilibrium state. Fig. 1*a*, above, shows a simple unimodal adaptive topography. Fig. 1*b*, facing page, shows a complex, multimodal topography. Initially similar populations diverge owing only to the influence of selection.

correlations among characters, that no genotype-environment interactions exist, and that mutation maintains a constant amount of heritable variation for each character. Further, assume that the fitness of each individual depends only on its own phenotype, not on the frequency of other phenotypes or the population density, and there is no environmental change. With these assumptions it can be shown that the change in the vector of mean values for each character is along the gradient of the logarithm of average fitness (Lande 1979). In other words, the mean phenotype in the population changes in the direction that maximizes the increase in the average fitness of the population. This is the sort of situation in which selection, and similar processes in the cultural system, ought to produce optimal adaptations in the straightforward manner depicted in elementary textbooks.

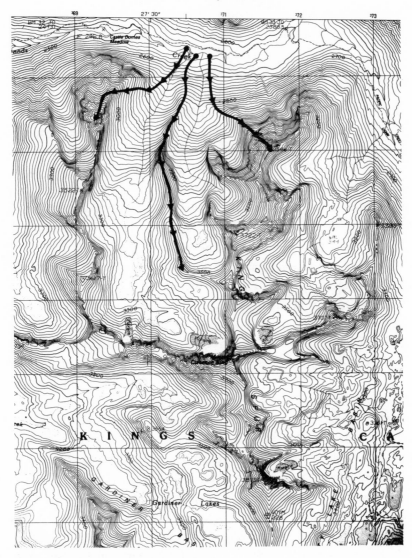

In this simple model the evolutionary trajectory of the population will be completely governed by the shape of average fitness as a function of mean phenotype. If the adaptive topography has a unique maximum then every population will evolve to the same equilibrium mean phenotype, independent of its starting position, and once there be maintained by stabilizing selection. On the other hand if there is more than one local maximum, different equilibrium outcomes are possible depending on initial condition. The larger the number of local maxima, the more path dependent the resulting trajectories will be (see fig. 1).

Unfortunately, we do not know what real adaptive topographies look like, and, as Lande (1986) has pointed out, there is little chance that we will be able to determine their shape empirically. In evolutionary texts, adaptive topographies are commonly depicted as a smooth three-dimensional surface with a small number of local maxima. However, if evolutionary "design problems" are similar to the engineering ones, this picture is misleading. Experience with engineering design problems suggests that real adaptive topographies are often extremely complex, with long ridges, multiple saddle points, and many local optima – more akin to the topographic map of a real mountain range than the smooth textbook surfaces.

A computer design problem discussed by Kirkpatrick et al. (1983) provides an excellent example. Computers are constructed from large numbers of interconnected circuits each with some logical function. Because the size of chips is limited, circuits must be divided among different chips. Because signals between chips travel more slowly and require more power than signals within chips, designers want to apportion circuits among chips so as to minimize the number of connections between them. For even moderate numbers of circuits, there is an astronomical number of solutions to this problem. Kirkpatrick et al. (1983) present an example in which the 5000 circuits which make up the IBM 370 microprocessor were to be divided between two chips. Here there are about 10^{1503} possible solutions! This design problem has two important qualitative properties:

A. It has a very large number of local optima. That is, there is a large number of arrangements of circuits with the property that any simple rearrangement increases the number of connections between chips. This means that any search process that simply goes uphill (like our model of genetic evolution) can end up at any one of a very large number of configurations. An unsophisticated optimizing scheme will improve the design only until it reaches one of the many local optima, which one depending upon starting conditions. For example, for the 370 design problem, several runs of a simple hill-climbing algorithm produced between 677 and 730 interconnections. The best design found (using a more sophisticated algorithm) required only 183 connections.

B. There is a smaller, although still substantial, number of arrangements with close to the optimal number of interconnections. That is, there are many qualitatively different designs that have close to the best payoff. In the numerical example discussed above there are on the order of sqrt(5000) ≈ 70 such arrangements.

Kirkpatrick et al. (1983) show that two other computer design problems, the arrangement of chips on circuit boards, and the routing of wiring among chips, have similar properties. These three computer design problems are not unlike evolutionary "design" problems in biology – the localization of functions in organs, the arrangement of organs in a body, and the routing of the nervous and circulatory networks – that are likely to generate complex adaptive topographies. Moreover, as anyone experienced with the numerical solution of real-world optimization problems will testify, these results are quite typical. To quote from the introduction of a recent textbook on optimization " . . . many common design problems, from reservoirs to refrigerators, have multiple local optima, as well as false optima, that make conventional [meaning iterative hill-climbing] optimization schemes risky" (Wilde 1978). Thus, if the analogy is correct, small differences in initial conditions may launch different populations on different evolutionary trajectories which end with qualitatively different equilibrium phenotypes.

It is important to see that this history-generating property does not depend on the existence of genetic or developmental constraints. At least as defined in Maynard Smith et al. (1985) there are no genetic or developmental constraints in the simple model of selection acting on a complex topography. Every combination of phenotypes can be achieved, and there is no bias in the production of genetic variation. Path dependence results from the facts that different characters interact in a complex way to generate fitness, and that the direction of natural selection depends on the shape of the *local* topography.

Of course, developmental constraints could also play a major role in confining lineages to historically determined bauplans, as many biologists have argued (e.g., Seilacher 1970). Further, complex topographies and developmental constraints may be related. Wagner (1988) hypothesizes, based on a model of multivariate phenotypic evolution, that fitness functions will generally be "malignant," and that developmental constraints act to make phenotypes more responsive to selection. By malignant Wagner means that the fitness of any one trait is likely to depend on the values of many other traits. For example, larger size may be favored by selection for success in contests for mates, but only if many traits of the respiratory, skeletal, and circulatory systems change in concert to support larger size. If phenotype is unconstrained, response to selection will be slow because of the need to change so many independent characters at once, whereas developmental constraints confine the expression of variation to a few axes which can respond rapidly to selection. Thus, the bill is a simple, rather constrained part of the anatomy of birds, yet selection has remodeled bills along the relatively few dimensions available (length, width, depth, curvature) to support an amazing variety of specializations. Developmental constraints may be a solution to the complexity of adaptive topographies, albeit one that limits lineages to elaborating a small set of historically derived basic traits as they respond to new adaptive challenges.

Path dependence can arise from the action of functional processes in a cultural system of inheritance as well. For example, decision-making forces arise when people modify culturally acquired beliefs in the attempt to satisfy some goal. If people within a culture share the same goal, this process will produce an evolutionary trajectory very similar to one produced by natural selection – the rate of change of the distribution of beliefs in a population will depend on the amount of cultural variation and the shape of an analog of the adaptive topography in which fitness is replaced by utility (the extent to which alternative beliefs satisfy the goal) (Boyd and Richerson 1985:chap. 5). The details of the transmission and selective processes are not crucial, as long as the processes that lead to change can be represented as climbing a complex topography.

It is unclear whether adding genetic constraints will increase or decrease the potential for path dependence. One sort of genetic constraint can be added by allowing significant genetic correlations among characters (Lande 1986). This assumption means that some mutants are more probable than others. As long as there is some genetic variation in each dimension, the vector of phenotypic means will still go uphill, but not necessarily in the steepest direction. The population will come to equilibrium at one of the local peaks, although this might be quite distant from the equilibrium that the population would have reached had there been no genetic correlations (Lande 1979, 1986). More generally, most genetic architectures do not result in Gaussian distributions of genetic values (Turelli and Barton, in press), and analyses of two locus models suggest that dynamics resulting from the combination of linkage and selection may create many locally stable equilibria even when the fitness function is unimodal (Karlin and Feldman 1970). This suggests that adding more genetic realism would increase the potential for path dependence. On the other hand, computer scientists (Holland 1975; Brady 1985) have found that optimization algorithms closely modeled on multilocus selection are *less* likely to get stuck on local optima than simple iterative hill-climbing algorithms. The issue of genetic constraints is still open.

The situation in cultural evolution is similar, even if not so well studied. On the one hand, many anthropologists stress the rich structure of culture. To the extent that such structure exists, path dependence is likely to be important. On the other hand, Bandura (1977), a pioneering student of the processes of social learning, argues that there is relatively little complex structuring of socially learned behavior. The many examples of cultural syncretism and diffusion of isolated elements of technology suggest his view ought to be taken seriously. Perhaps complex structure is most important in the symbolic aspects of culture, but symbolic variation may be only weakly constrained by functional considerations (Cohen 1974). According to Cohen, we have to use purely contingent historical explanations for things such as linguistic variation, while simple functional explanations suffice for economic, political, and social-organizational phenomena.

Long-term nonstationary trends in evolution can result if there is some process that causes populations to shift from one peak to another, and if that process acts on a longer time scale than adaptive processes like natural selection. So far we have assumed that populations are large and the environment is unchanging. With these assumptions, populations will usually rapidly reach an adaptive peak and then stay there indefinitely. They will not exhibit the kind of long-run change that we have required for change to be historical. Wright (e.g., 1977) long argued that drift plays an important role in causing populations to shift from peak to peak, and then competition among populations favoring the population on the higher peak. Chance variations in gene frequency in small populations could lead to the occasional crossing of adaptive valleys and the movement to higher peaks. Recently, several authors have considered mathematical models of this process (Barton and Charlesworth 1984; Newman et al. 1985; Lande 1986; Crow et al. 1990). These studies suggest that the probability that a shift to a new peak will occur during any time period is low; however, when a shift does occur it occurs very rapidly. If this view is correct, drift should generate a long-run pattern of change in which populations wander haltingly up the adaptive topography from lower local peaks to higher ones. It is also implausible that environments remain constant either in space or in time. As environments change, the shape of the adaptive topography shifts, causing peaks to merge, split, disappear, or temporary ridges to appear, connecting a lower peak to a higher one. Thus, populations will occasionally slide from one peak to another. As long as such events are not too common, environmental change will also lead to long-run change. Such change might appear gradual if there are many small valleys to cross, or punctuational if there are a few big ones.

Adding social or ecological realism to the basic adaptive hill-climbing model of evolution probably increases the potential for multiple stable equilibria. In the simple model, an individual's fitness depended only on its phenotype. When there are social or ecological interactions among individuals within a population, individual fitness will depend on the composition of the population as a whole. When this is the case, evolutionary dynamics can no longer be represented in terms of an invariant adaptive topography. However, they may still be characterized by multiple stable equilibria. Moreover, the fact that many quite simple models of frequency dependence have this property suggests that frequency dependence may usually increase the potential for path-dependent historical change.

Models of the evolution of norms provide an interesting example of how frequency dependence can multiply the number of stable equilibria. Hirshleifer and Rasmusen (1989) have analyzed a model in which a group of individuals interact over a period of time. During each interaction, individuals first have the opportunity to cooperate and thereby produce a benefit to the group as a whole but at some cost to themselves; they then have a chance to punish defectors at no cost to themselves. These authors show that strategies in which individuals cooperate, and punish noncooperators and nonpunishers, are stable in the game theoretic sense. However, they also show that punishment strategies of this kind can stabilize any behavior – cooperation, noncooperation, wearing white socks, or anything else. We (Boyd and Richerson, in prep.) show that the same conclusions apply in an evolutionary model even when punishment is costly. This form of social norm can stabilize virtually any form of behavior as long as the fitness cost of the behavior is small compared to the costs of being punished.

More generally, coordination is an important aspect of several kinds of social interactions (Sugden 1986). In a pure game of coordination it does not matter what strategy is used, as long as it is the strategy that is locally common. Driving on the left versus right side of the road is an example. It does not matter which side we use, but it is critical that we agree on one side or the other. This property of arbitrary advantage to the common strategy is shared by many symbolic and communication systems, and allows multiple equilibria whenever there are multiple conceivable strategies. In many other common kinds of social interactions elements of coordination and conflict are mixed. In such games, all individuals are better off if they use the same strategy, even though the relative advantages of using the strategy differ greatly from individual to individual, and some individuals would be much better off if another strategy were common. As long as the coordination aspect of such interactions is strong enough, multiple stable equilibria will exist. Arthur (1990) shows how locational decisions of industrial enterprises could give rise to historical patterns due to coordination effects. It is often advantageous for firms to locate near other firms in the same industry because specialized labor and suppliers have been attracted by preexisting firms. The chance decisions of the first few firms in an emerging industry can establish one as opposed to another area as the Silicon Valley of that industry. More generally, historical patterns can arise in the many situations where there are increasing returns to scale in the production of a given product or technology. Merely because the QWERTY keyboard is common, it is sensible to adopt it despite its inefficiencies.

Interactions between populations and societies (or elements within societies such as classes) can give rise to multiple stable equilibria. Models of the coevolution of multiple populations have many of the same properties as frequency and density dependent selection within populations, although the theory is less well developed (Slatkin and Maynard Smith 1979). The evolution of one population or society depends upon the properties of others that interact with it, and many different systems of adjusting the relationships between the populations may be possible. For example, Cody (1974:201) noted that competing birds replace each other along an altitudinal gradient in California, but latitudinally in Chile. Given the rather similar environments of these two places, it is plausible that both systems of competitive replacement are stable and which one occurs is due to accidents of history.

The stratification of human societies into privileged elites and disadvantaged commoners derives from the ability of elites to control high-quality resources and/or to exploit commoners using strategies that are similar to competitive and predatory strategies in nature. Insko et al. (1983) studied the evolution of social stratification in the social psychology laboratory. They showed that elites could arise in both an experimental condition that mimicked freely chosen trade relations and one that mimicked conquest. Elites were approximately as well off in both conditions, and insofar as they controlled things, would have no motivation to change social arrangements. It seems plausible that the diversity of political forms of complex societies could result from many arrangements of relations between constituent interest groups being locally stable. The distinctive differences between the Japanese, American, and Scandinavian strategies for operating technologically advanced societies could well derive from historic differences in social organization that have led to different, stable arrangements between interest groups, in spite of similar revolutionary changes in production techniques of the last century or two.

Social or ecological interactions may also give rise to dynamic processes that are sensitive to initial conditions, and have no stable equilibria. Lande (1981) analyzed a model of one such process, sexual selection in which females have a heritable preference for mates that is based on a heritable, sex-limited male character. According to his model, when the male character and female preferences are sufficiently correlated genetically, female choice can create a self-reinforcing "runaway" process that causes the mean male character and the mean female preference to either increase or decrease indefinitely, even in the presence of stabilizing selection on the male character. Selection cannot favor female variants that choose fitter

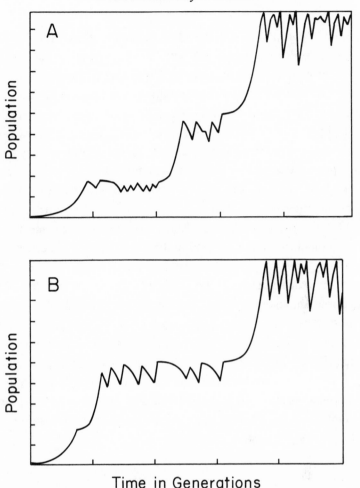

Figure 2. Both parts show the trajectories of population growth generated by the same model of social evolution for two slightly different initial population sizes. In fig. 2a, the society goes through three distinct phase of growth, while in fig. 2b, there are only two.

males (in the usual sense of fitter) because most females are choosing mates with an exaggerated character. The "sensible" female's sons will be handicapped in the mating game. The direction that evolution takes depends on the details of the initial conditions in Lande's model. His quantitative character will be elaborated in one direction or the other depending on how evolution drifts away from an unstable line of equilibria. Although the interpretation of this model is controversial, it is easy to imagine that the exaggerated characters of polygynous animals like birds of paradise and peacocks result from the runaway process. We (Boyd and Richerson 1985:chap. 8, 1987; Richerson and Boyd 1989b) have argued that quite similar processes may arise in cultural evolution when individuals are predisposed to imitate some individuals on the basis of culturally heritable characteristics. The use of some character associated with prestige (stylish dress for example) as an index of whom to imitate has the same potentially unstable runaway dynamic as Lande's model of mate choice sexual selection, and even casual observation suggests that prestige systems do follow contingent historical trajectories. Fashions in clothing, for example, evolve in different directions in different societies, often without much regard for practicality.

Perhaps the most clearly historical patterns of change result when social or ecological interaction lead to "chaotic" dynamics. For example, Day and Walter (1989) have analyzed an extremely interesting model of social evolution in which population growth leads to reduced productivity, social stratification, and eventually to a shift from one subsistence technology to a more productive one. The resulting trajectories of population size are shown in figure 2. Population grows, is limited by resource constraints, and eventually technical substitution occurs, allowing population to grow once more. The only difference between figures 2a and 2b is a very small difference in initial population size. Nonetheless, this seemingly insignificant difference leads to qualitatively different trajectories – one society shows three separate evolutionary stages, and the second only two.

Conclusion

Scientific and historical explanations are not alternatives. Contingent, diverging pathways of evolution and long-term secular trends can result from processes that differ only slightly from those that produce rapid, ahistorical convergence to universal equilibria. Late nineteenth and early twentieth century scientists gave up restricting the term "scientific" for deterministic, mechanistic explanation and began to admit "merely" statistical laws into the fundamental corpus of physics (very reluctantly in some cases – recall Einstein's famous complaint about God not playing dice with the universe to express his distaste for quantum mechanics). Similarly, historical explanations cannot be distinguished from other kinds of scientific explanations except that some models (and, presumably, the phenomena they represent) generate trajectories that meet our definition of being historical. These history-generating processes do not depend on exotic forces or immaterial causes that ought to excite a scientist's skepticism; perfectly mundane things will do. There are challenging complexities in historical processes. For example, even well-understood processes will not allow precise predictions of future behavior when change is historical. However, all the tools of conventional scientific methods can be brought to bear on them. For example, it should be possible to use measurement or experiment to determine if a process is in a region of parameter values where chaotic behavior is expected. At the same time, the historian's traditional concern for critically dissecting the contingencies that contribute to each unique historical path is well taken. Process-oriented "scientific" analyses help us understand how history works, and "historical" data are essential to test scientific hypotheses about how populations and societies change.

In the biological and social domains, "science" without "history" leaves many interesting phenomena unexplained, while "history" without "science" cannot produce an explanatory account of the past, only a listing of disconnected facts. The generalizing impulses of science require historical methods, because the phenomena to be understood are genuinely historical and because historical data are essential for developing generalizations about evolutionary processes. In return, generalizations derived from history and by the study of contemporary systems would seem to be essential for an understanding of particular cases. The amount of data available from the past is usually very limited, and the number of possible reconstructions of the past is correspondingly large. Some sort of theory has to be applied to make some sense of the of the isolated facts. Historians (e.g., Braudel 1972) and paleontologists (e.g., Valentine 1973) often cast their nets rather widely in search of help in interpreting the documents and fossils. McNeill (1986) advocates a "scientific," generalization-seeking approach to history much in this spirit. Consider the question of which of the potential history-producing processes we have discussed are most important in explaining the changes in human societies over the last few tens of thousands of years. Generalizing disciplines such as climatology and cultural ecology are certainly relevant to the task in general, and to the understanding of how particular societies changed in particular environments (Henry 1989). At the same time, because these historical societies faced Pleistocene climates and the transition to the Holocene, and because they developed a series of technical, social, and ideological innovations that are the foundation of modern human societies by processes that are not open to direct observation, the historical and archaeological record provide crucial data not available from ahistorical study. To the extent that the processes we have described are important, "science" and "history" cannot be disentangled as separate intellectual enterprises.

Darwinian models of organic and cultural evolution illustrate how little distinction can be made between the two approaches. Such models can produce historical patterns of change by a rather large number of different mechanisms. We have argued that historical change is distinguished by two attributes: the tendency of initially similar systems to diverge, and the occurrence of long-term change. Evolutionary models, including those which assume that selection or analogous cultural processes increase adaptiveness in each generation, readily generate multiple stable equilibria. Populations with similar initial conditions may evolve toward separate equilibria. Random genetic drift and analogous cultural processes coupled with environmental change may cause populations to shift from one equilibrium to another. It is plausible that peak shifting by populations (or the shifting of peaks due to environmental change) occurs at a slow enough rate to explain long-term secular trends.

Many anthropologists take as their task the explanation of differences among human societies, and suggest that most such differences are historical in character. If explanation of such variation is mainly historical, then anthropologists might reasonably ask, what is the point of Darwinian models of cultural change when historical or "contextual" explanations will be much more productive. The reasons are as follows:

First, the premise is often incorrect. Genuine convergences are common, and explaining them requires some theory based on common processes of cultural change. Perhaps the most spectacular cultural example is the convergence of social organization in stratified, state-level societies in the Old and New Worlds. For example, Cortez in 1519 found that Aztec society was quite similar to his own in important ways: it contained familiar roles, hereditary nobility, priests, warriors, craftsmen, peasants and so on. The bureaucracy was organized hierarchically. This convergence is remarkable because the Spanish and Aztec states evolved independently from a hunter-gatherer ancestry. The cultural lineages that resulted in these two states were without known cultural contact for several thousand years before state formation began in either (Wenke 1980).

Second, Darwinian models can make useful predictions. They can tell us why some forms of behavior or social organization are never observed and others are common. For example, kinship is an extremely common principle of social organization. Contrariwise, there would seem to be lots of advantages to a free market in babies – for the individual it would allow easy adjustment of family size, age composition, sex ratio and so on, and for society a division of labor in child rearing would allow better use of human resources. The sociobiological theory of kin selection explains why there are no societies with free trade in infants, and why kinship is generally an important feature of social organization. If most of the historic context is taken as given, Darwinian arguments can be very powerful heuristics. This is especially clear for genetic evolution. For example, given haplodiploidy, a theory based directly on the expected equilibrium outcome of natural selection can make surprising and extremely fruitful predictions about patterns of behavior in social insects. Who, for example, would have thought to connect sex ratio among reproductives and "slave making" in ant species? In recent years, similar ideas have been usefully applied to understanding human behavior. For example, Hill, Kaplan and their colleagues (reviewed in Hill and Kaplan 1988) have used theory from behavioral ecology to relate patterns of foraging, mate preference, and child care among Ache hunter-gatherers, and Borgerhoff-Mulder (1988) has explained variation in bride price among Kipsigis pastoralists in terms of parameters that predict future female fitness.

Finally, it is useful in and of itself to know that even the most strongly functional Darwinian models can give rise to historical change. The same processes that give rise to convergence in one case can generate differences in another given only small changes in the structure of the process or in initial conditions. Brandon (1990) argues that "why possibly" explanations are useful in evolutionary biology. By this he means explanations that tell us how some character *could* have evolved are useful even if we cannot determine whether the explanation is true. The theoretical models in population genetics provide a good example: Hamilton's (1964) kin selection models show how natural selection could give rise to self-sacrificial behavior. However, we usually do not know whether any particular case of altruism arose as a result of kin selection. The lack of *any* "why possibly" explanation would cast doubt on other aspects of our knowledge of how selection shapes behavior.

Understanding how adaptive processes could give rise to historical change is useful for analogous reasons. There is considerable evidence that people's choices about what to believe and what to value are affected by the consequences in material well being, social status and so on (e.g., Boyd and Richerson 1985). This view has a venerable history in anthropology (e.g., Barth 1981; Harris 1979), plays a foundation role in economics, and is taken for granted in many historians' explanations for particular sequences of events. If cultural change is affected by consequence-driven individual choice or natural selection, then it follows that there will be a process that will act to modify the distribution of cultural variation in a population in much the same way that natural selection changes genetic variation (Boyd and Richerson 1985:chaps. 4 and 5). The fact that functional processes like natural selection readily lead to history allows one to hold this view without having necessarily to search for external environmental differences to explain the differences among apparently similarly situated human societies.

Acknowledgments

We thank James Griesemer, Matthew H. Nitecki, Eric A. Smith, and two anonymous reviewers for most helpful comments on previous drafts of this paper.

Notes

1. This project is quite different from the better-known, classical studies of cultural evolution developed by Leslie White (1959) and other scholars in anthropology. This work focused de-

scriptively on the large scale patterns of cultural evolution rather than on the details of the processes by which cultural evolution occurs (Campbell 1965, 1975). The research tradition White represents derives from the progressivist ideas of Herbert Spencer, rather than from Darwin.

2. The additive genetic value of a particular individual for a particular character is the average value of that character for offspring produced when that individual mates at random with a large number of other individuals in the population. For example, the additive genetic value of a bull for fat content is the average fat content of all its offspring where mates were chosen at random. The distribution of genetic values is Gaussian when the probability that an individual has a given genetic value is given by the normal (or Gaussian) probability distribution. Genetic correlations exist when the distributions of genetic values for different characters are not probabilistically independent. For example, if bulls whose genetic value for size also tend to have a higher genetic value for fat content, then body size and fat content are genetically correlated. Genotype environment correlations arise when individuals with the same genotype develop different phenotypes in different environments.

References

Alexander, R. D. 1979. *Darwinism and Human Affairs*. Seattle: University of Washington Press.

Arthur, W. B. 1990. Positive feedbacks in the economy. *Scientific American* (February):92-99.

Bandura, A. 1977. *Social Learning Theory*. Englewood Cliffs, NJ: Prentice Hall.

Barth, F. 1981. *Process and Form in Social Life*. London: Routledge and Kegan Paul.

Barton, N. H., and B. Charlesworth. 1984. Genetic revolutions, founder effects, and speciation. *Annual Review of Ecology and Systematics* 15:133-64.

Borgerhoff-Mulder, M. 1988. Kipsigis bridewealth payments, 65-82. In *Human Reproductive Behavior: A Darwinian Perspective*, ed. L. Betzig and P. Turke. Cambridge: Cambridge University Press.

Boyd, R., and P. J. Richerson. 1985. *Culture and the Evolutionary Process*. Chicago: University of Chicago Press.

Boyd, R., and P. J. Richerson. 1987. The evolution of ethnic markers. *Cultural Anthropology* 2:65-79.

Brady, R. M. 1985. Optimization strategies gleaned from biological evolution. *Nature* 317:804-6.

Brandon, R. 1990. *Adaptation and Environment*. Princeton: Princeton University Press.

Braudel, F. 1972. *The Mediterranean and the Mediterranean World in the Age of Philip II*. Vol. 1. New York: Harper and Row.

Campbell, D. T. 1965. Variation and selective retention in sociocultural evolution, 19-49. In *Social Change in Developing Areas: A Reinterpretation of Evolutionary Theory*, ed. H. R. Barringer, G. I. Blanksten, and R. W. Mack. Cambridge: Schenkman.

Campbell, D. T. 1975. On the conflicts between biological and social evolution and between psychology and moral tradition. *American Psychologist* 30:1103-26.

Cavalli-Sforza, L. L., and M. W. Feldman. 1973. Models for cultural inheritance. I. Group mean and within group variation. *Theoretical Population Biology* 4:42-55.

Cavalli-Sforza, L. L., and M. W. Feldman. 1981. *Cultural Transmission and Evolution: A Quantitative Approach*. Princeton: Princeton University Press.

Cavalli-Sforza, L. L., and M. W. Feldman. 1983. Cultural versus genetic adaptation. *Proceedings of the National Academy of Sciences, USA* 90:4993-96.

Cloak, F. T., Jr. 1975. Is a cultural ethology possible? *Human Ecology* 3:161-82.

Cloninger, C. R., J. Rice, and T. Reich. 1979. Multifactorial inheritance with cultural transmission and assortative mating. II. A general model of combined polygenic and cultural inheritance. *American Journal of Human Genetics* 31:176-98.

Cody, M. L. 1974. *Competition and the Structure of Bird Communities*. Princeton: Princeton University Press.

Cohen, A. 1974. *Two Dimensional Man: An Essay on the Anthropology of Power and Symbolism in Complex Society*. Berkeley: University of California Press.

Collingwood, R. G. 1946. *The Idea of History*. Oxford: Clarendon.

Conklin, H. C. 1969. An ethnoecological approach to shifting agriculture. In *Environment and Cultural Behavior*, ed. A. P. Vayda. Garden City, NY: Natural History Press.

Crow, J. F., W. R. Engels, and C. Denniston. 1990. Phase three of Wright's shifting balance theory. *Evolution*. 44:233-47.

Day, R. H., and X. Walter. 1989. Economic growth in the very long run: On the multiple phase interaction of population, technology, and social infrastructure. In *Economic Complexity: Chaos, Sunspots, Bubbles, and Nonlinearity*, ed. W. A. Barnett, J. Geweke, and K. Schell. Cambridge: Cambridge University Press.

Diamond, J. 1978. The Tasmanians: Longest isolation, simplest technology. *Nature* 273:185-86.

Durham, W. H. 1976. The adaptive significance of cultural behavior. *Human Ecology* 4:89-121.

Eaves, L. J., A. Last, P. A. Young, and N. G. Martin. 1978. Model fitting approaches to the analysis of human behavior. *Heredity* 41:249-320.

Eldredge, N. 1989. *Macroevolutionary Dynamics*. New York: McGraw-Hill.

Elton, G. R. 1967. *The Practice of History*. London: Methuen.

Futuyma, D. J. 1986. *Evolutionary Biology*. 2d ed. Sunderland, MA: Sinauer.

Hallpike, C. R. 1986. *Principles of Social Evolution*. Oxford: Clarendon.

Hamilton, W. D. 1964. The genetical evolution of social behavior. *Journal of Theoretical Biology* 7:1-52.

Harris, M. 1979. *Cultural Materialism: The Struggle for a Science of Culture*. New York: Random House.

Henry, D. O. 1989. *From Foraging to Agriculture: The Levant at the End of the Ice Age*. Philadelphia: University of Pennsylvania Press.

Hill, K., and H. Kaplan. 1988. Tradeoffs in male and female reproductive strategies among the Ache, 227-306. In *Human Reproductive Behavior: A Darwinian Perspective*, ed. L. Betzig and P. Turke. Cambridge: Cambridge University Press.

Hirshleifer, D., and E. Rasmusen. 1989. Cooperation in a repeated prisoner's dilemma with ostracism. *Journal of Economic Behavior and Organization* 12:87-106.

Holland, H. D. 1984. *The Chemical Evolution of the Atmosphere and Oceans*. Princeton: Princeton University Press.

Holland, J. H. 1975. *Adaptation in Natural and Artificial Systems*. Ann Arbor: University of Michigan Press.

Ingold, T. 1985. *Evolution and Social Life*. Cambridge: Cambridge University Press.

Insko, C. A., R. Gilmore, S. Drenan, A. Lipsitz, D. Moehle, and J. Thibaut. 1983. Trade versus expropriation in open groups: A comparison of two types of social power. *Journal of Personality and Social Psychology* 44:977-99.

Jackson, J. B. C. 1988. Does ecology matter? *Paleobiology* 14:307-12.

Karlin, S., and M. W. Feldman. 1970. Linkage and selection: Two-locus symmetric viability model. *Theoretical Population Biology* 1:39-71.

Kirkpatrick, S., C. D. Gelatt, and M. P. Vecchi. 1983. Optimization by simulated annealing. *Science* 220:671-80.

Labov, W. 1972. *Sociolinguistic Patterns*. Philadelphia: University of Pennsylvania Press.

Lande, R. 1979. Quantitative genetic analysis of multivariate evolution, applied to brain:body size allometry. *Evolution* 33:402-16.

Lande, R. 1981. Models of speciation by sexual selection on polygenic traits. *Proceedings of the National Academy of Sciences, USA* 78:3721-25.

Lande, R. 1986. The dynamics of peak shifts and the pattern of morphological evolution. *Paleobiology* 12:343-54.

Levinton, J. 1988. *Genetics, Paleontology, and Macroevolution*. Cambridge: Cambridge University Press.

Lowe-McConnell, R. H. 1975. *Fish Communities in Tropical Freshwaters*. London: Longmann.

Lumsden, C. J., and E. O. Wilson. 1981. *Genes, Mind and Culture*. Cambridge: Harvard University Press.

Maynard Smith, J., R. Burian, S. Kauffman, P. Alberch, J. Campbell, B. Goodwin, R. Lande, D. Raup, and L. Wolpert. 1985. Developmental constraints and evolution. *Quarterly Review of Biology* 60:265-87.

McNeill, W. H. 1980. *The Human Condition: An Ecological and Historical View*. Princeton: Princeton University Press.

McNeill, W. H. 1986. A defense of world history, 71-95. In *Mythistory and Other Essays by W.*

H. *McNeill*. Chicago: University of Chicago Press.

Mitchell, W. A., and T. J. Valone. 1990. The optimization research program - studying adaptations by their function. *Quarterly Review of Biology* 65:43-52.

Newman, C. M., J. E. Cohen, and C. Kipnis. 1985. Neo-Darwinian evolution implies punctuated equilibria. *Nature* 315:400-401.

Pulliam, H. R., and C. Dunford. 1980. *Programmed to Learn: An Essay on the Evolution of Culture*. New York: Columbia University Press.

Raup, D. M. 1977. Probabilistic models in evolutionary paleobiology. *American Scientist* 65:50-57.

Reed, C. A. 1977. Origins of agriculture: Discussion and some conclusions, 879-953. In *Origins of Agriculture*, ed. C. A. Reed. The Hague: Mouton.

Richerson, P. J., and R. Boyd. 1989a. The role of evolved predispositions in cultural evolution: Or human sociobiology meets Pascal's wager. *Ethology and Sociobiology* 10:195-219.

Richerson, P. J., and R. Boyd. 1989b. A Darwinian theory for the evolution of symbolic cultural traits, 124-47. In *The Relevance of Culture*, ed. M. Freilich. S. Hadley, MA: Bergin and Garvey.

Rogers, A. R. 1989. Does biology constrain culture? *American Anthropologist* 90:819-31.

Rogers, E. M. 1983. *The Diffusion of Innovations*. 3d ed. New York: The Free Press.

Ruyle, E. E. 1973. Genetic and cultural pools: Some suggestions for a unified theory of biocultural evolution. *Human Ecology* 1:201-15.

Seilacher, A. 1970. Arbeitskonzept zur Konstruktions-morphologie. *Lethaia* 3:393-96.

Slatkin, M., and J. Maynard Smith. 1979. Models of coevolution. *Quarterly Review of Biology* 54:233-63.

Sugden, R. 1986. *The Economics of Rights, Co-operation and Welfare*. Oxford: Basil Blackwell.

Trigger, B. 1978. *Time and Traditions*. Edinburgh: Edinburgh University Press.

Turelli, M., and N. Barton. In press. The dynamics of polygenic characters under selection. *Theoretical Population Biology*.

Valentine, J. W. 1973. *The Evolutionary Paleoecology of the Marine Biosphere*. Englewood Cliffs, NJ: Prentice-Hall.

Valentine, J. W., and E. M. Moores. 1972. Global tectonics and the fossil record. *Journal of Geology*. 80:167-84.

Vermeij, G. J. 1987. *Evolution and Escalation: An Ecological History of Life*. Princeton: Princeton University Press.

Wagner, G. P. 1988. The significance of developmental constraints for phenotypic evolution by natural selection, 222-29. In *Population Genetics and Evolution*, ed. G. de Jong. Berlin: Springer-Verlag.

Wenke, R. 1980. *Patterns in Prehistory*. Oxford: Oxford University Press.

Westoby, M. 1989. Australia's high lizard density: A new hypothesis. *Trends in Ecology and Evolution* 4:38.

White, L. A. 1959. *The Evolution of Culture*. New York: McGraw-Hill.

Wilde, D. J. 1978. *Globally Optimal Design*. New York: John Wiley & Sons.

Wright, S. 1977. *Evolution and the Genetics of Populations*. Vol. 3. *Experimental Results and Evolutionary Deductions*. Chicago: University of Chicago Press.

Evolution and History:
History as Science and Science as History

Garland E. Allen

After reading Darwin's *On the Origin of Species* in December of 1860, Karl Marx wrote enthusiastically to his friend and collaborator Friedrich Engels (December 19): ". . . this is the book which contains the basis in natural history for our view" (Marx and Engels 1936:126). Just a week earlier (December 12), Marx had explained to Ferdinand Lasalle: "Darwin's book is very important and serves me as a basis in natural science for the class struggle in history. . ." (Marx and Engels 1936:125). And, according to one biographer, after reading the *Origin* Marx could talk of nothing else for months (Liebknecht, n.d.:106). Marx reread the *Origin* several times, and made a number of references to it in *Das Kapital*, particularly to the parallel between the evolution of animal adaptation and that of human technology (Heyer 1982:15). It is also well known that Marx sent a complimentary copy of the second German edition of *Das Kapital* to Darwin in the spring of 1873, and that Darwin penned a courteous, but noncommittal reply, claiming that he was not worthy of receiving and appreciating its import, given his lack of understanding of "the important subject of political economy" (Heyer 1982:16; Colp 1974:329).

It is curious that Marx, the bold political activist, philosopher, historian, and social scientist should have paid such enduring tribute to Darwin, the cautious naturalist who made a career out of avoiding as much controversy as possible, and who shunned philosophical discourse. Yet, as I will try to show, the similarities between Darwin's and Marx's work, and indeed even some of the details of their lives, is so striking that probing into it may well provide new insight into the thought of both men.

The parallel between the ideas of Darwin and Marx has been noted by a number of writers over the years, beginning with Marx's son-in-law, Edward Aveling, a biologist and popularizer of science, who must have been one of the few people who knew both men personally. Aveling wrote a student's introduction to Darwin (Aveling 1889), and an article, "Charles Darwin and Karl Marx" (Aveling 1897). In the intervening years a considerable body of literature, particularly by socialists and others who sought a rational basis for the principle of collectivity with which to counter the individualist claims of social Darwinists, pointed out clearly the similarity between Darwin's view of natural history and Marx's views of social history. In the early twentieth century Karl Kautsky sought to ground the ethical basis of socialism in Darwin's studies on the evolution of sociability in animals (Kautsky 1918). More recently, Jacques Barzun used a comparison between Darwin and Marx (throwing in Wagner for good measure) to blame both Darwinian natural science and Marxist social science for the rise of materialism in the nineteenth century and for what he saw as its logical consequence, World War II, in the twentieth (Barzun 1981).

None of these attempts looked as closely and as comprehensively as they might have at the many parallels in both ideas and methods of approach in the work of Darwin and Marx. To one degree or another, they all missed several of the most important points of commonality. Even Barzun, whose book, *Darwin, Marx and Wagner* (1981), is an intellectual *tour de force*, failed to see what I think are the main philosophical commonalities between Darwin and Marx, namely, their dialectical method of analyzing and understanding historical change.

One of the few recent attempts to deal clearly and in depth with the Darwin-Marx parallel is Paul Heyer's *Nature, Human Nature and Society. Marx, Darwin, Biology and the Human Sciences* (1982). Obviously sympathetic to his subject, Heyer presents a lucid exploration of the many common strains of thought in Darwin and Marx, stressing similarities where they exist but also differences that arise from their quite distinct areas of study. Heyer is one of the few modern scholars who has emphasized Marx's strong interest in the natural sciences of his day (most writers give Engels more attention on this score), documenting his considerable reading, and even writing, on mathematics, anthropology, geology, physiology and the philosophy of nature

(Heyer 1982:10-15). Heyer also correctly assesses the similarity in evolutionary thinking between Darwin and Marx. He sees their views of the historical process – both natural and social – as based on a common notion of *developmental*, as opposed to random, historical change. And he emphasizes that both thought the laws governing historical change could be discovered and studied scientifically.

Even Heyer, however, failed to explore in depth the philosophical dimensions of dialectical thinking inherent in the works of both Darwin and Marx. He discusses Marx's dialectical approach in a number of places, but does not mention a similar approach inherent in Darwin's work. Heyer even argues that while Marx enthusiastically accepted Darwin's general view of natural history, he "was never directly influenced by the great naturalist's method" (Heyer 1982:25). This may be true if what Heyer means is that Marx did not consciously and directly borrow his concepts of methodology from Darwin. My own sense is that Marx, through his interest in the natural sciences, quite independently came to similar ideas of Darwin, especially when applying those ideas to the study of historical processes.

I would like to explore what I see as several of the parallels inherent in the work of Darwin and Marx. In particular, I would like to examine what I think are their common views of history as an evolutionary or developmental process, and thus as a subject amenable to scientific inquiry. I would also like to explore what I see as a common, inherently dialectical way of understanding the dynamics of any kind of changing system.

There are two reasons that I find this subject interesting and important. One is that it provides an outstanding example of how two thinkers, working quite independently, came to similar views and similar ways of trying to understand the historical process. In other words, looking into the parallels in the work of Darwin and Marx provides an insight into the sociology of knowledge, the influence of a common cultural context on the formulation of ideas (a subject that is now of great interest to historians and sociologists of science). I cannot hope to elucidate the total range of causal factors that may have produced the remarkable parallels in Darwin's and Marx's work, nor can I demonstrate that these parallels are not the result of coincidence. But I do think they suggest some very interesting ways in which cultural factors affect the genesis of ideas and the formulation of theoretical constructs.

I do think there was truly something that these midnineteenth-century thinkers shared in the way of common context, which unites their approach to
explaining the world.

A second reason for pursuing the Darwin-Marx comparison is that I
think it can be useful in our own historical thinking today. At a time when
Marxism as a general method of historical analysis is under increasing fire,
and the socialist experiment around the world seems to have collapsed, it is
worthwhile, perhaps even crucial, to reexamine some of the most basic foundations of Marxist and socialist thought. The possible similarities between
Marxian and Darwinian approaches might well be an important means of
developing a revitalized Marxist theory of history. Prior to the recent, and
very rapid, dissolution of many socialist systems, various Marxist critics attempted to separate Marx's views of science, and particularly his scientific
approach to history, from his philosophical and social views. I am suggesting that just the reverse needs to occur: we need to reexplore the scientific,
and especially the evolutionary, basis of Marx's analysis of society and its
history in order to understand where socialist experiments of the twentieth
century have gone wrong, and how a more viable socialism might be forged
in the future. I think the Darwin-Marx connection is particularly useful here.
Scientific creationists aside, we have embraced Darwinism wholeheartedly
while largely rejecting the basic tenets of Marxism. A less naive and more
thorough understanding of Marx's approach to the history of society might be
gained by recognizing how similar, both overtly and covertly, the Marxian
view is to Darwin's view of the history of organic nature.

There are many difficulties inherent in making a broad scale comparison between such intellectual giants as Darwin and Marx. Both men had
long and highly productive careers; they changed their minds about a number
of issues, so that the early Marx (e.g., in the Economic and Philosophical
Manuscripts of 1844) is not the same as the later Marx of *Capital* (1867). To
counter some of the possible pitfalls of this approach, I will draw parallels
between Darwin and Marx at what are comparable periods in their careers,
namely, at the time they developed their boldest and most revolutionary
works in 1858-59, with the publication of *The Origin of Species* and *The
Critique of Political Economy*.

Another problem inherent in the present topic is that both Darwin's and Marx's ideas have been modified over the years by their followers, sometimes in ways that may seem to negate the original formulations. Since the focus of the present paper is more on making the comparison between Marx and Darwin in their own day (roughly between 1858 and 1875), rather than on evaluating modern schools of Marxist (or Darwinian) thought, I will not discuss current theories to any extent. I am aware, however, that modern Marxism, like modern Darwinism, is represented by a number of schools of thought, or camps, and that there is no single Marxist or Darwinian view today. Many of the basic ideas associated with both theories are still intact, and it is these, in their nineteenth-century versions, that I will deal with most explicitly.

In addition to the current problems Marxism is experiencing worldwide, my interest in the relationship between Marx and Darwin, or Marxism and Darwinism, has been stimulated by an increasing number of attempts in recent years among historians and philosophers of science, as well as among biologists, to revive the idea of an evolutionary approach to history. From E. O. Wilson's naive reduction of the social sciences to neo-Darwinian theory in his *Sociobiology, The New Synthesis* (1975), to the historically more sophisticated work of Robert Boyd and Peter Richerson (1985), Robert Richards (1988) and David Hull (1988), a renewed interest in Darwinian models of human history has been gaining attention. These recent attempts have been motivated by what I sense is a recognition of the pertinence of an evolutionary model to a broad-based historiography that tries to understand history as a *process* rather than merely as a sequence of events. I think these efforts can be enriched by taking a closer look at the common methodology inherent in the work of both Darwin and Marx, particularly the philosophy of dialectical materialism. While dialectical thinking is not so consciously developed by Darwin as by Marx, I argue that it is an element that clearly unites much of their approach to the world. This common methodological basis has not been recognized or used by those contemporary writers who set out to generate a Darwinian model of history. As a result those models, though intriguing, tend to be incomplete, reductionist, or oversimplistic. By drawing out the parallels in methodology more clearly, I think we can do better.

The Historical Background: The Common Context
of Darwin's and Marx's Methodology

Coincidence has a way of focusing our attention on larger issues. There are enough coincidences in the lives and work of Charles Darwin and Karl Marx to catch the historian's eye, as it did for Barzun, who first pointed them out. They were almost exact contemporaries, Darwin being born in 1809, Marx in 1818, while they died within a year of one another (Darwin in 1882, Marx in 1883). Both published the first full-fledged accounts of their theories in the same year, 1859 (Darwin's *Origin of Species* and Marx's *Critique of Political Economy*), both works being, in true nineteenth-century fashion intended as "abstracts" of larger works to follow. Both had wide-ranging interests, including political economy (Darwin was well acquainted with the works of Adam Smith, David Riccardo and, of course, Thomas Robert Malthus) and current natural science (Marx was familiar with the ideas and writings of Kepler, Laplace and Newton, as well as Schleiden and Schwann, T. H. Huxley, Helmholtz, Moleschott, and Liebig) (Heyer 1982:12). Even politically, Marx and Darwin shared some common ground in their opposition to slavery in the Caribbean and the United States. Such coincidences serve to underscore the deeper parallels in Marx's and Darwin's intellectual lives that I would like to discuss.

The most significant parallels, or common currents, in the work of Marx and Darwin include: (1) a developmental, evolutionary world view, including an antiteleological view of history, both natural and social; (2) a conviction that human beings are a part of nature in both the biological and social sense; (3) adherence to materialist explanations in general coupled with opposition to metaphysical or mystical causes; (4) use of a dialectical approach to explain the dynamics of change; and, (5) optimism and faith in progress achieved through dynamic change and struggle.

Darwin, Marx and History as Evolution

Marx, like Darwin, saw the world from an evolutionary point of view. For both change in natural processes was *developmental*. By these terms I mean that historical change – in the organic or the social world – comes about through a series of processes occuring both internal to and external to the system being studied (a natural population of organisms or a society). An evolutionary, or developmental, view of history is broader and more complex than either the idea of history as simple chronology, the sequence of antecedent to subsequent events, or of history as the unfolding of a "plan" (divine or otherwise). An evolutionary view of history does not rule out the effects of accidental change, for example, the assassination of a leader or the advent of epidemics, but it does not see such events as providing the main motive force for historical change. The social evolutionists (as adherents of an evolutionary view of history were called) in Marx's day – Herbert Spencer, Edward Tylor, Lewis Henry Morgan, among others – did not all agree on what the important factors were that brought about historical change, but they did agree that such processes were general ones, independent, at least to some degree, of time and place.

Social evolutionists in the nineteenth century sought to discover the laws of historical development that would provide the basis for understanding the past and even possibly for predicting the future. A brief example will make clear the sort of approach characterized by evolutionary or developmental views of history. An issue to be explained is the decline of feudalism (as an economic and social system) in the late Middle Ages, and its replacement by mercantile capitalism. Traditional histories of feudalism explain the system's decline by a variety of specific factors: bubonic plague in the fourteenth century, fiscal exhaustion of monarchies from high living, religious crusades, greed, continual petty warfare, or cyclical aging processes that carry societies, like individual organisms, through periods of youth, maturity and senescence. A developmental, or evolutionary view of history, as espoused for example by Marx, takes a different approach. Marx saw the decline of feudalism in the west as a result of changes that were an integral part of feudal society itself: the development of an improved agricultural technology that led to population growth without corresponding changes in land and tenant rights, leading ultimately to a surplus of labor, a resulting emigration of peasants and artisans away from the land to the towns, and thus an increase in numbers of people involved in alternative economic pursuit. New relationships emerged as a result – a commodity or mercantile economy that eventually evolved into modern capitalism.

According to the social evolutionists, including Marx, historical change is brought about by regularly acting laws whose existence can be discovered if only the proper methods of study are used. For Marx, then, social history could be a science as readily as natural history, but it could not be merely the application of laws or principles of natural history as such to human society. The "laws" of social evolution had to be discovered on their own, though the methods of investigating them might be very similar, if not identical to, those employed in investigating natural history.

The idea of "scientific laws" in history, as viewed by Marx, requires some elaboration. Marx's view of "laws" in the social sense is both similar to, and different from, Darwin's. In accord with the natural science tradition of his day, Darwin believed that once natural laws were discovered they would be expected to apply at all times and all places. Laws themselves do not evolve, only the entities governed by those laws. In organic evolution, for example, the mechanisms of heredity, variation, competition and selection as elaborated by Darwin were thought to have operated equally in creating the diversification of Cambrian, Ordovician, Cretaceous or Pliocene life. Likewise, those principles are operative today and apply as much to green algae as to bryozoans and elephants. Laws, then, once discovered, are fixed, to be modified in only limited ways to achieve greater accuracy.

Marx, however, appears to have held to a somewhat different conception of "law," at least as applied in the social sciences. For Marx, social and economic laws are not fixed for all times and places: they have an evolution of their own, very much related to historical conditions. The "iron law of wages," for example, enunciated by the classical economists and used by Marx in his analysis of capitalism, is a product of capitalist economics, and has meaning only in that context. It cannot be applied to chattel or feudal systems; indeed, its formulation might very well change from a primitive to an advanced capitalist system. The only lawlike entities – and he did not call these laws – that Marx held to be generally applicable throughout all phases of human history were the materialist conception of history (the belief that economic life is the ultimate driving force of society) and the labor theory of value (the notion that all value in human society, from primitive to modern, comess from human activity, or labor). Marx thus held a distinctly social view of what might be meant by "scientific law" or the attempt to view history "scientifically." He readily agreed that human social history could be studied as scientifically as natural history, but he was not naive enough (as were some of his contemporaries) to believe that the two were identical. Marx did not adhere to a positivist, Newtonian model of science, like so many of his generation. In this sense, as Heyer points out, he has been much misunderstood.

In attempting to treat history scientifically, Marx operated clearly within a major trend of his day. Althusser (1970:14) has noted that one of Marx's major intents was, in fact, to open up the "continent" of history to scientific investigation – to suggest both the content and the methodology by which history might be made more scientific and objective . For Marx, the purpose of the historian was to discover the natural laws of movement of modern society and to see "the evolution of the economic formation of society . . . as a process of natural history" ([1867] 1967:10). Such a goal can be naive or sophisticated, depending on how one goes about it. Marx was a penetrating and subtle thinker, and realized that to be scientific it is necessary to pay close attention to methodology, deriving methods that are appropriate to the subject being investigated. Even natural scientists of the midnineteenth century recognized that methods from one science, such as physics or chemistry, were not always directly applicable for studying problems in another, such as biology. Marx was ahead of many of his contemporaries among social scientists – for example, Herbert Spencer – in recognizing the importance of developing a methodology appropriate for the study of human society.

Like biological evolution, historical evolution is a unidirectional process. There have been, and will continue to be, new economic and social systems after modern capitalism, but there will never be a return to feudalism or its predecessor, chattel society. History does not repeat itself any more than organic evolution repeats itself. The earth might one day be populated again with large terrestrial vertebrates, but they will not be dinosaurs. Each period in the history of any system is a product of the periods preceding it; since later periods have more history behind them than earlier periods, the products of that history – particular species and their ecological associations, or particular economic and social systems – will be different. In some sense, then, every epoch is the product of all preceding epochs, making the conditions for the emergence of new historical developments (species, societies) at a later period necessarily different from those at an earlier period.

There are two important aspects of an evolutionary view of history that are important to mention in attempting to understand Marx's historical process. The first is that the view of developmental change outlined above is not teleological. There is no final goal, no utopian endpoint in historical evolution any more than there is in biological evolution. There is directionality in the biological or thermodynamic sense, but no necessary final goal. On the antiteleological aspect of Darwinian evolution Marx was most clear and appreciative. As he wrote to Lasalle in the same letter quoted earlier (1860): "Despite all deficiencies not only is the death blow dealt here for the first time to 'teleology' in the natural sciences but their rational meaning is empirically explained" (Marx and Engels 1936:125).

Marx was aware, of course, that human history has something more of the teleological element to it, even in its most evolutionary formulation, than the history of animal and plant species, since human beings are capable for formulating goals and striving to reach them. Marx was aware of this difference between humans and other animals; indeed, his entire political program was based on a faith in the ability of human beings to take charge of their destiny and, ultimately, to achieve their goals. The kind of teleology he opposed, in interpreting history, was that characterized by eighteenth- and early nineteenth-century writers who saw history as the unfolding of a plan – the working out of God's will or the inevitable passage of races or nations through a "life cycle" of youth, maturity, senescence and extinction. Any goal-directedness in history is, according to Marx, due to goals human beings set for themselves, rather than goals imposed on them by some external, metaphysical process. In this sense the term "evolution," applied to either natural or social history, was misleading, since it had been used in the eighteenth and nineteenth centuries in reference to embryonic development where the adult form was viewed as a literal unfolding of form from the fertilized egg. Many early naturalists used the term evolution, even in reference to the historical development of species, in this older sense as the unfolding of a plan, or a step-by-step progression through the great chain of being. Both Darwin and Marx were strongly opposed to any idea of historical developments as the unfolding of some inevitable plan.

There are two aspects of the evolutionary view of historical processes on which agreement between Marx and Darwin is less clear. The first concerns the question of whether evolutionary processes are open-ended, or ever reach a final or fixed state beyond which more change is not possible. For Darwin the answer is clear: evolution of adaptation never ceases – there is no point at which evolution stops. In contrast Marx appears to have seen the communist state as the final, or endpoint of social evolution. No sources give a clear, unambiguous answer, for Marx never suggests explicitly that there could be further social stages beyond communism. Such an attitude was, of course, common in the tradition of European utopian socialism, and while Marx held no liking for the utopians, he may have been unable to break away completely from their tradition.

A second aspect of the evolutionary view of history on which agreement between Darwin and Marx is less clear is the question of whether historical developments must occur in a certain sequence of steps, or "stages." This point is related to the teleological view of history as an "unfolding," but is nonetheless a different issue. For Darwin the matter was clear: there are no necessary stages through which any species *must* pass in its evolution. It was not inevitable that quadrupedal primates gave rise to bipedal humans, or that all bipedal animals had to pass through a quadrupedal stage in their ancestry. Evolutionary change is opportunistic, and any structure capable of variation can be modified for a later adaptation if conditions give it selective advantage. For Darwin, just as there was no endpoint to the evolutionary process, there were also no stages through which any species, or even higher taxonomic group (family, phylum) necessarily had to pass. There were, of course, certain constraints that made some evolutionary developments much more likely than others: quadrupeds, for example, were much more likely to give rise to bipeds than were earthworms, but that was only a matter of expediency and probability, not necessity.

For Marx, the question of the necessity of historical stages is more ambiguous. For generations, Marxists and Marxist scholars have debated this issue. Many have argued that Marx did hold to some notion of the necessity of historical stages and, given his early Hegelianism, such a view, even implicitly, is not unlikely. Certainly in his writings Marx described the history of human civilization in terms of a sequence of economic forms: chattel, feudal, capitalist and socialist (communist). It is not clear, however, that he thought such a sequence represented the only possible way that the changes could have occurred. Heyer is of the opinion that both Marx and Engels sought to develop a flexible historical theory, analogous to scientific theories, that was not committed irrevocably to fixed laws (Heyer 1982:25). My own reading of Marx supports this interpretation, though I must admit there is ambiguity in Marx's own writings on this question. While the chattel societies of the ancient world might have given rise directly, around 500 A.D., to mercantile capitalism, it is less likely that they would have developed such a highly individualistic economy out of the conditions that existed at that time. Feudalism, or some more rigidly hierarchical system like it, was a more likely system to have evolved from chattel societies (which were even more hierarchical in an economic sense than feudalism) than free-enterprise capitalism. There is a big difference between likelihood and necessity, however, and my own sense is that Darwin and Marx both appreciated that distinction more clearly than has been recognized.

Human Society As a Part of Nature

An aspect of the evolutionary world view on which both Darwin and Marx agreed was that human beings were a part of nature, not only in their physical but also their social and economic development. Although Darwin was perhaps more naive on this issue, and placed more emphasis on the biological basis of human instinct in the development of culture than did Marx, both men agreed that human society was an outgrowth, not merely an extension, of human biological evolution. Human beings were an integral and an historical product of nature. The point is clear in Darwin, especially in *The Descent of Man*, but it is equally clear in Marx. In volume 1 of *Capital* Marx wrote that his purpose was to discover the natural "laws of movement" in modern society and to view "the evolution of the economic formation of society . . . as a process of natural history" (Marx [1867] 1967, 1:10). He had made the same point earlier in 1844 when he wrote:

> History itself is a real part of natural history – of nature developing into man. Natural science will in time incorporate into itself the science of man, just as the science of man will incorporate itself into natural science: there will [then] be one science. (Marx [1844] 1972:142-43)

Marx even saw the explicit parallel between his own and Darwin's work as examples of "social" and "natural" history. In volume 1 of *Capital* he posed the very intriguing observation:

> Darwin has interested us in the history of Nature's technology, i.e., the formation of the organs of plants and animals, which organs serve as instruments of production for sustaining life. Does not the history of the productive organs of man, of organs that are the material basis of all social organization, deserve equal attention? (Marx [1867] 1967, 1:372; Heyer 1982:24)

It is the history of the technology of humans, their means and modes of production, that is the central object of Marx's investigation and a major aspect of understanding history. The parallel Marx saw here to Darwin's work is instructive. The study of evolution deals with physical (and, of course, physiological) adaptations, which to Marx are no more than an animal's or plant's *means of production* – that is, their tools and "technology" by which they make their living in nature. The importance of this comparison is to suggest that the study of human productive forces is just as central to the study of human history as the study of anatomical and physiological adaptations is to the study of animal and plant history (i.e., evolution). Darwin, for his part, sought to bring human beings, physically and culturally, into the natural realm. Although he made only one direct reference to human evolution in the *Origin*, he made the point the focus of *The Descent of Man* (1874) and *The Expression of the Emotions in Man and Animals* (1872). From the point of view of biological evolution, Darwin saw clearly that the human species had to be included – a point his religious critics noted with alarm. In addition, Darwin saw human cultural evolution as a product of biological evolution. He was clearly in tune with, if not highly knowledgeable about, the burgeoning anthropological work of his day, and was ahead of his time in viewing nonwestern cultures as equally well adapted to their own environments as European cultures were to theirs (Gruber 1981:181 ff). Human cultural practices were clearly adaptive – and those cultures that adopted less adaptive practices would perish at the hands of those that adopted more adaptive practices. For Darwin there was no question that human beings were an integral part of nature – both at present, as they used nature or natural processes for their own survival, and historically, as human cultures increased their ability to use nature to their own ends (survival). Darwin was one of the first naturalists to see human beings as both currently active ecological and historically active economic beings.

While Marx was sympathetic to a Darwinian view of social evolution as an outgrowth of biological evolution he recognized clearly that human history operated according to its own laws – those Marx identified primarily as having to do with organization of the forces of production – and could not simply be reduced to biological principles. Human history has its own level of organization, its own processes of adaptation – technological, economic, and social – that emerge from, but are not merely expressions of, biological processes. Marx's evolutionary view is thus markedly different from the crude, reductionistic efforts of nineteenth-century "social Darwinists" or twentieth-century sociobiologists. Heyer has pointed out that Marx's excitement on reading Darwin was perhaps more like that experienced when one encounters an "intellectual cousin," whose views complement one's own, as opposed to an intellectual ancestor who has formulated similar ideas (Heyer 1982:25). Both social Darwinists and sociobiologists fell into the reductionist fallacy: conflating biological and social inheritance into a single, indistinguishable process that portrayed social processes as biologically determined. Marx was inalterably opposed to such mechanistic and simple-minded views.

Darwin and Marx as Materialists

Both Marx and Darwin were materialists as the view was understood in the midnineteenth century. The evolutionary process, whether social or biological, resulted from the interaction of material elements and conditions. No abstract or metaphysical qualities were to be admitted as a cause for biological or social change. For Darwin, the material elements were, of course, the structures that made up the organism, including the chemical components (the hereditary counterparts were still unknown, but Darwin hypothesized they were hereditary units which he called pangenes). Natural selection was nothing more than the material interaction of concrete organisms with each other (competition) and with their physical environment. Even on the origin of life, on which he spoke privately though not publicly, Darwin had a strongly materialist outlook. In describing life forming through spontaneous chemical reactions among ammonia and various salts, Darwin wrote in a letter in 1871:

> But if (and oh! what a big if!) we could conceive in some warm little pond, with all sorts of ammonia and phosphoric salts, light, heat electricity, etc. present, that a protein compound was chemically formed ready to undergo still more complex changes, at the present day such matter would be instantly devoured or absorbed, which would not have been the case before living creatures were formed. (de Beer 1963:271)

In the same vein, Darwin, in describing thought, portrays it as a function of the structure of the brain, (explicitly, in marginal notes to a book he was reading in 1838) claiming this relationship to be the essence of his definition of materialism: "By materialism, I mean, merely the intimate connecting of kind of thought with form of brain – like kind of attraction with nature of element" (Gruber 1981:201). According to Gruber, material entities as the major cause of human action are invoked in passages in Darwin's "Old and Useless Notes" jotted down between 1837 and 1840. Criticizing the notion of "Free Will" as a human delusion, Darwin remarks, "As human beings we feel as though there is some incorporeal self controlling the actions of our bodies, but in fact even the mechanism of control represents the functioning of a part of the body, the brain" (Gruber 1981:215. He deals directly with the question "Was Darwin a materialist?" [Chapter 10], coming out clearly in the affirmative).

For Marx, of course, materialism was the core of his historical theory, what he called *historical materialism*. More philosophically attuned than Darwin, Marx developed his materialist theory consciously; it remains implicit in Darwin, but is nonetheless a common foundation for both theories of evolutionary change.

In Marx's scheme, the material basis for historical change is labor. The dynamic driving history is changes in the means and modes of production, including technology. For Darwin the driving force behind evolutionary change is physical variation of traits, providing changing means of interacting with the environment, or physical change in the environment leading to changed selective pressures. Darwin, as with all modern evolutionary ecologists, recognized that one cannot understand a species' role in the economy of nature, nor the reasons for its evolutionary change, without first and foremost understanding the material conditions of its life: what it eats and how it obtains its food, shelter, etc. – in modern terms – its "ecology." That question need not be the focus of every investigation, but it is a necessary foundation on which all other studies are built. Marx emphasized the same point, quite explicitly and forcefully, in *The German Ideology*:

> History is nothing but the succession of the separate generations, each of which exploits the materials, the capital funds, the productive forces handed down to it by all preceeding generations, and thus on the one hand continues the tradition activity in completely changed circumstances and, on the other, modifies the old circumstances with a completely changed activity. (Marx and Engels [1845-46] 1964:59)

Marx and Engel's materialist conception of history was partly a reaction to idealist and metaphysical views so common especially among early nineteenth-century German romantics who saw all events as the unfolding of some sort of divine or mystical plan. Marx particularly attacked Hegel for his notion that history was the gradual emergence of the "idea" or "spirit" at progressively higher levels of organization: earthly events gained their significance by contributing to the realization or actualization of this inherent "spirit" (Heyer 1982:49). By contrast, Marx and Engels sought to ground all historical change in concrete, material events taking place in the everyday world of labor and the social interactions it spawned. People in the commercial arena, like animals in nature's arena, are the product of their concrete circumstances, nothing more and nothing less.

For both Darwin and Marx the beginning point of all knowledge, of all investigation is the concrete, the examined empirical observations of nature. In the initially unpublished *Grundrisse*, written in 1857-58, Marx spelled out in somewhat convoluted form his notion of materialism in the study of human society:

> It seems to be correct to begin with the real and the concrete, with the real precondition, thus to begin, in economics, with, e.g., the population which is the foundation and the subject of the entire social act of production. However, on closer examination, this proves false. The population is an abstraction if I leave out, for example, the classes of which it is composed. These classes in turn are an empty phrase if I am not familiar with the elements on which they rest, e.g., wage labour, capital, etc. These latter in turn presuppose exchange, division of labour, prices, etc. For example, capital is nothing without wage labour, without value, money, price, etc. . . . [Developing abstractions from the concrete upwards] is obviously the scientifically correct method. (Marx [1859] 1973:100-108; quoted from Cohen 1978:411)

Darwin described himself, somewhat naively I suspect, as a Baconian inductivist. He clearly did not work in the absence of general theories, even at the outset of his career, but his selfcategorization does underscore his strong devotion to the concrete, observational basis on which his work so thoroughly depends. Both Darwin's and Marx's works are characterized by an enormous amassing of detailed observations, a feature that required that their ideas, however disagreeable to their critics, had to be taken seriously. Barzun noted, somewhat demeaningly, that for Darwin "facts impinged on his mind far more deeply and significantly than abstractions" (Barzun 1981:73). And, wrongfully, I think, Barzun accuses both Darwin and Marx (along with Wagner) of laying the foundations of a materialism that henceforth banished mind from European civilization, replacing ideas and spirituality with the concrete, material and banal.

Darwin, Marx and the Dialectics of Internal Change

Philosophically, both Marx *and* Darwin appear to be not only materialists, but dialectical materialists as opposed to mechanistic. As shown in figure 1, mechanistic and dialectical materialism share all the characteristics of materialism, but differ on a number of more specific points. Space and time do not permit discussion of all of the points of difference, but I have provided a more detailed analysis elsewhere (Allen 1980). I will focus here on only two features that particularly characterize dialectical materialism: how quantitative change leads to qualitative change; and how the most fundamental, and important, change in any system results from contradictory tendencies or processes within the system itself. Both of these features of dialectical thinking abound in the analytical methods of Darwin and Marx.

Dialectical thought grows out of the notion of dialog, or the presentation of two opposing points of view. In Hegelian terms, the dialectic represents a method of argument, of arriving at true ideas. Through the interaction and juxtaposition of two points of view (in Hegel's parlance, the "thesis" and "antithesis") a new, qualitatively different idea emerges (Hegel's "synthesis"). This first synthesis becomes the starting point for a new thesis and antithesis, leading to a second synthesis, and so on. Marx and Engels saw this basic method, cast in a materialist as opposed to primarily idealist or intellectual light, as a powerful tool for analyzing the causes of historical change. Dialectical thinking provided a way of asking certain questions about systems – of any sort – how they functioned or changed over time. Dialectics was not a method of thought that could be applied blindly or mechanically, and it was clearly not always applicable with equal validity to every situation. But as a general method of analysis, of understanding the interacting components of a system, it was a crucial feature of Marx and Engels, and, I will argue, Darwin's thinking.

The Change from Quantity to Quality. Marx, and Engels after him, developed the rudiments of a philosophical system, or school of thought, that specifically aimed, among other things, at describing and explaining the dynamics of changing – that is, evolving – systems. For Marx, one of the most important features of such systems was the shift from quantity to qual-

IDEALISM	MATERIALISM
Ideas are primary.	Matter is primary; the material world existed before humans came to know it.
Ideas determine our perception of reality.	Material conditions determine our perception of reality.
Primary ideas are never knowable.	All material reality is to some degree (but not to a final degree) knowable.
A reality outside of man does not necessarily exist (only perceptions of it exist).	A reality outside of man does exist.
Deals in metaphysics (seeks causes in the realm beyond physical reality).	Avoids as much as possible all aspects of metaphysical thinking.

MECHANISTIC MATERIALISM	DIALECTICAL MATERIALISM
The parts of a complex whole are separate and distinct.	The parts of a complex whole are all interconnected.
Study of a whole proceeds by study of individual parts.	Study of a whole proceeds by study of individual parts and their interactions.
Whole is equal to the sum of its individual parts (and no more).	Whole is equal to more than the sum of individual parts (parts + interactions).
Quantitative change leads to more quantitative change.	Quantitative change leads to qualitative change.
Changes are impressed on an object or process by outside objects and forces.	Changes originate from built-in contradictions, interacting with external objects and forces.
Atomistic.	Nonatomistic.

Fig. 1. Characteristics of idealism and materialism.

ity as any system undergoes developmental change. Social systems, for example, undergo all sorts of quantitative changes, as income taxes are raised or lowered, laws introduced to regulate work or commercial practices, and legislation passed to govern social relationships in matters such as discrimination, welfare, and the like. Such changes in practices and attitudes are quantitative in that they represent small, or gradual, changes that are still within the basic framework of the older, familiar practice (in T. S. Kuhn's terms, the older "paradigm"). Quantitative changes (for example, increasing the percentage of tax in a certain bracket, or extending a tax bracket by another $1000) modify but do not fundamentally alter existing circumstances. At some point, however, enough quantitative changes will have occurred that a qualitative change can be said to have taken place: for example, enough small modifications in a graduated tax system will yield equalized, rather than differential, real income – a paradigm that may be very different from the starting point of a system with highly differentiated income levels. The period of time during transition from quantitative to qualitative change is what we refer to as a "revolutionary period" – at least with respect to a specified change. Such transitional periods are relatively rapid in comparison to the longer period of quantitative change leading up to them. But it is crucial to recognize that revolutionary change does not occur all at once, nor does it totally obliterate all pre-existing conditions. A state may have become predominantly capitalist rather than feudal, or the majority of naturalists Darwinian rather than Platonic in their view of species, but elements of the old do remain in any qualitative change. The important point is that qualitative change does not come without quantitative change. Quantitative change is slow, gradual, and incremental; qualitative change – on the same time scale – is rapid, discontinuous, and nonincremental. Marx used the dialectical materialist as opposed to the primarily idealist, or intellectual, light, as a powerful tool for analyzing the causes of historical change. Thus, he could analyze the mounting tensions in the United States leading to the Civil War in terms of the contradiction between the need for southern growers to have cheap labor (slaves), and the need for northern industrialists to have an expanded market (i.e., a larger population with a salary) for their goods. This contradiction could not, in Marx's terms, continue indefinitely; it ultimately had to come to resolution through armed conflict and the destruction of the slave system in the south. The opposing forces of slavery on the one hand and northern industrial expansion on the other was not the only one Marx saw at work in the U.S. in the pre-Civil War period, but it was a major one. While this contradiction might have been resolved in other ways, for Marx and Engels, historically, armed struggle seemed empirically to have been the primary means. In the case of the American Civil War the struggle was between two segments of the bourgeoisie (southern growers and northern industrialists) rather than between two separate classes, but the dialectical process, involving the resolution of the internal to the expanding United States economy at the time, is the same.

In a dialectical process the most fundamental level of change in any system comes from *within* – that is, from the system's own internal contradictions. While the dialectical approach does not preclude the effects of external events, it does state that the first and most basic information we need for understanding the dynamics of any system comes from analysis of its own internal contradictory processes. Such an approach might go a long way, for example, toward reframing the current controversy in evolutionary theory as to whether a meteoritic impact at the end of the Cretaceous actually triggered mass extinctions, or only hastened the development of an already well-developed trend. The former would be an example of a mechanical approach – relying on an external agent of change – the latter a more dialectical approach, focusing on dynamics internal to the system, (that is, to the Cretaceous ecosystem as a whole). At any rate, for Marx, the primary contradictions in any society are to be found in the economic sphere: contradictions between the equality of socially based work and the inequality of division of the product of labor; between wages and profits; or, the need for oneself to pay low wages, but the need for others to pay high wages, etc. Such dialectical processes are the actual determiners of economic, and with it social and political, evolution in human society. It is the nature and extent of such contradictions that any historian must know first, before trying to understand the direction and rate of historical evolution that has taken, or is taking, place. Understanding the nature of those contradictions, and how they are being or not being resolved, provides a critical insight into the dynamics of change in any society: that is, why certain changes, and not others, occurred at a particular time. For example, to understand how and why fascism arose in Germany in the 1920s and 1930s, and the rate at which it grew, it is first and foremost necessary to analyze the opposing economic forces of failing profit rate and increased demands (trade union organizing and strikes) for higher wages in Weimar, Germany, and how those opposing needs or demands were viewed by German financiers, industrialists, and politicians (i.e., Germany's ruling class at the time). Without understanding these forces and their contradictory demands on economic and political policy, the phenomenon of fascism becomes difficult to explain except as a unique, metaphysical event, as in Erich Fromm's claim that the German people have a sadomasochistic longing for submission to a dominant leader (Fromm 1965) or William L. Shirer's view that fascism was a product largely of Hitler's personality (Shirer 1960). These are all particularist, and essentially abstract causes, lending no insight to the social processes under investigation.

I contend that Darwin was also a subtle, but pervasive, dialectical thinker. The very mechanism of natural selection itself involves a fundamental dialectic: between inheritance (exact replication) and variation (inexact replication). With one or the other of these components alone, there can be no evolution; with both present, evolution becomes inevitable, and stasis impossible. Darwin also saw many other dialectics in nature: between a species' degree of specialization and of flexibility, between organism and environment, between ornamentation as a sexual attraction, and ornamentation as an advertisement to predators, or between competition and cooperation both within and between species. To take one example, Darwin saw that organisms are able, through natural selection, to adapt to their environments. Implicit, but not so explicit in Darwin's formulation of this relationship is its reciprocal, dialectical nature. Just as species are changed by the environment, so the evolution of adaptations by organisms changes the environment. Thus organisms mold their environments much as a gymnast molds the surface of a trampoline. Sewall Wright's adaptive peaks on an ecological landscape are not permanent structures, but are eroded away and nonadaptive valleys are filled in by the action of living organisms. The gymnast and the trampoline become the two opposing parts of a dialectical process in which each affects the other to produce an outcome (a resolution or synthesis), namely, the acrobatics of the jumper. In the evolutionary process, the trampoline metaphor stands in stark contradiction to the idea of the organism reacting to a fixed and external landscape. Not only do organisms adapt to environments, but environments adapt to the activities of organisms ("adaptation" is used in two very different senses here).

One crucial advantage to the dialectical mode of thinking is that it focuses attention on the *dynamics* of change within a system. Opposing forces, or tendencies, do not produce a stable or static system, but one that is always changing. A dialectical approach provides one way of understanding how and in what direction evolutionary change – biological or social – occurs. In historian's terms, it goes one step beyond merely seeking antecedent events. It provides a more general causal analysis of the flow from antecedent to subsequent states in society. Moreover, analysis of a number of such changes provides, through this common methodology, a way to uncover general laws of historical development. It suggests, for example, that when the rate of profit falls (quantitative change) beyond a certain limit in a capitalist system, profound (qualitative) changes are likely to come quickly on its heels – unless the contradiction can be quickly resolved. While not providing the historian with a crystal ball, a dialectical method of analysis does provide some level of predictive power. It provides a view of the large sweep of history, both from the present into the past, and from the present into the future.

An aspect of the dialectical process that has intrigued Darwinians and Marxists alike is the concept of struggle – class struggle for Marx, inter- and intraspecific competition for Darwin. Both may be said to be ideas taken from midnineteenth-century socioeconomic history, including the extension to colonialism (a form some have equated with interspecific competition). Certainly the two ideas share the same social origins and refer to processes that seem to occur in the real world. And, I would argue, both do represent a dialectical process, a confrontation between opposing or contradictory processes. I would not make a case for this aspect of dialectics being central to the Darwinian or Marxian methodology, although it is one example of that thinking. Through class struggle or competition (either interspecific or intraspecific) in the organic world, change does occur – and ultimately qualitative change (new socioeconomic forms, or new species, respectively). The struggle that both Darwin and Marx incorporated into their world views was an expression of their similar dialectical approaches to dynamic processes. That dialectical approach was, in its turn, brought to the fore by nineteenth-century economic and social developments (industrial revolution, colonial conquests, etc.).

Darwin, Marx and Optimism in Evolutionary Progress

One final issue on which it is important to make clear the similarities and differences between the original Darwin and Marx, and their modern followers, is that of evolutionary progress. Both Darwin and Marx saw some progressive change inherent in the evolutionary process. For Darwin, progress clearly demonstrated by the fossil record could be seen in the gradual filling of available niches with more complex and better adapted forms. For Marx, progress could be seen in the transition from precapitalist to capitalist to socialist economic organization. Yet Darwin was well aware of the dangers inherent in thinking that modern or complex forms are necessarily *better* than ancestral or simpler forms. Marx was also aware that capitalism, for all its faults as he saw them in 1859, was better in some respects for a larger number of people than feudalism or chattel society had been. Both thinkers, however, felt that progress was inevitable in their respective worlds. Modern-day Darwinians certainly deny any idea of "progress" in the history of life other than, perhaps, the very general trend of organisms to spread over the globe in the past 4.5 billion years. Any idea of progress in the old eighteenth- or nineteenth-century sense is taboo in evolutionary thinking. Present-day Marxists, on the other hand, still retain a sense that historical change is progressive, a view that I think is valid if "progressive" is understood as nonteleological. With human beings and their ability to formulate goals for the future and to improve the quality of their lives, the occurrence of real progress is not likely to be merely a matter of chance. Thus, while it may not be proper to speak of organic evolution as progressive, it is more justifiable to speak of social evolution as progressive – or perhaps as *progressing*. Needless to say, backward steps in social evolution do not preclude the possibility that history can show an overall progressive turn.

Conclusion: Toward a New Historiography

The striking similarity of many of Marx's and Darwin's views provides the basis for an interesting historical juxtaposition. However, my ultimate objective is to go beyond merely an interesting juxtaposition, and raise the question of how the similarity between Marxism and Darwinism can be used to throw light on the historian's methodology. I think this juxtaposition can be useful, especially given the recent attempts by David Hull and by Robert Richards to fashion an evolutionary model of history. If that enterprise has any validity, and I think it does, it seems to me that it would be greatly enhanced by a deeper understanding of the Darwin-Marx comparison.

Let me focus on Hull's intriguing attempt at evolutionary history in his recent *Science as a Process. An Evolutionary Account of the Social and Conceptual Development of Science* (1988). In this highly informative work, Hull presents an evolutionary model of history in which Darwinian competition and struggle are the main processes by which ideas in science are tested, and by which they are judged successful or wanting. In Hull's explicitly evolutionary language, ideas (species) show variations (some successful, some not), are accepted (survive) or rejected (die out), form lineages, become extinct, and so forth. The proponents of theories, the individual scientists, of course, are the actual competing agents whose activities largely determine the fate of given ideas. Individual scientists attempt to gain adherents to their ideas (theories), that is students, protégés or followers, and thus improve their own "inclusive fitness." The arenas for competition include the pages of journals, professional meetings, editorial boards and committees, funding agencies, review panels and the like. Hull suggests that scientific merit is not always *the*, or even, *a* major factor in determining the success of an idea. Nonepistemic, sociological or institutional factors ultimately may be the more important arbiters of success, at least in the short run. Hull's account is illustrated with several examples, the most extensive and detailed being the debates that took place in the field of taxonomy from 1950 to 1980 between so-called cladists, who emphasized branch-point similarities (but not true phylogeny) as the basis of classification, and pheneticists who rejected all notions of ancestry in favor of grouping organisms solely by overall similarities.

Hull meticulously researched the development of the controversy between these groups, using archives from journals, society meetings, and the like to trace the fate and fortune of each school of thought. He emphasized not only the intellectual content of the debate, but its sociological, institutional and contextual basis, suggesting that the issues were resolved, or at least decided upon, on the basis of many factors other than scientific merit. Power struggles within professional societies, for space in journals, for control of professional meetings, for students and funds, formed the main arenas of debate, which at times became highly personal and vindictive.

Hull's model to account for how and why such debates take place is an evolutionary one – specifically Darwinian. By Darwinian, what Hull seems to emphasize most is competition and struggle, a kind of Spencerian or sociobiological account for how science develops. Hull explicitly uses metaphors from Darwinian theory – "inclusive fitness" (researchers and the ideas they champion) as determined by the number of "progeny" (graduate students or younger colleagues) they win over to their ideas, and "resource utilization" (funds, lab space, institutional control). With his model, Hull hopes to show that ideas in science are like species, they evolve through being tried out in the competitive arena of scientific societies, journals, etc, with some winning out (surviving) and others failing. Ideas show divergence (speciation), phyletic modification, extinction, etc., all described in the language and conceptual framework of Darwinian theory.

Intriguing as this model is, it seems to me that Hull's account could have been greatly expanded and made even more inclusive by incorporating elements of a more Marxist-Darwinian historiography. This would have allowed him to treat even more thoroughly the sociobiological aspects of the debates – their institutional, socioeconomic aspects – than he did with his present model (and Hull does not ignore those factors at all – he is concerned to include them). Where Hull's model seriously goes astray is that it conflates what "is" with what "probably ought to be" – that is, while pointing out that there might be other ways of doing science (cooperative, collective, etc.), Hull concludes that the competitive model might be best after all. He thus fails to take into account some of the more important social factors contributing to the prevalence of the competitive model of science, and its original derivation from the socioeconomic sphere, and thus its dependence on cultural context for its legitimacy. Moreover, Hull nowhere suggests that this model can change – that there is nothing "writ in stone" about how science *must* be done. This is where his model comes too close to sociobiology for comfort – it suggests a level of fixity about human behaviors and practices (customs, if you will) that is not truly evolutionary in perspective.

Where Hull's lack of evolutionary perspective would have profited from a consideration of the Darwin-Marx perspective is exactly at the level where the application of biology to human society leaves off, namely, in the rules or "laws" of social development. If Marx is correct that social laws – perhaps less like scientific laws – themselves evolve, then the study of history should be aimed as much at discovering the laws of human history as at the ways in which these laws themselves undergo change. If laws of social development, that is, the rules by which our behavior is governed, evolve, then there is no fixed process of science – only the process that has evolved, through conscious and unconscious effort, up to this point in time. Hull's model, for all its apparent evolutionary basis, is actually quite static from the sociological point of view. I argue that Hull would possibly have developed a more dynamic view – in keeping with his own professed evolutionary perspective – of the history of science by considering the historiographical lessons to be gleaned from the Darwin-Marx parallels. At the very least, the parallel would have underscored one of Marx's main points: while human social evolution is a part of nature, it is not merely an extension of nature. Human society is subject to its own laws of evolution, which evolve along with the larger society of which they are a part.

I would thus suggest that Hull's case is a particularly good example of how modern historiography of science could be enriched by a closer familiarity with a Marxist perspective, but particularly one that has been synthesized with Darwinism. The fact that Hull's work aims to present a Darwinian view of history makes it all the more likely that his approach could profit from a knowledge of the Darwin-Marx parallel. History can, I think, be more scientific, but not by borrowing ideas directly from science in a mechanical way. The whole of society is much greater than the sum of its parts as a result of the higher level of organization inherent in human society. Thus, a model of social evolution that fails to incorporate this principle becomes naively reductionistic, ultimately providing little real insight into our collective historical experience.

References

Allen, G. E. 1980. Dialectical materialism in modern biology. *Science and Nature* 3:43-57

Althusser, L. 1970. *For Marx*. New York: Random House.

Aveling, E. 1889. *Darwin Made Easy*. London: Progressive Publishing Co.

Aveling, E. 1897. Charles Darwin and Karl Marx. *New Century Review* 1(June):20-31.

Barzun, J. 1981. *Darwin, Marx and Wagner. Critique of A Heritage*. 2d ed. Chicago: University of Chicago Press.

Boyd, R., and P. J. Richerson. 1985. *Culture and the Evolutionary Process*. Chicago: University of Chicago Press.

Cohen, R. 1978. Karl Marx, 403-17. In *Dictionary of Scientific Biography*. Vol. 15. New York: Scribners.

Colp, R. J. 1974. The contacts between Karl Marx and Charles Darwin. *Journal of the History of Ideas* 35:329-38.

Darwin, C. [1859] 1964. *On the Origin of Species by Means of Natural Selection, or the Preservation of Favoured Races in the Struggle for Life*. Facsimile of 1st ed. Cambridge: Harvard University Press.

Darwin, C. [1872] 1970. *The Expression of the Emotions in Man and Animals*. Chicago: University of Chicago Press.

Darwin, C. 1874. *The Descent of Man*. 2d ed. London: John Murray.

de Beer, G. 1963. *Charles Darwin*. London: Thomas Nelson and Sons.

Fromm, E. 1965. *Escape from Freedom*. New York: Avon.

Gruber, H. 1981. *Darwin on Man*. 2d ed. Chicago: University of Chicago Press.

Heyer, P. 1982. *Nature, Human Nature and Society. Marx, Darwin, Biology and the Human Sciences*. Westport, CT: Greenwood Press.

Hull, D. L. 1988. *Science as Process. An Evolutionary Account of the Social and Conceptual Development of Science*. Chicago: University of Chicago Press.

Kautsky, K. 1918. *Ethics and the Materialist Conception of History*. Chicago: Charles H. Kerr.

Liebknecht, W. n.d. *Reminiscences of Marx and Engels*. Moscow: Foreign Languages Publishing House.

Marx, K. [1844] 1972. *The Economic and Philosophical Manuscripts of 1844*. D. Struik, ed. New York: International Publishers.

Marx, K. [1859] 1970. *Contribution to the Critique of Political Economy*. New York: International Publishers.

Marx, K. [1859] 1973. *Grundrisse: Foundations of the Critique of Political Economy* (Rough Draft). Translated, with a Foreword by M. Nicolaus. Middlesex, England: Penguin Books, Ltd.

Marx, K. [1867] 1967. *Capital: A Critique of Political Economy*. Translated by S. Moore and E. Aveling. New York: International Publishers.

Marx, K., and F. Engels. [1845-46] 1964. *The German Ideology*. Moscow: Progress Publishers.

Marx, K., and F. Engels. 1936. *Correspondence, 1846-1895*. Translated by D. Torr. New York: International Publishers.

Richards, R. 1988. *Darwin and the Emergence of Evolutionary Theories of Mind and Behavior*. Chicago: University of Chicago Press.

Shirer, W. L. 1960. *Rise and Fall of the Third Reich: A History of Nazi Germany*. New York: Simon and Schuster.

Wilson, E. O. 1975. *Sociobiology, The New Synthesis*. Cambridge, MA: Harvard University Press.

Evolution of Scientific Theories and the Tension in Ecology

Lawrence B. Slobodkin

In our imagination, both private and public, words can become magical. Sometimes certain words are assumed to have empirical power and not merely empirical denotations. Lawrence (1964) has analyzed the history of the "cargo cults" on the island of Papua-New Guinea. Their adherents sought to explain the obvious differences between native poverty and the material wealth of the various European, American, and Australian missionaries, soldiers, planters, and government officials. It did not seem to correlate with differences in virtue, beauty, piety or hard work. The members of the cargo cults made the superficially reasonable speculation that the critical factors which brought cargo to the foreigners was that they had appropriate relationships with overseas deities and also appropriate docking and landing facilities in New Guinea. They, therefore, constructed docks and "landing strips" – flat strips of ground delineated by lanterns – reorganized their religious life to some approximation of that of the foreigners and waited for the cargo to arrive. They were repeatedly disappointed when nothing arrived. Response to these disappointments was to once again reorganize their rituals and their arrangements of rocks and lanterns.

Unfortunately, applying a word like "airport" to a field in a jungle does not make airplanes land on it. Similarly, coining a name for a field of interest and asserting it to be a science does not make it a science, despite the virtue, intelligence, and industry of its advocates, nor does borrowing the name of a science and using it in a strange context draw that context into the science.

There is a distressing echo of cargo–cult thinking in the coining of hopeful neologisms such as "systemology" or "cosmetic science" and in the free application of such terms as "evolution" to human history or "artificial intelligence" to computerization of data banks. Part of this careless use of terms is related to modern advertising theory and is anything but naive. Consider the birth of many of the institutions called "universities" during the past several decades, which at best were colleges with inflated titles. This is not a new problem. It was discussed by Plutarch.

The dangers of misapplication of terms are not necessarily permanent. The people of Papua-New Guinea have now developed a more sophisticated understanding of aviation and economics, and have proper airfields. Likewise, some of the renamed colleges are at least in some areas the match for any of the older universities, but clearly it was not the word "university" that produced the substance of universities. Also, it must be decided case by case when a denotation of a scientific theory in a particular context is or is not useful. Nevertheless, it is important to be aware that both street words and jungle fields and instant universities require an infrastructure of both material objects and formal meanings before they will attract valuable things. Terms normally laden with particular technical associations may be dangerous when used in other settings unless it is clearly understood that their role in the new setting must be independently established and cannot be assumed to be analogous to their more technical role.

"Evolution" and "Change"

Within biology "evolution" refers to the set of descriptive facts, general biological processes and environmental circumstances which are involved in the "theory of evolution." This includes the actual history of changes in organisms, that is, paleontology or phylogeny, in which both nonbiological circumstances and biological processes and properties are significant, and a more theoretical type of evolutionary study which primarily focuses on the mechanisms and processes assumed to be basic and invariant over a larger or smaller group of organisms and set of circumstances, for example, genetics, physiology, and ecology.

Biological evolution is a consequence of the complex interactions between these mechanisms and processes and particular environmental circumstances. Note that the circumstances may be in part a consequence of past evolutionary history – as, for example, the oxygenated atmosphere and the carbon-rich sediments – or of current biological properties such as organisms actually seeking particular qualities in their environments. I will return to the problem of the domain of evolutionary mechanisms and processes later.

The technical term "evolution," as used in biology, carries all the wealth of ecology, paleontology, population genetics, and systematics in its domain. On the other hand it says nothing about areas for which these concepts are irrelevant. The term "evolution" has also a general or "street" usage in which it is almost synonymous with the word "change," even if the change has no connection with biological processes. One may refer to the evolution of manners or customs, languages, machines, or art. Although this usage is grammatical, there is no formal analogy between the street term and the technical biological term.

But is the biological theory of evolution quite irrelevant to the evolution of such cultural properties as, for example, artistic styles? It is possible to consider that accumulated knowledge transmitted to offspring is another form of inheritance, whose formal differences from genetic transmission can be rigorously defined. It is also necessary for the completeness of evolutionary theory to consider how and when the biological properties of learning ability and memory do, or do not, have selective advantage.

This is a particularly sensitive area since there is an obvious and recurrent temptation to take problems of cultural "evolution" as a springboard for speculation about "explanations" of human history, with all the attendant political and philosophical problems. As recently as the 1970s, polemical dispute on questions of free will, genetic determinism, and the role of Marxism in biology spewed forth a torrent of acrimony in the biological profession. It would not be an intellectual service to return to these problems. It is, however, germane that much of the debate floated on a stream of fluid terminology.

Cautious discussions of the role of the theory of evolution in the development of learning ability, cultural transmission, and even discussion of biological aspects of human intellect are possible. Some of this is in the form of verbal theorizing (e.g., Slobodkin 1983). Some is more formal. Boyd and Richerson (1983) have demonstrated, at least within the bounds of some simplifying assumptions, what kinds of environmental circumstances would lead to the evolution of learning capacity and cultural transmission. This type of research provides hints of how historical change and evolution may interact, but does not sanction more than a metaphorical connection between the two.

A lasting contribution of analytic philosophy, from Boole to Nagel, was to establish clearly that words born of rigorous formulations, although they may sound like street language, are really constrained by their genesis. They carry in one sense more and in another sense much less meaning than their street homophones. To confound uncritically technical and street meanings of "evolution," as if the use of the term evolution instead of the less technically loaded terms "change" or "history" provides some of the theoretical strength of evolutionary theory, is curiously similar to the construction of isomorphs of airports by followers of cargo cults. Nevertheless, there are elements of the biological theory of evolution which may be shared by other uses of the term evolution so that the informal sense of the word is not devoid of meaning.

Recently Hull (1988) has discussed the "evolution" of scientific thought, documenting the fact that at any given moment at the forefront of scientific advance, there are likely to coexist several more or less incompatible theories, schools or paradigms, most of which will vanish in the course of time. Hull felt these selective or competitive interactions to be reminiscent of the processes of selection and competition that occur among organisms in biological evolution.

Hull's analysis is important as a corrective to the naive position that the history of science is about only the relative quality, in some abstract sense, of scientific theories and ideas. He amply demonstrates, in particular cases, that ideas and theories are attached to people and schools which occur in a real world context in which there is competition and sometimes even direct struggle. At least in the short term, the history of science is determined by this selective process.

Sciences may also subdivide in a way reminiscent of speciation and also may become extinct. These similarities seemed strong enough for Hull to refer to "evolution" of scientific theories, rather than mere "history" or "change." This is a highly suggestive metaphor but less than a complete analogy.

I will ask how sciences become extinct, how they may originate and, with particular reference to my own specialty of ecology, what are the barriers to their healthy development, from the standpoint of their intellectual content, without focusing on the social and political mechanisms analyzed by Hull. I will use the terms "evolution," "extinction," and "origination," simply as convenient metaphors without any intention of invoking evolutionary mechanisms.

The Extinction of Sciences

Sciences can become extinct either by becoming so profoundly transformed as to be unrecognizable or by leaving no (intellectual) descendants. Some fields of study that have vanished from the list of respectable sciences did so because they never succeeded in meeting the basic standards for predictive power. Phrenology, cheiromancy, graphology, and astrology share the property of existing now only as charlatan-ridden vestiges of initially sincere attempts to predict human character and behavior on the basis of various kinds of physical evidence. Today, adherence to the validity of these pseudo-sciences betrays superstitious ignorance of what science is. Eminently respectable sciences may also vanish because they are no longer interesting, in the sense that their subject matter no longer has uniqueness and cohesion.

Pharmacognosy, the study of medicinal products derived from plants, has vanished from most American and European universities. This was once a standard department in medical schools but the dictionary of the word processor I am using to prepare this paper has no clue to its meaning. While it is still the case that more than half of our pharmaceutical products are either derived from plants or were originally discovered in plants, the role of medical school professors of pharmacognosy has all but vanished, except in Africa, and perhaps other parts of the third world. Ethnobotanists, with affiliations to botany and anthropology, deal with the uses of plants in folk medicine. Together with organic chemists, pharmacologists, and biochemists they fill the niche of the pharmacognostics, except in countries in which herbal medicine is the only economic recourse.

Sciences may become uninteresting as research areas because they have been too successful. The adjective "classical" often has this meaning. Sciences that are classical in this sense, for example, Euclidian geometry, Mendelian genetics, and parts of Newtonian mechanics, have been so successful in their area that they have pretty well exhausted it of any likelihood of surprises. They may hang on to a place in a curriculum by dint of their practical importance, such as human anatomy or comparative anatomy, or their capacity to surprise elementary students, or their usefulness as background for more advanced students. To become classical and elementary is the most dignified old age a science can attain. Some old sciences shrivel from ennui. The survival of a science in full youthful vigor depends on its attracting investigators. A major appeal of living science is its capacity to provide surprises.

Sciences may also be made moribund by nonscientific agencies. The New York Times of May 10, 1989, reported on its first page that several major universities are retrenching science departments simply because of lack of funds. It may be argued that funding is a sign of interest and that a failure to attract funds is an indicator of morbidity, but the fate of genetics in the Soviet Union under Stalin demonstrates that more pernicious forces may be responsible for attempts to destroy sciences from outside the scientific community. Genetics was vital enough to return. Can one be sure that sciences which for the moment lack this vitality deserve to die?

The Origin of Sciences

The Splitting of Academic Units. Sciences can appear as well as disappear. The most obvious way in which this occurs is by the amassing of sufficient new information, or a sufficiently new formal theory or viewpoint, to burst the bound of some preexisting parental science. My doctorate was given by a department of zoology which included a range of students and professors studying everything from the biochemical basis of egg fertilization, the formation of feathers, and enzymology of respiration to the fate of phosphorus in lakes and the systematics of water fleas. Even with this breadth, there was a sense of regret that botany and zoology had become separated.

Sixteen years later, in 1967, I founded the first independent department of ecology and evolution, and in the subsequent years many other departments with a similar name were established. Ecology-and-evolution, taken together, are a new science with all the ancillary machinery that goes with distinct sciences. The growth of diversity within ecology-and-evolution may break this new science at the hyphens, resulting in separate departments of ecology and of evolution but that is still in the future.

I had considerable misgivings about establishing a separate department, since excessive fragmentation of knowledge, and more specifically excessive narrowness of training, seems deplorable. In fact, modern students of ecology-and-evolution tend to be narrower in their biological knowledge than their teachers. I was convinced of the need for a split from a general biology department by considering my own incapacity to judge the quality of the work of a young investigator in biochemistry or embryology and the clear incompetence of biochemists and embryologists and some geneticists to evaluate the quality of ecologists and evolutionists. In the ensuing two decades, while I still regret the narrowness of our training, the wisdom of making the split has been manifested by the fact that bitter battles over promotion, curriculum, and more important, resources, have broken out in almost all departments of biology which have resisted splitting. The fact that there exists a department with a name does not guarantee intellectual quality. If the work of ecologists and evolutionists is worthwhile, their segregation into a separate science department was correct. If not, these departments will vanish. The definition of intellectual quality is not obvious, nor is it free of the kinds of political considerations discussed by Hull.

One problem that besets ecologists and evolutionists in their struggle with their colleagues from other sciences is that they do not generate funding at anything like the rate of biochemists and health scientists, who are supported by the National Institute of Health. There is no corresponding agency for ecology and evolution, despite the practical importance of applied ecology and the obeisance paid to ecology by politicians during election campaigns. This is a serious issue which I and others have addressed elsewhere (Langenheim 1988; Slobodkin 1988 *inter alios*). Also, in an administrative sense ecologists and evolutionists are seen, and see themselves, as working in new sciences. Darwin was the beginning or at least a major beginner of the science of evolution. Although study of the subject matter of ecology began in human prehistory, clear definition of the field as a scientific discipline is post-Darwinian (Sheail 1987; McIntosh 1985).

The Empirical Foundation for the Origin of Sciences. There are two fundamental preconditions for the origin of recognizable sciences. There must be a social and intellectual structure in some human population which will permit focusing on some definable subject matter. There are also a necessary set of natural preconditions. I will explain.

Could scientific ecology and evolution, as contrasted with speculation, anecdote or pure compilation of observations in the style of Pliny or Lucretius, have begun several centuries earlier? Obviously this is a possible event, and one can only speculate about what might have triggered earlier development. This would be an academic game up to a point.

If we push back far enough we can defend at least two answers to the question: What is the earliest possible date when ecology might have started? An almost trivial answer is that certainly the earliest period for the development of any science, considered as a discrete body of knowledge, is when humanity had evolved sufficient intelligence to make scientific assertions. Recall Thomas Browne's "Science is the debt we owe to God for the gift of intellect." (Browne 1643).

Saying that human intellectual evolution was a prerequisite to science does not differentiate among sciences. Assuming that there was no limit of this sort – perhaps adopting the viewpoint of an extraterrestrial academy of science observing the earth through its four- to six-billion-year history – it would still be the case that the possibility of originating each science comes into existence at a particular time, dependent on the stage of development of the earth.

This simple statement focuses attention on the two separate senses of the assertion that "Sciences evolve." Not only is there an intellectual and sociological history to the complex of institutions, viewpoints, theories and people which are subsumed under the particular name of a science, but also there are certain prerequisite circumstances of the natural world that must have existed before the science itself can begin its evolution.

In an earlier symposium of this series I was deeply impressed by an astrophysicist who described the "very early history of the universe after the

Big Bang." Initially "all we can safely say is that our current concept of space and time has no real meaning" for the first 10^{-43} seconds (Schramm 1980). Ignoring the question of how one measures that time interval when time has no meaning, the statement clearly implies that the subject matter of those sciences that rely on measurement of space and time had yet to evolve. Not until it was 10^{-6} seconds old could the universe contain neutrons and protons. As the universe continued to cool and expand it generated chemical elements, and thereby the possibility of studying chemistry.

This was chemistry under constraints of high ambient temperature, oddities of radiation and radioactive decay. Certainly not all compounds were possible under these conditions and the evolution of chemistry did not end at its birth. The much later birth of geology was contingent on the evolution of chemistry and the cooling of the earth. This cooling was a consequence of an orderly sequence of physical events but cannot be attributed to an evolution in physics.

That is, there were times and places in cosmic, and later terrestrial, history in which preexisting natural circumstances not only generated changes but generated new sets of regularities in the way change occurred. These sets of regularities are the subject matter of the discrete sciences, waiting for biological evolution to produce the intellects that could discover them. Of course, all of the social sciences which take humanity as subject matter only became possible with intelligent humanity (Slobodkin 1980).

I believe that what I am saying here is similar to the assertion by Newell and Simon (1976) that each science is characterized by the "essential nature of the system it studies. These characteristics are qualitative – the cell doctrine in biology, plate tectonics in geology . . . – and establish a frame within which more detailed, often quantitative studies can be pursued." It is the relative temporal constancy of these qualitative properties that make sciences possible, although not all possible frames are equally interesting.

Why Isn't Ecology Like Biochemistry?

The natural laws of what we now call physics gave birth to the laws of chemistry by a process of natural changes. This process shared its irreversible property with biological evolution. Like evolution, or other historical changes, I suspect that it might have transpired in another way under slightly different circumstances. If the mass of the proto-Earth had been greater there would have been less degassing, with consequent differences in geology, and presumably in phylogeny and paleontology.

The science of biology can be thought of as beginning either with the occurrence of the prerequisites for the origin of life, or at the time of development of the first organisms for which evolution would be valid in something like the modern technical sense of the term. It seems safe to say that once the development of the world had reached this point the mechanisms of evolution (selection, mutation, speciation, etc.) themselves had evolved, much as the laws of chemistry evolved earlier. It might be difficult to assign a clean border to the temporal extent of biological laws but by the time of the first eukaryotes we would clearly be in the domain of modern biology.

As evolution proceeds, many properties of organisms remain invariant. With some exceptions and minor modifications the genetic molecular machinery that evolved in the first eukaryotes are shared still by all their descendants. Most respiratory enzymes, much of the gene transcription process, sperm morphology, visual pigments and many other properties have varied relatively little compared with external morphology, behavior, food preferences and social behavior. The relatively invariant properties shared by a preponderance of organisms are what permit most of the subsciences of biology to be reasonably orderly, but it is just these highly variable aspects of organisms which are the subject matter of ecology.

Since biology is too large to be viable as a single science it has, within the past hundred years, been divided into variously defined subdisciplines. This can be done in a variety of ways. A process common to all organisms may be abstracted for consideration, as say biochemistry, genetics, membrane physiology or evolution, or the class of all organisms may be subdivided creating botany and zoology on the coarse level or acarology, pomology, or bryology if finer subdivisions are made. Both coarse or fine patterns of subdivision produce reasonably coherent blocks of information. The field of ecology does not neatly fit this scheme (Slobodkin 1988).

In genetics, biochemistry, and most other sciences the general competence and interests of a research worker are sufficiently specified by stating the name of a field and perhaps some subspecialty. By contrast, even in modern ecology it is customary actually to name a teacher or a specific university in order to describe properly the attitude and approach of a research worker (Langenheim 1988). This is reminiscent of certain branches of psychiatry. Sciences in which intellectual genealogy is that important may be thought of as less well developed.

Intellectual genealogy may always retain some importance since there are obvious political and social advantages and disadvantages related to where and with whom one studied. It loses importance to the degree that subject matter and theory are sufficiently unified so that there is general consensus as to what constitutes important problems and how these should be solved. But this is a description of how intellectually revolutionary sciences are reduced to the status of technical routine. If this reduction can be easily made, the science has lost its frontier. If it cannot be made at all, the science may be suspected of being vacuous.

The history of ecology has recently been the focus of serious attention (Sheail 1988; McIntosh 1987). There are several subdisciplines within ecology, some as old as ecology itself. To predict the probability of survival of the field the interaction among these must be understood. Ecology, in its early sense of descriptive natural history, lays claim to just those aspects of biology that makes organisms different, while theoretical ecology must focus on commonalities among organisms, and applied ecology is concerned with an array of problems ranging from fisheries management and water purity to global warming and landscape esthetics. Obviously there is internal tension in the field, which threatens its survival. These tensions have existed since the field began to show independent organizational life eighty years ago. How could a field come into existence under a unitary designation with these centripetal properties?

In the nineteenth century microbiology crystallized around medicine while botany and zoology did not. The science of ecology grew from botany and zoology, and is only now developing concern for smaller organisms. Ecology crystallized around a combination of felt social needs in fisheries, range and game management, which are now taught and practiced in an engineering mode. It also focused on more general concerns about the environment as expressed in various popular books (Carson 1962; Ehrlich 1960;

Sears 1945, *inter alios*, which were not trite when they first appeared).

Ecology received strong impetus in the nineteenth century because it, like genetics, was needed to develop the theory of evolution. There was, in addition, an impetus and unifying force in ecology from an almost poetic or religious concern with a Romantically reified sense of "nature" (McKibben 1989), often intertwined with politics and nationalism (Slobodkin and Loya 1980). This has been accompanied by a series of metaphorical simplifications derived from mathematics, economics and other areas which served to focus research schools up to the present.

Ecology, like medicine and geology, is a field defined by its subject matter rather than by its intellectual competence to deal with that subject. On the other hand, physics and mathematics, and to a lesser degree chemistry, can abandon certain areas as not falling within their purview, simply on the basis of their incapacity to deal with them. It has been said that physics is the science of answerable questions. This is not completely true, but recall the relegation of turbulent flow to hydrologists while laminar flow remained in physics and mathematics until new conceptual schemes permitted more elegant and, therefore, physicslike, analyses.

Like medicine, ecology cannot dismiss phenomena from consideration because they are difficult. This has been discussed elsewhere (Slobodkin 1988). In one critical way ecology differs from medicine. Medicine has a clear focus on one species. Specialization involves some ailment, structure or function of that species or the study of some other species because it is either pathogenic or significant nutritionally or a model for human biology. Recently the New York Times (January 15, 1989, sect. I, p. 23 and January 26, 1989, sect. II, p. 8) carried an account of a dispute at major medical schools about academic legitimacy of a specialty in Emergency Medicine; opponents claimed that severely specialized knowledge was necessary for treatment and advocates asserted that specializations lack the breadth of knowledge to make the full range of diagnoses needed under emergency conditions nor to provide the mix of treatments needed before the specialists' knowledge can come into full play. Even veterinary medicine suffers from the fact that while mammals differ only slightly in their properties they do differ, so that expertise developed on dogs may or may not relate to cattle. Ecology has some multiple of 10^6 species to deal with. To study one species very deeply is criticized as a lack of generality, nevertheless, to attempt generalizations over an array of species, however defined, results in loss of precision.

I now return to the previous discussion of evolving natural laws. I suggested that as the history of nature unfolds with time there are not only changes in the state of nature but that certain states of nature result in the genesis of new laws of change that alter all subsequent changes. The chemistry of the earth's surface produced the beginnings of life, definable in chemical terms. From the moment of its appearance, life not only altered the earth's chemistry but also persisted in repeating a set of processes peculiar to itself. These processes are the laws of biology that now occupy biochemists, molecular biologists and, to a lesser degree, cell physiologists. The evolutionary process then produced variations among kinds of organisms – each sharing in the general properties of life, but each also having its own special set of regularities in the context of its own ecological situation and biological endowments. Evolutionary changes occur if, and only if, the organisms differ both in their genetic properties and in the degree to which they and their descendants can survive and reproduce in the environmental context.

We cannot easily imagine a different physics, and it is almost as hard to imagine a very different system of chemistry. The elementary organic chemistry lecturer's assertion that we can imagine a silicon-based organic chemistry is an affirmation of the power of chemistry to predict events in a possible but highly hypothetical world different from our own or about a set of laboratory synthesis that might be undertaken. However, given what we know of physics and chemistry it does not seem as difficult to imagine a world with radically different geology and certainly we have an immediate knowledge of different ecologies.

The previous paragraph consists of truisms, which lead directly to the conclusion that the rate of evolution will fluctuate as a function of environmental events and of the particular biological properties of the organisms concerned, including their rate and pattern of mutation. (The general pattern that evolutionary change occurs in fits and starts is accepted by most biologists, regardless of their acceptance or rejection of the full panoply of "punctuated equilibrium" doctrines.) Between the intervals of relatively rapid evolution, each species is following a set of regularities of its own, slightly different from other species. These regularities are discovered by the committed naturalist focusing on a small number of reasonably similar species. It is because his discoveries are about particular species that the naturalist is condemned for lack of generality. It is because each species follows its own set of regularities that the ecological generalist or theoretician is condemned for imprecision. This contributes to the difficulty of ecological progress.

Conclusions

Both the state of the world and the state of the science which describes it change with time. Science changes its focus, its organizational structure, and its conclusions as a consequence of social and political events. But also nature itself goes through historic and developmental changes from which emerge previously inconceivable phenomenological regularities, which can act as foci for scientific inquiry. In particular, the evolutionary history of particular species, or perhaps even populations, leads to the development of regularities in their relation to their environment. If the number of kinds of organisms on earth were very much smaller, their careful description would be generally agreed to be scientifically meritorious.

Because species are numbered in the millions, focus on an excessively small subset of species is seen as a trivial pursuit unless the species in question are pests, pathogens or otherwise of medical relevance, or unless the descriptive process can be seen as a model for future analysis of more important species. Careful study of the way that particular single species deviate from broad generalizations is, however, critically important to ecological understanding. There is no correct single way to solve the difficulties of science. A balance between the general and the specific is needed in all scientific fields, particularly those in which the subject matter cannot be selected for the theoretician's convenience and there is the possibility that evolution-like changes have actually occurred, permitting subareas of the subject matter to be following different natural laws.

The "evolution of sciences" is not within the subject matter domain of biological evolution, but there are, nevertheless, patterns and regularities in how both social and natural sciences change. Understanding of these patterns may aid our understanding as both participants in, and audience for, science.

Acknowledgments

William Wimsatt and Dan Dykhuizen kindly read drafts of this paper and contributed criticism and ideas. Nicky Etkin discussed pharmacognosy with me.

References

Boyd, R., and P. Richerson. 1983. The cultural transmission of acquired variation: Effects on genetic fitness. *Journal of Theoretical Biology* 100:567-96

Browne, T. 1643. *Religio Medici*. London: Printed for Andrew Crooke.

Carson, R. 1962. *The Silent Spring*. Boston: Houghton Mifflin.

Ehrlich, P. 1960. *The Population Bomb*. New York: Ballantine Books.

Hull, D. L. 1988. *Science as a Process: An Evolutionary Account of the Social and Conceptual Development of Science*. Chicago: University of Chicago Press.

Langenheim, J. H. 1988. The path and progress of American women ecologists. *Bulletin of the Ecological Society of America* 69:184-97.

Lawrence, P. 1964. *Road Belong Cargo: A Study of the Cargo Movement in the Southern Madang District, New Guinea*. Manchester: Manchester University Press.

McIntosh, R. 1985. *The Background of Ecology: Concept and Theory*. New York: Cambridge University Press.

McIntosh, R. 1987. Pluralism in ecology. *Annual Review of Ecology and Systematics*. 18:321-41.

McKibben, B. 1989. Reflection (The end of Nature). *New Yorker Magazine*, Sept. 14:147-85.

Newell, A., and H. Simon. 1976. Computer science as empirical inquiry: Symbols and search. *Communications of the Association for Computer Machinery* (March, 1976)

Schramm, D. 1980. The astrophysical framework of life, 13-37. In *Crises in Ecological and Evolutionary Time*, ed. M. H. Nitecki. New York: Academic Press.

Sears, P. 1940. *Deserts on the March*. New York: Simon and Schuster.

Sheail, J. 1987. *Seventy-Five Years in Ecology*. Oxford and New York: The British Ecological Palo Alto Society, Blackwell Scientific Pub.

Slobodkin, L. B. 1980. Listening to a symposium – A summary and perspectives, 269-88. In *Crises in Ecological and Evolutionary Time*, ed. M. H. Nitecki. New York: Academic Press.

Slobodkin, L. B. 1983. The peculiar evolutionary strategy of man. *Boston Studies in Philosophy of Science* 71:227-48.

Slobodkin, L. B. 1988. Intellectual problems of applied ecology. *Biosciences* 38:337-42.

Slobodkin, L. B., and Y. Loya. 1981. Israel, 549-59. In *Handbook of Contemporary Developments in World Ecology*, ed. E. J. Kormondy and J. F. McCormick. London: Greenwood Press.

CONTRIBUTORS

Garland E. Allen received his doctorate from Harvard University in the history of science. He taught at Harvard, and is now Professor of Biology at Washington University in St. Louis. He is also a Trustee of the Marine Biological Laboratory at Woods Hole. Allen's main interest is history of biology in the post-Darwinian period, and he has published extensively on the history of evolution, genetics, and eugenics. Currently he is working on a social history of the American eugenics movement, 1900-1950, and a comparative study of Darwin, Marx, Wagner, and Freud.

Robert Boyd has a doctorate in ecology and population biology from the University of California, Davis. He has been a consultant on energy and resource policy for the California State Assembly and the California Energy Commission. Boyd, with Peter Richerson, began to use ideas from population biology to explore the relationship between culture and human evolution, and they coauthored *Culture and the Evolutionary Process.* Boyd is Professor in the Department of Anthropology at the University of California at Los Angeles.

Marc Ereshefsky received his undergraduate degree at the University of California, Berkeley, and his doctorate in the philosophy of science at the University of Wisconsin, Madison. After a post-doctoral fellowship in the Department of Philosophy at Northwestern University, he is now Assistant Professor in the Department of Philosophy at Washington University in St. Louis. Ereshefsky has published papers on the species problem, the concept of individuality in evolutionary theory, and macroevolutionary theory.

Douglas J. Futuyma did his undergraduate work at Cornell University and received his doctorate in zoology at the University of Michigan. He is Professor of Ecology and Evolution at the State University of New York at Stony Brook. Futuyma's papers have concentrated on the analysis of mechanisms of coevolution and its effects on community structure, and on the genetic and ecological dynamics of coevolution of terrestrial plants and herbivores. He is the coeditor of a book on coevolution and the author of *Science on Trial: The Case for Evolution* and the textbook *Evolutionary Biology*. He has served as editor of *Evolution* and as president of The Society for the Study of Evolution.

David L. Hull did his undergraduate work at Illinois Wesleyan University and received his doctorate in the history and philosophy of science at Indiana University. He is Professor of Philosophy at Northwestern University, where he was formerly chairman of the Department of Ecology and Evolutionary Biology. Hull is past president of the Society of Systematic Zoology and the Philosophy of Science Association, and is an editor of the Science and its Conceptual Foundations Series of the University of Chicago. He is author of three books, *Philosophy of Biological Science, Darwin & His Critics,* and *Science as a Process,* and over 100 papers on the history of biology and on the philosophy and sociology of science, particularly evolutionary biology and systematics.

David B. Kitts is a vertebrate paleontologist, geologist, and historian who received his doctorate in zoology from Columbia University. He has taught biology at Amherst College and the University of Oklahoma, where he is David Ross Boyd Professor Emeritus of Geology and the History of Science, and Adjunct Professor of Philosophy. Kitts is best known for his work on the structure of historical knowledge, Cenozoic mammals and stratigraphy, and the philosophy of geology and evolutionary theory. He is the author of numerous papers and *The Structure of Geology*.

Rachel Laudan received a degree in geology at the University of Bristol and her doctorate in history and philosophy of science at the University of London. She has taught history of science and technology at Carnegie-Mellon University, the University of Pittsburgh, Virginia Tech, and is now Professor in General Science and History at the University of Hawaii. Her major research interest has been the history and philosophy of geology, resulting in articles on geology from the eighteenth century through plate tectonics and the book, *From Mineralogy to Geology: The Foundations of a Science 1650-*

1850. She is also editor of *The Nature of Technological Knowledge: Are Models of Scientific Change Relevant?* Her current focus is eighteenth- and nineteenth-century scientists' uses of history as they struggled to forge an image of science.

Doris V. Nitecki did her undergraduate work at Maryville College and received an M.A. from the University of Chicago. She is an Associate in the Department of Geology at the Field Museum. She is coeditor of *The Evolution of Human Hunting*, and coauthor of two bibliographies on fossil algae.

Matthew H. Nitecki is Curator of Fossil Invertebrates in the Department of Geology at the Field Museum and in the Committee on Evolutionary Biology at the University of Chicago, where he did his master's and doctoral work in paleontology. He also holds a faculty appointment in the College of the University of Chicago. Nitecki has written or edited about 150 papers, including twelve books, on paleobiology of Paleozoic fossils, history and sociology of science, and theoretical evolutionary biology.

Peter Richerson did his undergraduate and doctoral work at the University of California, Davis. He is Professor of Ecology in the Division of Environmental Studies and a Director of the Institute of Ecology at the University of California, Davis. He is also a consultant to the National Water Commission. Richeson has published on human ecology, the theory of cultural evolution, plankton community ecology, and tropical limnology. He is coauthor with Robert Boyd of *Culture and the Evolutionary Process*.

Robert J. Richards received his doctorate in history of science from the University of Chicago, where he is now Professor in the departments of History, Philosophy, and Psychology, and the College. He is also chairman of the Committee on the Conceptual Foundations of Science at Chicago. Richards has written extensively on the history and philosophy of biology and psychology. He is the author of the recently published *Darwin and the Emergence of Evolutionary Theories of Mind and Behavior* and is now working on an Ernst Haeckel volume.

Michael Ruse received his undergraduate degree at the University of Bristol and his doctorate at McMaster University. He is Professor of Philosophy at the University of Guelph, and an authority on the philosophy and history of evolutionary biology. A fellow of the Royal Society of Canada, he is the author of numerous papers and several books, including a trilogy on Darwinism: *The Darwinian Revolution, Darwinism Defended* and *Taking Darwin Seriously*. Currently he is writing a volume on evolutionary progress.

Lawrence B. Slobodkin did his undergraduate work at Bethany College in West Virginia, and his doctoral studies in zoology at Yale. He has worked for the U.S. Fish and Wildlife Service, Bingham Oceanographic Laboratory, University of Michigan, and the State University of New York at Stony Brook, where he is now Professor of Biology. He is past president of the American Society of Naturalists, and has published over 100 papers, books, and monographs on theoretical and experimental population ecology, evolutionary strategy, ecological planning and decision making with reference to environmental management, the biology of hydra, and aquatic toxicology. He is now writing a book on the intellectual role of simplicity and minimalism.

INDEX

DATE DUE